Confidence and Character

Confidence and Character

The Religious Life of George Washington

JAMES A. PINGEL II

WIPF & STOCK · Eugene, Oregon

CONFIDENCE AND CHARACTER
The Religious Life of George Washington

Copyright © 2014 James A. Pingel II. All rights reserved. Except for brief quotations in critical publications or reviews, no part of this book may be reproduced in any manner without prior written permission from the publisher. Write: Permissions. Wipf and Stock Publishers, 199 W. 8th Ave., Suite 3, Eugene, OR 97401.

Wipf and Stock
An Imprint of Wipf and Stock Publishers
199 W. 8th Ave., Suite 3
Eugene, OR 97401

www.wipfandstock.com

ISBN 13: 978–1–62564–836–5

Manufactured in the U.S.A.   11/18/2014

For Dad—whose love of history, westerns,
and God rubbed off and inspired a little boy.

Now it shall come to pass in the latter days
that the mountain of the LORD's HOUSE
shall be established on the top of the mountains,
and shall be exalted above the hills;
and peoples shall flow to it.
Many nations shall come and say,
"Come, and let us go up to the mountain of the Lord,
to the house of the God of Jacob;
He will teach us His ways,
and we shall walk in His paths."
For out of Zion the law shall go forth,
and the word of the LORD FROM JERUSALEM.
He shall judge between many peoples,
and rebuke strong nations afar off;
They shall beat their swords into plowshares,
and their spears into pruning hooks;
nation shall not lift up sword against nation,
neither shall they learn war anymore.

But everyone shall sit under his vine and under his fig tree,
and no one shall make them afraid;
for the mouth of the LORD OF HOSTS HAS SPOKEN.
For all people walk each in the name of his god,
but we will walk in the name of the LORD OUR GOD
forever and ever.

Micah 4:1–5 (KJV)—Washington's most frequently referenced Bible verse. He referred to the "under his vine and under his fig tree" phrase almost fifty times in his correspondence.

Contents

Illustrations

Preface

For over two centuries, historians have almost universally lauded the character of George Washington. This study started out as search to discover *why* his character was so impressive and striking—both in the eyes of his contemporaries and subsequent historians. Researching the why question led to others: *How* was his character shaped and nurtured? *What* inspired or informed his character?

America's greatest founding father spoke or wrote about character almost 1,500 times in his correspondence. Yet many Washington biographies ignore, suppress, manipulate, or do not adequately explain, the foundations or inspiration of his reputable character. Certainly he wanted to earn the affection and admiration of his fellow man and retain an enduring legacy. But does a desire for fame fully explain the almost universal praise of Washington's character—both by contemporaries and subsequent historians? Biographer Ron Chernow notes that Washington is the most elusive and "interior of the founders." Contemporaries "*felt* the inner force of his nature" and sensed his "unseen power."[1] Enquiring minds want to know what made this indispensable man tick.

The divergent portrayals of Washington's religious faith also piqued historical inquiry and curiosity. On the religious spectrum, Washington ranges from an aloof, disinterested deist to a devout evangelical Christian. No other founding father has been so widely debated and acutely disputed for his precise religious beliefs.

These historiographical curiosities prompted two guiding questions: Might the inner force and unseen power in Washington emanate directly from his religious faith? If Washington's integrity and honor were so evident and esteemed by family members and contemporaries alike, why are his religious beliefs disputed or portrayed so differently among historians and biographers even yet today?

1. Chernow, *Washington*, xix–xx.

Preface

While no one can be completely sure about what resides in a man's heart and mind, the historical evidence strongly suggests that the primary source of Washington's character formation and leadership proficiency was his Christian faith and confidence in God. This religious faith was embedded and evident in almost all of his vocations and consistently throughout the entirety of his life. To be sure, religion was not the only force that shaped and influenced his character and worldview. Yet, Washington's religious inspiration remains the most underappreciated and significantly underrated aspect of his consequential life.

Since character is often destiny in leadership, America's first national hero provides a convincing and compelling life study. Indeed, Washington's faith grounded him in his private life and helped propel him to achieve grand accomplishments in public life. He left an indelible and enduring legacy for his family and countrymen. We can still learn from his life and leadership legacy today.

Acknowledgments

I want to thank Peter Jonas for his guidance throughout the early research and writing process of this work. Peter is a published and renowned author on the impact laughter has on student learning. I benefitted greatly from his guidance and leadership, and I am sure he laughed a lot as he read and critiqued my initial drafts.

I want to thank my wife, Michelle, whose patience and encouragement gave me the confidence to see this project through to fruition. Like Martha was for George, asking her to be my bride was the best decision of my life. George and I definitely married up.

Finally, I thank God for giving me the opportunity to write and publish. So many people in the world are unable to read, or live in impoverished areas where books and the Internet are not accessible, or face other monumental challenges that inhibit their ability to participate in research and scholarship. God has given me more than I deserve. Any mistakes and errors that remain in this work are my own, but whatever is found to be of value in this book are truly gifts from God.

Introduction

On a cold February winter night, in 1778, General George Washington took a brief leave of his officers and troops, who were encamped at Valley Forge, Pennsylvania, and set off for a quiet, discreet location in the woods to pray. Washington, like many of his soldiers, was tired. For almost three years, the Continental Army had waged a war for independence against British Redcoats and Hessian soldiers. The army had suffered several setbacks during the war, some of them embarrassing and humiliating. Yet, somehow, the General and his army still survived.

As Washington prayed, Isaac Potts, owner of the house the General was using as a headquarters at Valley Forge, passed by the grove where he heard and saw the Commander in Chief down on one knee praying earnestly. Potts froze in his tracks, unwilling to disturb the Virginian until his prayers and devotions were completed. When he returned home, Potts told his wife Sarah what he had observed.

"Sarah, my dear! Sarah! All's well! All's well! George Washington will yet prevail!" he exclaimed.

"What's the matter, Isaac?" she replied. "Thee seems moved."

"Well," Isaac answered, "if I seemed moved, tis no more than what I am. I have seen what I never expected." Potts continued: "I always thought the sword and the gospel utterly inconsistent; and that no man could be soldier and a Christian at the same time. But George Washington has this day convinced me of my mistake."[1] Indeed, as a Quaker, Potts had been opposed to the war. From that day forward, however, he became a Revolutionary.

On May 6, 1982, at his National Day of Prayer Proclamation, President Ronald Reagan asserted that

> the most sublime picture in American history is of George Washington on his knees in the snow at Valley Forge. That image personifies a people who know that it is not enough to

1. Weems, *Life of Washington*, 181–82.

depend on our own courage and goodness; we must also seek help from God, our Father and Preserver."[2]

While the Isaac Potts's story was apocryphal, many contemporaries did witness and observe Washington in public and private prayer. Picture by John C. McRae. (Courtesy of the Mount Vernon Ladies' Association)

To this day, in the halls of the United States Congress, a private chapel features a stained glass window—called "Washington's Gethsemane"—which depicts the General kneeling at Valley Forge praying to God presumably for his soldiers, the Revolutionary War effort, and his country.

The story of Washington on bended knee at Valley Forge was first told by Reverend Mason Locke Weems, better known as Parson Weems, at the dawning of the nineteenth century and remains a highly disputed historical reference. Some historians and biographers have soundly criticized Weems for fabrications of the Washington legend. Potts, they note, had not yet purchased the farm where the incident allegedly occurred, nor had he married yet.[3] Moreover, Weems is the same hagiographer who told the even more infamous story of young George chopping down his father's cherry tree and is, critics argue, not credible. Many early biographies of Washington fail to mention the Potts or the cherry tree stories at all.

2. McDowell, *Apostle of Liberty*, 89.
3. Henriques, *Realistic Visionary*, 176.

THE DEIST

The Potts story, or non-story, aptly represents the conflicting portrayals of Washington's religious faith over the past two centuries. Washington's personal beliefs, no doubt, would have been more discernible and clear had he firmly declared his deepest convictions in a religious treatise as Jefferson did. Historians often lump him with other founding fathers, such as Thomas Paine, Thomas Jefferson, James Madison, and Benjamin Franklin, who were outspoken about their deistic beliefs.

Eighteenth-century deism was a religious perspective, motivated primarily by the Enlightenment, where reason reigned over revelation as a driving force for human advancement. Nature superseded Scripture as a way to understand and approach God. While they had no organized sect, creed, form of worship, or recognized leader, deists cast off almost everything peculiar to orthodox Christianity. They believed that the Bible—presented as the truth or the absolute, infallible Word of God—had been corrupted and distorted by men who had inserted superstitions and supernatural revelations. Biblical miracles—which implied a perfect God, theological dogma, mystery, and religious authority were ridiculed, disdained, or eliminated in a deistic worldview. Deists believed in God, but denied the divinity of Jesus, original sin, the Incarnation, the atonement of Christ, the faith-giving work of the Holy Spirit, and the Triune God—all major teachings and pillars of orthodox Christianity.

For the deist, everything was explainable, rational, and provable. Anything incomprehensible or above reason, such as divine revelation, was deemed irrational and illogical. Thus, the Bible was attacked for alleged superstitions and fabrications, supposed miracles, and the God-breathed infallibility claim. Jefferson admired much about the New Testament, for example, but literally cut out many supernatural references—including the resurrection and miracles of Jesus—so that he could reduce Christianity to reason alone. Only if emotion, mystery, enthusiasm, and fantasy were eliminated could one's mind be free. A rational thinker was a freethinker.

Critical of the basic foundations of Christianity, deists purported that God had created the universe but had not intervened in the daily operation of the world since creation. No miracles would be forthcoming in the future either. God, the watchmaker, created a world that could be elucidated, utilized, and perfected by humankind. All divine work had been completed during creation. The deist God was a distant deity, not a personal one.

This aloof, detached God directly countered the Judeo-Christian tradition, which taught that humans could have a close personal relationship with God, and that God had spoken to humankind directly through the

Holy Scriptures and the Incarnation. Deists did not find any redemptive reason to read the Bible, pray, get baptized, receive Holy Communion, or adhere to the doctrines and sacred teachings of the organized church. Paine's deistic *Age of Reason,* published from 1794–95, relentlessly attacked Christianity for its supernatural accounts and denigrated the prophets—referring to them as mere poets. Only foolish people believed in miracles and the theology of the orthodox, Christian church. While some deists read the Bible, they were not people of the book. Their God was a naturalistic God.

Deists believed the Creator bequeathed all human beings a moral faculty to make virtuous decisions and live a moral life. God rewarded and punished human beings based on their enlightened decisions and good works. God-given reason could be used to solve all human problems and promote human progress, even to the point of perfection. Natural theology—the scientific study and examination of God's creation using reason and rationality—ruled the deist worldview.

Some biographers, especially those in the twentieth century, select evidence to paint Washington a deist. They argue that the words "Jesus," "Christ," or "forgiveness of sins" are almost nonexistent in his voluminous writings. Washington may have believed in God, but a distant God whom he referred to as "Providence" or "Governor of the Universe." He allegedly refused to partake of Holy Communion or bow when praying in church, appeared disinterested in religious dogma and doctrine, and eschewed any public proclamations of his fidelity or submission to the Triune God. He may have attended church throughout his life—and more frequently as President—but this was only for social necessity, formality, and for the good governance of the nation. Washington supposedly viewed the afterlife forlornly and with dour grimness. During his last few harrowing and painful hours of life on earth, he died stoically but without adhering to any last rites or traditional Christian sentiment. Washington, they conclude, seemed rather dull in his piety and genuinely disinterested in religion.

The deistic Washington, however, is inaccurate and a slipshod depiction when one meticulously examines the totality of his words, deeds, and testimony of family members and contemporaries. Upon reconsidering ample and compelling historical evidence, some biographers have recently tried to depict the Father of His Country as a warm deist, "theistic rationalist,"[4] "Anglican-affiliated Deist,"[5] "lukewarm Episcopalian,"[6] or

---

4. Ibid, 185.
5. McDonald, "A Leader," 40.
6. Ellis, *His Excellency,* 45.

"Deistic Episcopalian."[7] They concede that Washington prayed regularly and believed in an active, intervening God—two beliefs which do not conform to the standard deistic worldview. Warm deists, they contend, could accept the Holy Scriptures as truth as long as they conformed to reason and rationality. Outwardly conforming and accommodating, warm deists attempted to balance and reconcile revelation and reason in their worldview.

Many founders did adhere to both deistic and Christian worldviews. The Scientific Revolution, after all, was propelled by Christian scientists who believed that the universe was designed after an orderly and heavenly Creator. Nature could be studied, comprehended, and developed for humankind's benefit and progress. Therefore, enlightened Christians could defend their faith using reason as well as revelation. For warm deists, the Newtonian vision or conception of the world meshed nicely with deistic devotion to reason and rational thought.

Moreover, the bloody and brutal religious wars in Europe, which dominated much of sixteenth, seventeenth, and eighteenth centuries, compelled many founding fathers to temper and restrain their religious zeal and affirmation in public. "Christian Deism"[8] provided a safe middle ground on the religious continuum for those who desired to be renowned as scientifically enlightened and religiously observant citizens.

Washington never claimed to be any kind of deist. This would have been a false rendering and out of character for the Virginian. For while Benjamin Franklin proudly proclaimed to be a deist in his autobiography and Jefferson wrote two treatises articulating his deistic worldview, Washington's religious soul was revealed in his daily Christian walk—in thought, word, and deed. The historical record shows that almost all his contemporaries and associates had no doubt that he was a devout Christian, a perception and assessment that Washington never felt necessary to rectify.

CHARACTER

A man who prided himself on integrity and reputation, Washington wrote about character approximately 1,500 times in his letters. He desired to be a man of fortitude and integrity, and peers recognized his remarkable veracity and moral fiber in every aspect of his life. As a farmer, for example, Washington worked hard to produce the best crops possible. Indeed, his reputation for quality goods became so well known that any barrel stamped "George Washington, Mount Vernon," was exempted from regular

7. Holmes, *Faiths*, 65.
8. Walker et al., *History*, 579.

inspection in the West Indies.[9] Fellow Virginian, James Monroe, insisted that he "never doubted the perfect integrity of Genl. Washington, nor the strength, or energy of his mind." He admired the General—who exerted his "best faculties, on all occasions, in support of his character & fame."[10] Years after Washington's death, Supreme Court Justice, John Marshall, asserted that Washington's character itself was "one of the most interesting, perhaps the most interesting events in the history of the human race."[11] Gouverneur Morris, a founder and delegate to the Constitutional Convention, praised Washington's "steady persevering Industry," his "Self Command," which was of a "higher Grade," and how he, "at any moment," could "command the Energies of his Mind to a Cheerful Exertion" despite his sometimes "violent" passions.[12] Tobias Lear, Washington's personal secretary, explained that the General was "the only man of an exalted character" who had "not lost some part of his respectability (right to respect) by an intimate acquaintance." After having "lived with him near two years," and receiving "many marks of his affection and esteem," Lear had observed Washington in every occasion "which a man is placed in his family"—having "drank with him constantly, and almost every evening played cards with him . . . ." Lear declared that "I have never found a single thing that could lessen my respect for him." Washington's "honesty, uprightness, and candor in all his private transactions have sometimes led one to think him more than a man."[13]

Numerous contemporaries lauded Washington's character and integrity. He was modest, selfless, and honest. They admired his fortitude, firmness, and courage. "I thought him a perfectly honest Man, with an amiable and excellent heart," contended John Adams in the middle of the Revolutionary War, "and the most important Character at that time among Us."[14] Chevalier de La Luzerne, French Minister to the United Colonies during the war, insisted that Washington's character was the most "eminent" of the Revolutionary generation.[15] "There was in him that assemblage of qualities which constitutes real greatness," William Linn, DD, eulogized shortly after Washington's death. "He was not tinsel, but gold; not a pebble, but a diamond; not a meteor, but a sun." If compared with "the sages and heroes of

9. McDowell, *Apostle of Liberty*, 21.

10. Monroe to John McLean, December 5, 1827, in Hamilton, *Writings of Monroe*, 7:129–30.

11. Marshall to William T. Dwight, August 7, 1827, in Hobson, *Papers of Marshall*, 11:50.

12. Morris to John Marshall, June 26, 1807 in ibid., 7:54.

13. Flexner, *George Washington*, 3:54.

14. Adams Autobiography, December, 1777, in Kaminski, *Founders*, 476.

15. Chevalier de La Luzerne to Comte de Vergennes, March 29, 1783, in ibid., 484.

antiquity, he would gain 'by comparison'" being free of their blemishes and uniting "the excellences of them all."[16]

The more time people spent with Washington, the more impressed they became with his inner composition. "I admire him more each day for the beauty of his character and his spirit," Marquis de Lafayette commented to a friend.[17] "Every noble and sensitive soul must love the excellent qualities of his heart." Washington's "honesty, his candor, his sensitivity, his virtue in the full sense of the word are above all praise."[18]

Even while admitting and acknowledging Washington's temper, contemporaries complimented the Virginian's extraordinary self-discipline and efforts to manage and control this conspicuous personality flaw. They recognized his ability to function under great duress as well as his propensity for rebounding from terrible disappointments. Thomas Paine, for example, specifically commended the General's resolve and fortitude in dealing with difficulties and overcoming long odds.[19] John Adams and Jefferson, among others, hailed Washington's deliberate and thoughtful decision-making. No one ever described him as being blithe, careless, or reckless.

Jefferson's observations are intriguing given the rupture that occurred in their relationship near the end of Washington's life. Both before and after their falling-out, Jefferson praised and applauded his contemporary's character. After the Constitutional Convention concluded in 1787, Jefferson was concerned that the executive branch had been made much too powerful. However, he found solace in the realization that Washington would, in all probability, become the nation's first chief executive. The Constitution would not need to be "altered during the life of our great leader," Jefferson maintained, "whose executive talents are superior to those I believe of any man in the world." He was confident in Washington's "perfect integrity," and further asserted that the man's talents and "weight of character" were "peculiarly necessary to get the government so under way as that it may afterwards be carried on by subordinate characters."[20]

After Washington passed away, Jefferson continued to extoll the character of "my illustrious countryman, Washington," especially the "moderation of his desires . . . strength of judgment . . . support for the laws and

---

16. M'Guire, *Religious Opinions*, 375.

17. Lafayette to Duc d'Ayen, December 16, 1777, in Kaminski, *Founders*, 477.

18. Lafayette to Baron von Steuben, March 12, 1778, in ibid., 478.

19. Paine, "The American Crisis," December 19, 1776, in ibid., 474.

20. Jefferson to Francis Hopkinson, March 13, 1789; Jefferson to David Humphreys, March 18, 1789, in Oberg, *Papers of Jefferson*, 14:651, 679.

liberties of our country" and "his will."[21] In 1814, Jefferson explained that Washington's mind was

> great and powerful, without being of the very first order; his penetration strong, though not so acute of that of a Newton, Bacon, or Locke; and as far as he saw, no judgment was ever sounder. It was slow in operation, being little aided by invention or imagination, but sure in conclusion . . . He was incapable of fear, meeting personal dangers with the calmest unconcern. Perhaps the strongest feature in his character was prudence, never acting until every circumstance, every consideration, was maturely weighed; refraining if he saw a doubt, but when once decided, going through with purpose, whatever obstacles opposed. His integrity was most pure, his justice the most inflexible I have ever known, no motives of interest or consanguinity, of friendship or hatred, being able to bias his decision. He was, indeed, in every sense of the words, a wise, a good, and a great man . . . On the whole, his character was, in its mass, perfect, in nothing bad, in a few points indifferent; and it may truly be said, that never did nature and fortune combine more perfectly to make a man great.[22]

Contemporaries were fascinated and captivated with Washington's rectitude and moral fortitude. While Washington "did not possess that rapidity of decision which distinguishes many men of genius," Marshall explained, he "never yielded principle" nor "sacrificed his judgment on its altar" to obtain "popular favor" or public acclaim. Washington's "firmness of character added to acknowledged virtue" enabled him "to stem a torrent which would have overwhelmed almost any other man" and save his country.[23]

The Virginian's character was recognized and extoled during his lifetime, and in the decades that followed, as something singular and special. "The character of Washington," wrote Reverend E. C. M'Guire in 1836, is "justly considered the property of his country and, in a measure, of the civilized world." His "*greatness* and *goodness*" was "seldom found to exist in the same human being."[24] Poet Robert Frost explained, "George Washington was one of the few people in the whole history of the world who was not carried away with power." Napoleon Bonaparte lamented, on his deathbed,

---

21. Jefferson to Earl of Buchan, July 10, 1803, in Peterson, *Jefferson: Writings,* 1135.

22. Jefferson to Walter Jones, January 2, in ibid., 1318–19.

23. John Marshall to Timothy Pickering, March 15, 1827, in Oberg, *Papers of Jefferson,* 10:411.

24. M'Guire, *Religious Opinions,* iii.

that the French people "wanted me to be another Washington,"[25] and realized he fell far short of the American's "moderation, disinterestedness, and wisdom."[26] The Duke of Wellington described the Washington as having "the purest and noblest character of modern time—possibly of all time."[27] Nathaniel Hawthorne once wondered aloud if anyone "had ever seen Washington nude?" He "had no nakedness," and "was born with his clothes on, and his hair powdered, and made a stately bow on his first appearance in the world."[28]

World leaders continue to acclaim Washington's character today. Nelson Mandela once told President George W. Bush that the people of South Africa wanted him to run for a third presidential term in South Africa, but he had declined. "I told them that I want African leaders to see that it's okay to retire," Mandela explained lamenting the fact that too many African warlords and strongmen abused their people and refused to give up power. Bush complimented the Nobel Peace Prize winner by comparing him to Washington, who refused to become king. "Your country was lucky that he was that kind of man," Mandela told Bush. "Africa doesn't have enough of them."[29]

The Bush family has a special fondness for Washington's historical legacy. President George H. W. Bush placed his family's Bible on top of the Washington Bible at his 1989 swearing-in ceremony, the bicentennial of the United States first inauguration (the Bible was specially transported under Masonic guard from New York to Washington). "With the advantage of hindsight," George W. Bush told reporter, Bob Woodward, "it is easy to take George Washington's success for granted." America's path to freedom was a struggle and no sure thing. The Continental Army "stood on the brink of disaster many times," noted Bush, "but his will was unbreakable."[30]

In his memoirs, George W. Bush acknowledged the harsh criticism a president receives and how one's character is severely tested especially during tough times. He noted how the first President of the United States once wrote that as long as he made decisions based on principle and led with conviction, "no earthly efforts" could deprive him of inner peace. "The arrows of malevolence, however barbed and well pointed, never can reach the most vulnerable part of me" the 43rd president quoted the first. "If they

---

25. Smith, *Patriarch*, 359.
26. Herold, *Age of Napoleon*, 123.
27. Lillback and Newcombe, *Sacred Fire*, 112.
28. Borden, *Great Lives*, 1–2.
29. Rice, *No Higher Honor*, 637–38.
30. Woodward, *War Within*, 330–31.

are still assessing George Washington's legacy more than two centuries after he left office," insisted Bush, "this George W. doesn't have to worry about today's headlines."[31]

Even from an early age, Washington recognized his life story would be one for the history books. In a time where printed material was the primary mode of communication, there were few things he valued more than his papers and personal correspondence. Early in the Revolutionary War, while bracing for General William Howe's assault on New York, the General ordered a box of his papers to be transported to Philadelphia for safe keeping. He even had a special chest with strong hinges attached to secure them. He also instructed his cousin, Lund Washington—the overseer or manager of affairs at Mount Vernon, to take care of Martha first but then secure his papers second. Martha eventually gathered her husband's documents and crammed them in a trunk for removal and safe-keeping in case British armies would make a surprise visit to Mount Vernon. During the eight years of war, Washington was forced to move his headquarters, often under adverse conditions, almost 170 times.[32] Yet he was determined to keep his papers with him. He also asked Congress to hire secretaries to copy his wartime correspondence demanding beautifully bounded papers with precise writing for the documentation.

Washington restricted even his closest friends and acquaintances from seeing or getting access to his papers asserting that they had to be properly archived and prepared for public scrutiny. David Humphreys, who served as an aid to the General during the Revolutionary War, approached Washington, in 1784, wanting to write the General's biography. Washington cautiously agreed but only allowed his wartime associate to review his papers at Mount Vernon and only under his close supervision. Humphreys eventually gave up the project, among other reasons, because of Washington's meticulous and mettlesome insistence to review and edit everything he wrote.

History laments that Martha, according to family tradition, burned almost all correspondence between she and her husband. Only two letters between Martha and George survive and remain in existence (discovered in a writing desk many years after George and Martha's deaths—Martha must have missed them when burning the others). Lund Washington's correspondence with George was also destroyed by Lund's widow, according to her husband's wishes, after his death.

A meticulous paper handler and filer, Washington literally and deliberately preserved almost every scrap of paper belonging to him—including

---

31. Bush, *Decision Points*, 121–22.

32. Fowler, *American Crisis*, 225.

diaries, letters sent and received, accounts, and other day-to-day transactions—as if they represented his very identity. In 1786, before he became President, Washington began editing his own papers eliminating or changing awkward constructions, faulty grammar, misspellings, and other errors. After his presidency, he also made deletions, insertions, and substitutions in many of his writings. As years passed, he took considerable time to arrange his papers in chronological order and by name and subject. Washington fully realized he was literally making history and that his correspondence, in addition to his public accomplishments and conspicuous achievements, would be meticulously reviewed and examined for decades to come.

That he was intentional and took such deliberate care to mention God so frequently in his correspondence, then, is significant. Washington was not a theologian, priest, or pastor, yet he referred to "God" approximately 150 times, "Providence" some 270 times, and "Divine" almost one hundred times in his writings. Moreover, he often spoke of God by other honorific titles—the "invisible hand," "Governor of the Universe," "Giver of Life," "All-wise disposer of events," to name a few, approximately ninety different times. Heaven was acknowledged around 130 times in his correspondence, and he composed over one hundred prayers.[33] God and religion were central in his life and never far from his thoughts.

THE CHRISTIAN

Washington spoke, wrote, and lived as a Christian his entire life. He was baptized, raised, educated, married, and buried in the traditions of the Anglican and, later, Episcopal Church. When he became a surveyor and vestryman in colonial Virginia, Washington signed mandatory oaths—conformity required by the Church of England and established by law—which endorsed the Anglican teachings found in *Thirty-Nine Articles of Religion* and *Book of Common Prayer*. Never, at any time throughout the rest of his life, did Washington ever recant or disown these oaths.

Unlike deists, such as Franklin or Jefferson, who occasionally attended Christian churches but denounced the divine teachings of Scripture and church doctrine, Washington neither wrote, spoke, or lived as a deist nor did he publicly or privately disown orthodox Christian teachings. He did, however, commend and esteem chaplains who sent him sermons critical of deism and the deistic espousals of individuals such as Paine.[34] While he certainly exhibited a propensity for unity and harmony amongst different

33. Lillback and Newcombe, *Sacred Fire*, 556, 713.
34. Ibid., 386.

denominations, he had little incentive to act or be something or someone he was not. Washington was a practicing Christian man.

His religious beliefs must be analyzed and considered in proper historical context. He is best labeled a Latitudinarian—an Anglican Christian who believed in orthodox Christian teachings and rationalism. Appealing to reason and intellect rather than emotion, the Latitudinarian movement took place primarily within the Anglican Church in the seventeenth and eighteenth centuries. Repulsed by nearly two centuries of religious warfare in Europe, which culminated in the Thirty Years War and English Civil War, Latitudinarians, later known as Broad Church Episcopalians, emphasized the reasonableness of Christianity, downplayed creedal and special religious language, and saw a middle ground between Protestantism and Catholicism. They were broadminded in the way they spoke about the Christian faith, particularly in the public square, and gave theological room or latitude to those who disagreed with the established church and even some church doctrine deemed of lesser importance. Latitudinarians emphasized and highlighted commonalities shared among the many Christian denominations rather than their differences. Washington displayed this unifying, harmonious attitude toward different religious denominations throughout his entire life.

Latitudinarians simplified or limited their doctrine to a few core beliefs, but orthodox Christian teachings—such as revelation of God's Word, the divinity and resurrection of Christ, the forgiveness of sins, the indwelling Holy Spirit, to name a few—remained fundamental in their biblical worldview. While they desired harmony between different Christian denominations and sects, they did not abandon the infallibility and sacredness of Scripture.[35]

Washington's reverence for the Bible is manifest throughout his life. His birth and baptism were recorded in a large family Bible. He ordered Bibles for his stepchildren with their names inscribed in gold as well as a music book containing a new version of Psalms and hymns (set for the spinet for his stepdaughter). Out of the forty-seven books he acquired for his stepson, eleven of them concerned the subject of religion or the Bible. He purchased a book entitled *Sermons on the Lords Prayer* in 1772. He hired a Scottish immigrant, Walter Magowan, to tutor his stepchildren in the Greek New Testament. Washington's teenage signature was found on Theodore Beza's (a famous Protestant reformer) Latin Bible in his library. His stepchildren's school textbooks, as well as his own childhood textbooks, often

---

35. Thompson, *Good Providence*, 4–5; Lillback and Newcombe, *Sacred Fire*, 307–8; Novak and Novak, *Washington's God*, 121.

addressed biblical themes. He asserted that the Bible should be rigorously taught in American schools. He willed Reverend Bryan Fairfax—a close boyhood friend from Virginia who served as his pastor in Alexandria—a three volume English bishop's Bible from Bishop Thomas Wilson of Sodor and Mann. Elizabeth Washington, wife of cousin Lund—who was Washington's overseer and manager, broke an unwritten social understanding by distributing Bibles to the slaves of Mount Vernon, an activity that would have been prohibited on many plantations. Washington listened to clergy give sermons, read Scripture lessons, and recited liturgy during Anglican worship services. He read the Bible to his family before church, on Sunday evenings, and in front of many contemporaries. He even subscribed and invested in Reverend John Brown's new "Self-Interpreting Bible" in 1792, which provided copious notes and commentary on the Word of God, when many other atheist or deistic founding fathers did not. Throughout Mount Vernon, pictures and portraits hung illustrating biblical events, evangelistic sentiment, and followers of Christ living out their faith. An inventory of Washington's library at his death revealed fifty volumes dealing with religion and religious matters, 170 sermons, and many other additional short works which were labeled as sermons or political sermons. He bound these and wrote his name in each of the binders. Micah 4:4—that everyone should sit under their own vine and fig tree with no fear because God would be with them—was the most frequent Bible passage cited in his writings (almost fifty times). Washington's papers, which he so meticulously and intentionally preserved, demonstrate a profound appreciation and reverence for the Word of God.[36]

Washington's biblical literacy was extensive and intimate. Scripture passages and Bible stories permeate his correspondence. He believed in an active, caring, intervening God, not a deistic one. He repeatedly spoke of "the wondrous works of Providence," the "bountiful Providence" which never failed him, the "inscrutable" deeds and prevailing "finger" of God, and the "astonishing interpositions" of his Heavenly Father. Washington frequently praised and gave God credit for his accomplishments, and noted how the "allwise disposer of events" watched over his daily walk and worked out the providential plan according to his purposes. Miracles could and did happen with regularity. God did intervene in his own time, in his own way, and in the daily lives of his children.

Washington was a remarkably consistent and dedicated church-goer throughout his entire life, especially considering the historical and

36. M'Guire, *Religious Opinions*, xv, 9, 154, 168, 349; Meade, *Old Churches*, 162, 184, 245–46; Thompson, *Good Providence*, 39, 50, 62, 71; Lillback and Newcombe, *Sacred Fire*, 316–17, 395; Novak and Novak, *Washington's God*, 15.

geographical context. Typical travel time to the closer of his two home parishes was, at minimum, an hour-and-a-half horseback or carriage ride. Pohick Church in Truro Parish and Fairfax Parish (later Christ Church) in Alexandria were seven and ten miles from Mount Vernon respectively.

Documentation reveals that Washington attended church one to two times a month, more frequently during his presidency. He may have even gone to church more often since diaries and correspondence do not always record routine or regular events.[37] Even if he worshipped twice each month, this was an impressive and pious church attendance record considering the geography and historical context of the era. Colonel William Byrd II, for example, was regarded as religiously observant man. Even though he lived only a half mile from his church, he attended divine worship just 50 percent of the time, and only one time when his own congregational pastor was absent. Often there were too few ministers to staff Anglican churches every Sunday. In pre and post-Revolutionary Virginia, an Anglican preacher occupied the pulpit approximately once a month. With a low supply of pastors, parishioners often settled for subpar preachers when they did hold worship services. Turnout suffered when a congregation's pastor did not preside over the divine service. In the early 1780s, Pohick Church was primarily manned by itinerant preachers. Christ Church, even in the 1790s, held services only once a month.[38] There were many Sundays, in many perishes across the Virginia landscape, where divine worship did not or could not take place due to the shortage of preachers. When this occurred, Washington stayed home and read sermons, written and sent to him by primarily Anglican ministers, to his family at Mount Vernon.[39]

Long trips over wilderness lands, poor roads, wintery or hot and humid weather, sweltering or unheated churches (for fear of fire in a wooden church), and disease outbreaks were other formidable impediments which might explain why Washington attended church only twice a month in Virginia as opposed to his more frequent church attendance when his military and presidential duties placed him in or next to the urbanized centers of New York and Philadelphia. Saint Paul's Church (later Trinity Church) in New York and Christ Church in Philadelphia not only provided steady pulpit supply every Sunday, but better roads and shorter distances to travel which made it easier for people to attend worship services.

As America's first hero, Washington was showered with adulation and veneration wherever he went. During his presidency, for example,

---

37. Thompson, *Good Providence*, 53.

38. Ibid., 53, 56–57.

39. Lillback and Newcombe, *Sacred Fire*, 259–70.

awe-struck parishioners and spectators engulfed him with his every appearance at worship. Leaving church, the President would simply nod at his admirers as they parted before his exit.[40] As he aged, and especially in retirement, one can understand how this public notoriety to behold the man would weigh and burden his psyche and physical health as well as intrude on the comfort and peaceful refreshment that divine worship might otherwise bring.

Pastors praised his faithful and reverential worship attendance. Washington's diaries show that he went to church and occasionally fasted for the remainder of the day—a commitment not performed by someone who was not serious about his faith. Sometimes he would attend two different church services on a Sunday. The pastor of Pohick Church, Lee Massey, whom Washington had urged to enter the ministry after an unsuccessful and short-lived law career, reported that Washington was one of the most faithful and generous of his parishioners, a leader in the church for years. The tall Virginian even bowed his head at the mention of Jesus in the apostolic creeds.[41]

Anglican worship services were reverential and non-charismatic. In almost every worship service, liturgy was read from the *Book of Common Prayer*. Public and corporate confession of sins preceded an absolution from the minister. After reading or singing from the Psalms, the Old and New Testament Scriptures were proclaimed and followed by responsive readings and prayer. Then the Nicene or Apostles Creed was recited. The sermon usually came at the end of the worship service. Four times a year, the Ante-Communion would take place, which prepared attendees for the distribution of the Lord's Supper. Like most orthodox, Christian divine services, ritual and repetition not only grounded the parishioner, but divulged a dependence as well as comfort in one's Christian faith.[42]

The Sabbath was a holy day for Washington. When visitors stayed at Mount Vernon, he did not neglect worship, but brought guests with him to church. Moreover, he refrained from fox hunting, one of his favorite recreational activities, and did not receive visitors on Sundays out of respect for the Sabbath.[43] Sundays were for worship and meditation, catching up on correspondence, and spending time with family.

Not only did Washington worship faithfully, but he also served as a vestryman at two parishes—Fairfax Parish and Pohick Church—regularly

---

40. Chernow, *Washington*, 646.

41. Meade, *Old Churches*, 247; Schroeder, *Maxims of Washington*, 274–75, 297, 309.

42. Thompson, *Good Providence*, 50.

43. Meade, *Old Churches*, 248.

participating in business meetings and taking the lead in executing projects for the betterment of the congregation and church polity. An Anglican vestry was usually made up of the minister and twelve gentlemen. Some of their responsibilities included: levying taxes to pay the minister's salary, creating and executing the church budget, maintaining the church property, supplying the bread and wine for Holy Communion Sundays, and caring for the poor in the community. Each vestryman had to take an oath of allegiance and conform to the doctrine and discipline of the Church of England.

There were some ministers who did not know Washington and wanted more public signs and confessional displays of his Christian orthodoxy. Overall, however, ministers admired him for his faithfulness. Washington, in turn, greatly esteemed ministers for their vocation and friendship. He would correspond frequently with many clergymen throughout his lifetime.

Biographers have also scrutinized Washington's Holy Communion practice, or lack thereof. Anglicans of the eighteenth century generally administered and partook of Holy Communion only four times a year on "Sacrament Sundays." According to Eleanor "Nelly" Parke Custis Lewis, the General's adopted granddaughter, Washington did receive the holy sacrament prior to the Revolution. Beyond the Revolutionary era, Major Popham and General Porterfield claimed they witnessed Washington communing in New York City when he was President. Elizabeth Hamilton, wife of Alexander, told her family that she communed with President Washington on the day of his first inauguration. Bishop William Meade and Reverend E. C. M'Guire reported on Washington's communing practices too. In addition to these testimonies, oral histories suggest the General communed in a Presbyterian Church in Morristown, New Jersey during the Revolution as well as at a German Reformed church in Germantown, outside of Philadelphia, during his presidency. Almost no one would expect an Anglican to commune at a Presbyterian table due to tensions dating from the English Civil War of the 1640s—where Puritan Congregationalists and Presbyterians fought against Anglican Loyalists. If Washington did commune as such, there must have been something there to make the story not only plausible but credible and noteworthy.[44]

Reverend Dr. James Abercrombie chastised Washington from the pulpit during one of his sermons, at Christ Church in Philadelphia, for not taking communion and setting a bad example for other parishioners. Washington apparently never attended the church on a communion Sunday again. Abercrombie's reproof might have been repayment for the President's decision to deny him the Treasurer of the Mint post in 1792, before he

44. Meade, *Old Churches*, 254; Lillback and Newcombe, *Sacred Fire*, 405–36.

became a priest.[45] Washington reportedly later told an unnamed senator that that if he communed he would be accused of zealotry and misusing his influence and power as a government official.[46]

The Abercrombie incident may explain why Washington might not have attended church every Sunday, especially communion Sundays. Moreover, participating in Holy Communion presented a delicate situation for an Anglican Christian and patriot leader. Perhaps the hero of the American Revolution made a political calculation that he should abstain from communing with the head of the Anglican Church, the King of England.[47] Washington may also have refrained from communing regularly because he felt unworthy to receive it, either as a general who contributed to bloodshed in war or as a slaveholder. His unwillingness to indulge in hypocrisy indicates the worldview and acknowledgement of a Christian sinner, not a deist.

Washington had a deep reverence and appreciation for communion, and he supplied wine to Pohick Church for the sacrament. He gave money, along with his friend George William Fairfax, for the crimson hangings, as well as a gold leaf for gilding religious inscriptions, on the altarpiece when the new church was built at Pohick in the early 1770s. He purchased the pew closest to the communion table. Moreover, he referred to the "cup of blessing" in public and private writings, a phrase revealing his impressive comprehension and veneration of Scripture. In short, the preponderance of evidence suggests that Washington communed as an Anglican throughout most of life, though he may have done so less frequently during and after the Revolutionary War.

As opposed to his participation in Holy Communion, there is little doubt about Washington's prayer life. Numerous accounts exist—from family members, military associates, and other contemporaries—of Washington's active prayer life—both in public and private. Unfortunately, many officers, such as General David Cobb and General Robert Porterfield, who served with him during the Revolutionary War, have had their statements discounted in the historical record because they told, rather than wrote, their testimonies of their General's prayer habits.[48]

Family members testified about the General's prayer life in detailed accounts. Nelly Parke Custis Lewis, Martha's youngest granddaughter, said that he faithfully prayed in the evening and before breakfast. During the Revolutionary War, Major George Lewis, Washington's nephew, had to wait

---

45. Saint Peter's Church, "Venerable Dr. Abercrombie," 1.

46. Thompson, *Good Providence,* 78–79.

47. Cousins, *In God,* 47; Lillback and Newcombe, *Sacred Fire,* 425.

48. Thompson, *Good Providence,* 92–97.

to deliver messages to the General until he was done praying. His younger brother, Robert Lewis, lived a short time with Washington's family during his presidency and inadvertently walked in on the President while he was praying and studying the Bible. Hannah Bushrod Washington, the General's sister-in-law, witnessed his tearful emotion and ardent prayers at the bedside of her aunt and his stepdaughter, Martha Parke Custis, as the young woman neared death in 1773.[49]

In numerous letters and diary entries, he wrote about prayer and offered up many prayers for friends and associates. His writings contain over one hundred written prayers. In addition, he often took part in fasts (fasting usually included refraining from food and praying to God for heavenly strength). Staff members—who worked under Washington as aide-de-camps, cabinet members, officers, etc.—knew that their Commander in Chief expected prayers to be included in his correspondence. During the French and Indian War, and especially later during the Revolutionary War, officers frequently witnessed the General on his knees in private prayer. In 1771, he ordered from London "A Prayr Book with the new Version of Psalms and good plain type, covd. With red Moroco, to be 7 Inchs. long 4 ½ wide, and as thin as possible for the greatr. Ease of caryg in the Pocket."[50] The pocket-sized 1662 *Book of Common Prayer* taught prayer and worship from a traditional Anglican and orthodox Christian perspective. This book was used by the parish priest or liturgical lay-reader every Sunday in Anglican worship services, and the one Washington read from when conducting British General Edward Braddock's torch-lit funeral service after the disaster at Monongahela during the French and Indian War. Thomas Comber's *Short Discourses upon the Whole Common-Prayer; Designed to Inform the Judgment, and Excite the Devotion of Such as Daily Use the Same* and Sir Matthew Hale's *Contemplations Moral and Divine*, books read by Washington since his youth, only served to nurture and deepen the personal relationship between Washington and God over time. Visitors of Mount Vernon commented on the General's prayer life before and after meals and at the beginning of his day.[51]

Just as Washington's prayer life reveals an intimate relationship with God, so too does his many different designations for the Almighty. Washington used over one hundred remarkably diverse titles for God throughout

---

49. Ibid.

50. Washington Invoice to Robert Cary & Company, July 18, 1771, in Fitzpatrick, *Writings of Washington*, 3:61.

51. M'Guire, *Religious Opinions*, 137, 156, 168; Thompson, *Good Providence*, 91–100; Novak and Novak, *Washington's God*, 143–74; Lillback and Newcombe, *Sacred Fire*, 351–76.

his correspondence, almost as if he did not want to reprise the same title a second time. Honorific titles for God, such as "the Great Author of the Universe" or the "Great Disposer of Human Events," exhibit a depth of theological vocabulary and articulation as well as a tender understanding of God.

Furthermore, the different titles he used for God were in vogue among orthodox Christian ministers of his day. Many eighteenth-century Christian ministers referred to God as the "Allwise Disposer of Events," the "Governor of the Universe," "Providence," and other names. Dr. John Witherspoon, for example, a devout Presbyterian and President of the College of New Jersey (later known as Princeton University), once preached a sermon entitled "The Dominion of Providence over the Passions of Men." In the sermon, Witherspoon thanked "God, the Supreme Disposer of events, for His interposition on our behalf . . . ."[52] Reverend Samuel Miller, a Presbyterian, sent Washington a sermon in which he refers to God as "the supreme Arbiter of nations," "the grand Source," "the Deity himself," "the Sovereign Dispenser of all blessings," "the Governor of the universe," and "thou exalted Source of liberty" (Washington had this sermon bound in his sermon collection). The point is Washington spoke and wrote as other Christians did in his day. Moreover, the verbs he used to describe an active, intervening Providence are congruent with the orthodox interpretation of the Triune God—who sent his son into the world to intercede and redeem it.[53]

The charge that Washington did not refer to Jesus Christ specifically in his writings has also been misconstrued. He had, in fact, a thorough knowledge of the Bible and heard Gospel accounts of Jesus's life and words regularly in church throughout his life. That the General did not write about Jesus as a great moral teacher, even as deists like Jefferson, Madison, or Franklin did, does not indicate indifference to Christianity's essential figure any more than Washington's neglect to write about "no taxation without representation" signifies his disinterest in the tax issue during the Revolutionary period. On the contrary, when taken in the context of his lifelong adherence to the teachings of the Anglican Church, the evidence suggests that Washington was exceedingly intentional and disciplined in eschewing and refraining from using the words "Jesus" or "Christ" in his public and private correspondence and speaking.

Washington's reticence to write or use the words "Jesus" or "Christ" makes sense in proper historical context. Practicing eighteenth-century Anglicans, especially Latitudinarians, believed that Jesus was a sacred name and should be referenced only in worship settings. Christians, after all, were

52. Lillback and Newcombe, *Sacred Fire*, 593.

53. Ibid., 40–41.

commanded not to take or use God's name in vain. A book Washington studied voraciously during his childhood, the *Rules of Civility,* reinforced this understanding. Rule 108 insisted that, "When you speak of God or his attributes, let it be seriously and with reverence." Outside of worship, Washington refrained from speaking the holy name of Jesus Christ. This was a display, not of rejection, but reverence to the Savior and devotion to Anglican teachings. A similar comparison is how observant Jews have historically eschewed speaking the name Jehovah (YHWH). Latitudinarians believed deists, like Paine, profaned Jesus's name by using it often and irreverently.

The alleged silence about Jesus Christ does not disprove Washington's Christian faith nor augment the argument for the deist Washington. His diaries, for example, have not a word about the historic debates at the Constitutional Convention in 1787, and yet we know he was there.[54]

If Washington's silence on Jesus makes him a deist, does his silence on deism make him a Christian? Despite the fact that most of his contemporaries believed him to be a Christian, one of the main assertions for the deist Washington is based on silence. Yet the argument from silence cuts both ways, for there is no evidence that he was a deist in any his writings or public utterances. Deists such as Paine or Jefferson, for example, referred to Jesus as a great moral leader, teacher, or virtuous man. Nowhere in Washington's letters does any kind of humanistic reference to Jesus and his teachings, direct or implied, exist.[55]

Of course, Washington spoke of Jesus, as well as Jesus's own words in the Scriptures, every Sunday he attended divine worship. Anglican churches, including those Washington attended, made use of "reredos" during the worship service. Reredos were large wall plaques located behind the altar. These plaques were usually fastened to three panels—one each for the Apostles's Creed, Lord's Prayer, and the Ten Commandments. Since books and printing were expensive in colonial America, reredos saved unneeded budgetary expenditures for congregations while providing the essentials of the Children's Catechism and Anglican *Book of Common Prayer* for the entire congregation. Every Sunday Washington worshipped in an Anglican church, he recited the words on the reredos—which spoke of the Triune God, forgiveness of sins, and resurrection of Christ.[56]

Furthermore, Washington *did,* in fact, make reference to Jesus Christ in his writings. There are a few instances where he literally spelled out the name of Jesus. More often, however, within the Anglican tradition of

54. Ibid., 55.

55. Eidsmoe, *Christianity and the Constitution,* 138.

56. Lillback and Newcombe, *Sacred Fire,* 44–47.

eschewing Jesus's name, Washington instead referred to the Savior by various names. He frequently used "our gracious Redeemer," "Divine Author of our blessed Religion," "the great Lord and Ruler of Nations," "the Judge of the Hearts of Men," "Divine Author of Life and felicity," "the Lord, and Giver of all victory, to pardon our manifold sins," "the Lord, and Giver of Victory," "Giver of Life," and other names to denote Christ. In addition, he made repeated references to the Gospel message and the Bible as a whole.

Numerous contemporaries, close friends, and associates believed that Washington was a devout Christian. Clergy of all Christian denominations called him their friend. His family professed his Christian faith. Even his political adversaries acknowledged Washington's obvious religious beliefs. For example, Reverend Jonathan Boucher—minister of the Episcopal Church at Annapolis, Maryland and private tutor to John Parke Custis, son of Martha Washington, during the 1760s and early 1770s—opposed colonial independence and returned to England in 1775. He knew Washington intimately and wrote of the General in 1776: "In his moral character he is regular, temperate, strictly just and honest . . . and I always thought, religious; having heretofore been pretty constant an even exemplary in his attendance on public worship in the Church of England."[57]

Not only did Washington write as a Christian, he behaved and acted like one. The generosity he exhibited toward relatives, friends, and neighbors was awe-inspiring. When the downtrodden came to Mount Vernon looking for help, servants and workers were instructed to help and give aid. Washington not only gave financially and generously to his local churches for construction projects and operational expenditures, he also supported numerous other charities including those which were created to proselytize and spread Christianity among Native American groups. Furthermore, he was especially magnanimous and compassionate in supporting widows and children of families who lost their fathers.

After his death, hundreds of eulogies given in his honor illuminated Washington's Christian faith and life of service. "He had a deep sense of religion impressed on his heart—the true foundation-stone of all moral virtues," according to Jonathan Mitchell Sewall. "He was a firm believer in the Christian religion," and made sure that "no secular business could be transacted with him on the day set apart by Christians for the worship of Deity." Washington was "a member of the Episcopal Church," and "constantly attended public worship of God on the Lord's Day" and communed regularly. "For my own part, I trust I shall never lose the impression made on my own mind beholding in this house of prayer the venerable hero . . . bending in

---

57. Johnson, *Washington: Christian*, 256–57.

humble adoration to the God of armies, and great Captain of our Salvation." Sewall added: "Let the deist reflect on this, and remember that Washington, the savior of his country, did not disdain to acknowledge and adore a great Saviour, whom deists and infidels affect to slight and despise."[58]

Throughout his earthly life, Washington received the "applause of mankind," and a "wealth of honours," orated Timothy Bigelow, but "he never forgot that he was mortal, and destined to another state of existence. *In him religion was a steady principle of action.*" His faith "taught him fortitude in danger, patience under misfortunes . . . and even humility in the full swell of prosperity."[59]

Captain Josiah Dunham, of the 16th U.S. Regiment of the Continental Army, noted Washington's embrace of "the tenants of the Episcopal Church" and "every denomination of the followers of Jesus."[60] Major William Jackson, aid-de-camp to General Washington, praised the "inestimable character" of his former commander who "blended the glories of the Hero and the Statesman" and mingled them with "the milder radiance of religion and morals . . . ."[61] Washington's virtues, according to Reverend John Thornton Kirkland, "were crowned with piety" and devoutness. "To Christian institutions he gave the countenance of his example."[62] The Honorable David Ramsey commented on Washington's steady worship attendance, support of clergy, and "respectful mention of Providence" in all his public acts. "He was far from being one of those minute philosophers who believe that 'death is an eternal sleep,' or, of those, who, trusting to the sufficiency of human reason, discard the light of divine revelation."[63] Throughout his life, "what Heaven had made necessary, Washington complied with cheerfully . . . with resignation and tranquility in the hands of the Father of mercies, to whom he had ever been accustomed to look up," explained Dr. Joseph Blyth. The Virginian "had walked piously before his God."[64]

Washington had been a warrior, statesman, and friend of the people his entire life, but also an "advocate of religion," according to John Davis. His character had been influenced "by the more permanent and operative principle of religion: by firm and active persuasion of an All-Seeing,

58. Ibid., 251–52.

59. M'Guire, *Religious Opinions*, 368.

60. Johnson, *Washington: Christian*, 253.

61. M'Guire, *Religious Opinions*, 391.

62. Johnson, *Washington: Christian*, 252–53.

63. Ibid., 253–54.

64. M'Guire, *Religious Opinions*, 382–83.

All-Powerful Deity."[65] Washington lived "impressed with a sense that he derived all from God, and that all should be devoted to his service," ruminated William Linn.[66] Timothy Dwight, President of Yale College, acclaimed Washington's "exemplary and edifying attention to public worship, and his constancy in secret devotion," prayer, and Bible study. "I shall only add that if he was not a Christian, he was more like one than any man of the same description whose life has been hithero recorded."[67]

During his long career of public service, Washington taught the nation "that the foundation of national policy can be laid only in the pure and immutable principles of private morality," insisted Jeremiah Smith. Moreover, the Virginian faithfully practiced the Christian faith and "publicly professed the religion in which he was educated . . . his life affords the best evidence of the purity of his principles, and the sincerity of his faith." Smith respected the "genuine mildness" of Washington's religious worldview and disposition. "He was neither ostentatious, nor ashamed of his Christian profession. He pursued in this, as in everything else, the happy mean between the extremes of levity and gloominess, indifference and austerity. His religion became him."[68]

Contemporaries did not come forth to dispute these portrayals and testimonials. The evidence had been clear and conspicuous. America's Indispensable Man, as labeled by one biographer,[69] consistently lived and led as a Christian throughout his sixty-seven year life. His religious faith grounded him daily, informed his worldview, and shaped his character. Moreover, his relationship with God inspired an inner confidence that propelled him to make courageous decisions, execute and produce lasting achievements, and establish an exemplary legacy for the country he so dearly loved. Washington's religiously inspired and character-driven life then is worth examining from beginning to end and for all times.

---

65. Ibid., 369–70.

66. Ibid., 373.

67. Johnson, *Washington: Christian*, 255.

68. Ibid., 254–55.

69. Flexner, *Indispensable Man*.

PART I

Young Virginian

1

Upbringing

According to the family Bible at Mount Vernon, George Washington was born to Augustine Washington and Mary Ball, on February 11, 1732, on his father's estate near Pope's Creek in Westmoreland County, Virginia. (The new Gregorian calendar, which replaced the old style, or Julian calendar, was implemented in the mid-eighteenth century and moved the birth date to February 22, 1732.) Two months after birth, Augustine and Mary, both faithful followers of the Church of England, had their eldest son baptized, on April 5, 1732, by Reverend Roderick McCullough at the family home.[1]

The Washington Family Bible notes that George Washington was born "about 10 in the morning" on February 11, 1731/32, according to the Julian calendar then in use. When England adopted the Gregorian calendar in 1752 (which we still observe today), this date changed to February 22, 1732—the day Washington considered to be his birthday. (Courtesy of the Mount Vernon Ladies' Association)

1. McDowell, *Apostle of Liberty,* 34.

Young George descended from a long history of dedicated churchmen. His great-great-grandfather, Reverend Lawrence Washington, was a clergyman in the Church of England. His great-grandfather, John Washington, settled in Virginia in 1657 and founded "The Parish of Washington" on his own estate in Prince William County. In his will, John Washington not only designated an erection of a tablet of the Ten Commandments and King's Arms to the church, but also provided a Christian testimony on the full remission and forgiveness of sins found only in Jesus Christ. John's son, Augustine, George's father, similarly expressed his Christian faith in his will. An active member in parish affairs, Augustine Washington became a vestryman in Truro Parish when young George was just three years old. On his mother's side, Grandfather Ball was also an Anglican vestryman, while George's uncle, Joseph, took an active lead in educating young men for the ministry.[2]

When George was three years old, the family moved to the Little Hunting Creek region of their lands and settled in Prince William County. In 1739, Augustine Washington gave the Little Hunting Creek plantation (which would eventually be named Mount Vernon) to his oldest son and George's older half-brother, Lawrence, and moved the rest of the family yet again to another plantation, called Ferry's Farm, near Fredericksburg, Virginia. Life on the Rappahannock River was tragically interrupted for eleven-year old George, however, when his father suddenly died after catching a cold riding his horse in a severe storm. George would, eerily, die in a similar manner many years later.

The legacy and impact that Augustine Washington left on his son is difficult to definitively ascertain due to limited historical sources. Many stories about Augustine and George have been relegated to legend because they cannot be confirmed by multiple sources, and also because they are told in Parson Weems's hagiographic *The Life of Washington*. One such account has Augustine encouraging George to share an apple with his siblings insisting that God would bless his generosity with an overabundance of fruit in the future. Observing a bountiful apple orchard the following fall, young George learns the lesson of Christian generosity. In another well-known story, George cannot tell a lie and confesses to cutting down his father's favorite cherry tree. His forthrightness earns the commendation of his father. Yet another episode has father tracing his son's name with a stick in a garden and sowing seeds in the lettered furrows. A few weeks later, when the cabbage seeds sprout and the growth spells out GEORGE WASHINGTON, young George comprehends the creative power of the Grand Designer, how

2. Ambler, *Washington and the West*, 6; Johnson, *Washington: Christian*, 16–17.

God makes his plans and purposes manifest in the lives of his followers, and that everything he possessed is a gift from God.[3]

John C. McRae's picture highlights Parson Weems's famous and legendary story. Washington's father, Augustine, died when young George was only eleven. However, while the cherry tree story is questionable, the influence Augustine had on his son—from the physical genes to his religious upbringing—was significant. (Courtesy of the Mount Vernon Ladies' Association)

We do know that Augustine was extremely active in local affairs and firmly established his family as one of good standing in the community. A successful entrepreneur, he acquired extensive land holdings and invested in enterprises such as the Quaker-initiated Principio Iron Company.[4] Augustine was also an active church vestryman who made sure his family worshipped regularly.

Although the evidence is limited, the relationship between father and son seems to have been a close one. After Augustine's sudden death, George received his father's prayer book, *Short Discourses upon the Whole Common-Prayer. Designed to Inform the Judgment, and Excite the Devotion of Such as Daily Use the Same*, which was written by Reverend Thomas Comber in 1712. Washington not only signed his name in this book, at the age of thirteen, but he also carefully inscribed his father's name nine times as well as many of his father's monograms. Augustine and Mary both frequently

3. Thompson, *Good Providence*, 19.
4. Jones, *Washington*, 1.

assigned their son reading lessons on the Lord's Prayer, the church cat-echism, and other religious topics.[5]

Although his father's name is mentioned only twice in all of his corre-spondence, George inherited much more from his father than a magnificent physique.[6] The hard-working, community-minded, entrepreneurial spirit that his father possessed was evident and prominently exhibited in George's life. So, too, was the heritage and importance of faithful church attendance and an active parish life.

While the record on Washington's father is limited, we know more about his mother, Mary Ball Washington. Mary was wed to Augustine at the age of twenty-three, which was old for colonial times and may indicate a feisty and independent personality.[7] George was the first of six children she gave birth to in seven short years. Compensating as an overwhelmed mother of six young children, Mary brought order and energetic oversight to her own home. She also had a temper[8]—a personality trait that would be suitably displayed throughout her eldest son's life too.

As years would pass, and as her son's stature increased, Mary would feel neglected and grow jealous of her most famous child. George was popular amongst his countrymen and seemed primarily dedicated to their well-being instead of hers. Moreover, there are indications Mary had Loy-alist leanings and may have suffered from an early onset of dementia by the end of the Revolutionary War. In 1781, she petitioned Congress for an emergency pension implicitly suggesting that no one was tending to her needs. Whether she meant to embarrass her son or not, George confided a few years later that his mother "still continues to give me pain."[9] Yet George devotedly served his mother throughout the duration of her life. He gave her money, provided her loans even though she often reneged on payments, squired his elderly mother to the Fredericksburg ball after the American victory over the British at Yorktown, and eventually purchased a house for her in Fredericksburg, Virginia.[10]

During her childrearing years, however, Mary asserted a strong will, self-reliance, and selflessness, and George honored her as a dutiful son. When he was fourteen, she discouraged him from accepting a proffered

5. Thompson, *Good Providence*, 16–20; Eidsmoe, *Christianity and the Constitution*, 128.

6. Johnson, *Washington: Founding Father*, 6.

7. Chernow, *Washington*, 5.

8. Unger, *Unexpected Washington*, 11.

9. Washington to John Augustine Washington, January 16, 1783, in Fitzpatrick, *Writings of Washington*, 26:43.

10. Chernow, *Washington*, 396, 422–23.

midshipman's post in the Royal Navy. Despite his enthusiasm for the venture and the prestige that accompanied admission in the British navy, George responded to his mother's tender love and concern by turning down the offer to join and serve.

Whatever pain she brought to her most famous son later in life, Mary faithfully taught and successfully passed on the Anglican faith to her children. Daily, she would go to the same secluded area—a spot occupied by shade trees and rocks—for private devotion and prayer. She persistently drilled her children in the catechism of the Anglican faith. On Sunday evenings, she would read aloud sermons from the Bishop of Exeter, provide biblical illustrations, or recite the Bible to her loved ones. A book of sermons, published in 1717, called *The Sufficiency of a Standing Revelation in General, and the Scripture Revelation in Particular . . . In Eight Sermons, Preached in the Cathedral Church of St. Paul, London*, by Offspring Blackhall, was put in George's possession during his youth. He signed the sermon series twice at the age of eight or nine. In addition, Matthew Hale's *Contemplations: Moral and Divine*, which Mary read almost daily to her children, was found well-worn and much-marked in Washington's personal library after his death. Mary gave the book to her son as a memorial of her love and bears her written inscription. The lessons advocated on stewardship and humility in Hale's book are especially noteworthy because these traits became prominent and salient in George's adult life. Mary did not hesitate to implore the aid of Jesus in the raising of her children, and friends and associates considered her a dedicated Christian. In her will, she testified to the remission of sins "through the merits & mediation of Jesus Christ, the Saviour of mankind."[11]

One legendary story portrays George's attempt to ride an untamed Arabian colt. After he finally mounts the horse, a terrible struggle ensues in which the horse falls, breaks a blood vessel in the neck, and tragically dies. When George confesses to the entire episode, Mary expresses joy and affirmation of her son's truth-telling.[12]

Despite her petulance and irritability as she aged, George never forgot his mother's love for him and the Christian upbringing she provided. While away for long durations during the Revolutionary War, Washington had his good friend, Marquis de Lafayette, call and check on his mother. After the war, George rode out to visit her frequently, even on the coldest of days. He urged her to move in with him or one of her children. In his letters to her, he

---

11. Thompson, *Good Providence,* 19–20; M'Guire, *Religious Opinions,* 47–48, 54, 68; Eidsmoe, *Christianity and the Constitution,* 129; Ambler, *Washington and the West,* 4–5.

12. M'Guire, *Religious Opinions,* 37–39.

called her "My Revered Mother" or "Honored Madam."[13] That he modeled and embraced her practice of reading sermons, the *Book of Common Prayer*, and devotional works to his own family at Mount Vernon, just as she had done for him and his siblings, reveals the religious legacy she cultivated and the considerable impact she had on her son's biblical worldview and faith development.

While Washington's mother provided stability and a religious anchor in the household, George became especially close to his older half-brother, Lawrence, especially after his father's untimely death. In many ways, Lawrence had the biggest impact on his little brother's upbringing and ascension in colonial Virginia. Lawrence not only took George into his home, but also looked after his social development and education. He taught him the life of a plantation gentleman and how to be a successful businessman. Lawrence's British schooling, commission in the king's army, and estate—named after the British commander he served under in the Cartagena campaign of 1740–1741 (Mount Vernon)—greatly impressed the younger Washington. Since his father's death stymied the opportunity for a British education, George's lack of a formal education was more than offset by the opportunity to spend much of his teenage years at Mount Vernon under the guidance and tutelage of his polished, older half-brother. He became George's idol.[14]

Lawrence's marriage to Anne Fairfax, daughter of Colonel William Fairfax, paved a road of promise and future success for George. The prestigious and extremely wealthy Fairfax family owned practically all of northern Virginia. When Lawrence and Anne lost newborns in 1744, 1747, and 1748, George became their de facto son, the only child the couple would ever raise. The tutoring and gentlemanly grooming Lawrence provided his younger step-brother only intensified as time passed, and Anne taught George to love music and dance.[15]

Lawrence and George took a trip together to Barbados, in 1751, hoping that the tropical climate might help Lawrence fight the tuberculosis that was ravaging his body. Instead, George contracted smallpox—a blessing in disguise since inoculation against smallpox would keep him healthy and immune from the malady during the Revolutionary War. While George would survive the bout with his deadly disease, Lawrence died a year later.

With Lawrence's passing, George lost a mentor, brother, close friend, and hero. He refused to rename Mount Vernon when he rented it from Lawrence's widow, Anne, in 1754. The residence became George's outright

13. Lillback and Newcombe, *Sacred Fire*, 105, 245–46.

14. Higginbotham, "Revolutionary Asceticism," 146.

15. Unger, *Unexpected Washington*, 14.

property in 1761, according to the dictates of Augustine's will, after Anne Fairfax Washington died.[16]

At twenty-one years of age, George had lost his father and older half-brother. As a result of Lawrence's death, he acquired Mount Vernon as well as other surrounding plantations and considerable assets. By Virginia gentry standards, the inheritance was not magnificent but enough that he would now be considered a planter of significance.

The connection with the Fairfax family provided a rich social life and a unique opportunity for Washington to associate with the upper echelon of Virginian society. George assumed Lawrence's duties as a director of the Ohio Company. Moreover, in a gesture of great fondness for Lawrence and the entire Washington family, Colonel William Fairfax lobbied Virginia Governor, Robert Dinwiddie, to appoint George to succeed Lawrence as the colony's adjutant general, which had the responsibility for recruiting and training the state's militia. The assignment would eventually catapult Washington onto the world stage and on toward a historic military career.

The Fairfaxes were devout, practicing Anglican Christians whom George often accompanied to church.[17] George William Fairfax, the oldest of the children who befriended Washington, served as a vestryman and church warden at Pohick Church from 1757 to 1773. Even after he moved to England, he stayed in touch with Washington until he died in 1787. Shortly after his death, George received a letter from an Englishman who had witnessed Fairfax's "Firmness of Mind & christian patience with which he sustained his Malady . . . to the last." Fairfax's Christian faith should "alleviate their sorrow for his Departure."[18]

Reverend Bryan Fairfax, youngest of the Fairfaxes, was pastor of Christ Church in Alexandria of which Washington was a member. One of his sermons focused exclusively on the doctrine of eternal life by faith in Christ's redeeming work on the cross.[19] A neighbor, confidant, and frequent foxhunting comrade (but not on the Sabbath), Bryan and George remained life-long friends even after Lord Fairfax chose the Loyalist side during the Revolutionary War. Their correspondence reveals an intimate and considerate relationship. Washington asked Reverend Fairfax to officiate his nephew's (George Augustine Washington) funeral in April of 1793 and willed him a three volume Bible.

---

16. Jones, *Washington*, 8.

17. Meade, *Old Churches*, 106, 109, 245–46; Thompson, *Good Providence*, 171–73.

18. Samuel Athawes to Washington, July 20, 1787, in Abbot and Twohig, *Washington: Confederation Series*, 5:264.

19. Lillback and Newcombe, *Sacred Fire*, 835–43.

Washington had a special relationship with the Fairfax family and owed much of his early success
in Virginia society to their benevolence. He and Reverend Bryan Fairfax loved to foxhunt together
and retained a close, lifelong friendship. Fairfax family members were devout Anglican Christians.
Lithograph by G. P. Putnam & Co. publishers. (Courtesy of the Mount Vernon Ladies' Association)

The Fairfaxes successfully encouraged Washington to become a surveyor when he was only sixteen years old. Accompanying George William
Fairfax and a surveying party in 1748, young Washington explored the
Shenandoah Valley of Virginia and was first exposed to the colonial frontier.
By the time he was eighteen, he earned enough money to purchase 1,200
acres of land. At his death, Washington would own more than 45,000 acres
of carefully selected land in Kentucky, Virginia, Pennsylvania, and Ohio.[20] In
1749, Washington was appointed a public surveyor, a state job that required
an oath to the Church of England. Pay was good with much Fairfax land to
survey and few surveyors in existence. For almost three years, Washington
made a profitable living thanks to the Fairfax connection.

On the very first page of his surveyor's notebook, Washington wrote
an interesting biblical reference: "If you can't find it in the book of Ezekiel,
look for it in Israel." The citation makes sense only to those with an intimate
familiarity of the Bible. According to the book of Joshua (chapters 13–21),
the nation of Israel had been marked out with specific borders, as a surveyor
would surely appreciate. Moreover, the book of Ezekiel (chapters 40–48)
concludes with a remarkable survey having been implemented to establish

20. Abbot, "George Washington," 200.

the boundaries of New Jerusalem. Just as those biblical lands needed to be plotted and organized, Washington found a similar calling in surveying the frontier of the New World.[21]

While Washington's informal education—thanks to the special attention received from Lawrence and the Fairfax family—served and prepared him for life as a plantation gentleman, his formal education should not be overlooked or disdained. Some of the details of Washington's early formal education are vague—history records unnamed tutors or teachers of nearby parishes. Nevertheless, he was educated in the context, and under the influence, of the Anglican Church.

Washington was a student at Reverend James Marye's church school in Fredericksburg—which started in 1740. Marye, a French Jesuit turned Anglican priest and rector of St. George's Church in Fredericksburg, was known for his evangelical views and earnest piety. Tradition holds that Master Hobby, sometimes identified as William Groves, who served as a parish sexton of a nearby field school in Fredericksburg, also taught Washington and was highly regarded by his pupils. Much later, when he was an old man, Hobby allegedly boasted that he was the one who helped propel the Virginian to glory and fame. Whoever directly instructed young Washington, the evidence shows he learned in a setting and environment that continually taught the Apostles's Creed, the Ten Commandments, the doctrine of the Trinity, the Lord's Prayer, and the sacraments according to the tenets of the Anglican Church.[22]

When he was twelve, one of Washington's homework assignments was to write a will (frontiersmen needed experience writing legal documents in case a lawyer could not be found). His "Form of a Short Will" not only exhibited a moving writing style but a boy who understood the core teaching of orthodox Christianity. On his assignment, he "Principally and first of all" recommended his "Soul to God Who gave it hoping for salvation in and through the merits and mediation of Jesus Christ . . . ."[23]

An inquisitive, diligent student whose passion for active sports and military discipline were conspicuously displayed in interactions with schoolmates, Washington formed friends into companies, marched, and fought make-believe battles, always placing himself as the commander. Yet he also played the peacemaker and arbiter of his classmates' conflicts and struggles.[24] His running, jumping, wrestling, throwing, and other feats of

21. Lillback and Newcombe, *Sacred Fire,* 108–09.

22. Ibid., 115–17.

23. Ibid., 128.

24. Sparks, *Life of Washington,* 5–6.

sport impressed and foreshadowed the striking athleticism and physical appearance peers and contemporaries would remark upon later in his life. As an adult, he would demonstrate considerable skill playing horseshoes, cracking walnuts between thumb and forefinger with his massive hands, and becoming one of America's greatest horsemen of the age.

Already showing leadership skills at a young age, young George made the most of his limited formal schooling. Engraved by John Dainty. (Courtesy of the Mount Vernon Ladies' Association)

Washington's informal and formal education revolved around books. Agriculture, military manuals, and biographies of military leaders were prominent topics of interest, but so was religion. His library was filled with religious books and sermons, which he read from youth until the day he died. A tear-soaked *Short Discourses upon the Whole Common-Prayer,* designed to teach a person how to use the *Book of Common Prayer* and which included one part of the earliest surviving signatures of the founder (he was thirteen years old at the time), was discovered in his library after his earthly passing. So, too, was a publication of a series of sermons, entitled *The Sufficiency of a Standing Revelation,* and a school book, *The Travels of Cyrus,* both of which upheld the revelation and inerrancy of Scripture while refuting deism and atheism. A "Christmas Poem"—which articulated historic Christian teachings concerning Christ's death and resurrection, as well as the human and divine nature of Christ—is also found in Washington's handwriting. He may have copied the orthodox Christian poem from the February 1743 issue of *Gentleman's Magazine*. Other textbooks found in his library indicate that his Christian tutors provided a thorough and well-rounded Christian education. By the time of his death, Washington's personal library consisted of nearly 750 books, almost every one of which he had read. While he had less formal education than other founding fathers such as Franklin, Jefferson, and Madison, Washington was self-motivated and one of the most completely self-made heroes America has ever had.[25]

The *Rules of Civility and Decent Behavior in Company and Conversation*, a collection of 110 maxims of table manners and rules for conversation, written by Jesuit scholars in 1595, also made a substantial impression on Washington. The maxims were taught in his first year of study under Reverend James Marye. Washington copied the maxims from a London magazine. Some of the dictums promote signature leadership qualities, habits, and biblical precepts that would come to characterize the man: carry a serious countenance for serious matters; be conscientious; respect others; make actions speak louder than words; lead by example; think before you speak; and speak of God only with earnest reverence.[26] The *Rules of Civility* implicitly imparted that leaders were always on stage and, therefore, must be conscientious and intentional about acting their part appropriately.

The lessons taught in the *Rules of Civility* melded nicely with his Latitudinarian approach to the Christian faith. He never spoke or wrote about God irreverently. In his correspondence and interactions with others, he was careful not to offend. Instead, whether he was writing or speaking to someone, he shaped his remarks to be winsome and agreeable. Benjamin Rush once noted that Washington copied a simple letter two or three times even after he made just one mistake. He wanted things just right and harmonious. He listened more than he spoke, and let his outward actions exhibit his inner convictions. A leader on a stage, he was cognizant and sensitive how his words and actions would affect the feelings of others.[27]

By the time he turned twenty-one, Washington had learned much about his family's Anglican heritage and the life expected of a disinterested, Virginia planter. Physically, he stood six feet, three and a half inches—tall by contemporary standards. Men and women both admired his physique. Jefferson said that his physical stature was "fine" and "exactly what one

25. Lillback and Newcombe, *Sacred Fire*, 118–121; Johnson, *Washington: Founding Father*, 8; Smith, *Patriarch*, 6.

26. Ellis, *His Excellency*, 9; Connell, *Faith*, 7–30; Smith, *Patriarch*, 6; Lillback and Newcombe, *Sacred Fire*, 122–25.

27. Wood, *Radicalism*, 191; Flexner, *Washington*, 1:23.

would wish, his deportment easy, erect and noble." Washington was the "best horseman of his age, and the most graceful figure that could be seen on horseback."[28] A superb athlete and extraordinary graceful dancer, Washington's physicality, if not his public speaking, would always be a part of his allure and leadership charisma.[29]

In addition to the physical, he had also grown intellectually and spiritually. Born into a religious, Anglican family, he endured his father and brother's tragic deaths while reaping the benefits of their landed fortunes, social connections, and religious heritage. The education he received from Anglican clergymen, tutors, and family members, as well as his own self-study of the Bible and other religious works, nurtured his faith and confidence while providing a sound foundation for his worldview. He would learn to lean on his faith and his God in the upcoming frontier adventures and impending clash with France.

---

28. Peterson, *Jefferson: Writings*, 1319.

29. Wood, *Revolutionary Characters*, 33; Henriques, *Realistic Visionary*, 15.

2

Frontier Foundations

Even though he had risen in Virginian society, Washington remained a highly restless, ambitious young man. Like most Virginian plantation owners, he wanted to expand his land holdings and increase his wealth. No doubt the loss of his father, Augustine, and older step-brother, Lawrence, as well as the "love and applause of Country,"[1] motivated him to make a name for himself.

While other contemporaries and founding fathers, such as Madison, Jefferson, Hamilton, went to college during their late teens and early twenties, Washington went to war. In 1753, the French had pushed south from Lake Erie toward the Forks of the Ohio River Valley (the confluence of the Allegheny, Monongahela, and Ohio Rivers and the site of present-day Pittsburgh). In yet another power struggle for New World supremacy, both France and Great Britain claimed areas of Virginia and Pennsylvania as their own.

Governor Dinwiddie dispatched Major Washington to the Ohio country to deliver a warning to French encroachers and to retrieve a scouting report of the situation. The trip to Fort Le Boeuf, near Lake Erie, was risky and dangerous. Washington braved unbearably cold temperatures, untracked forests, and fickle Indian allies. He almost died during two separate incidents—first when he survived an assassination attempt by an Indian guide and, second, when his raft capsized into the icy Allegheny River.

The French were polite but refused to obey the British request to leave the territory. Washington returned to Dinwiddie with valuable information on the French expedition. He also reported that new Native American

---

1. Washington to Adam Stephen, May 18, 1756, in Abbot and Twohig, *Washington: Colonial Series,* 3:158.

tribes would support England in the impending conflict. Washington published a journal on his mission and received considerable commendation in America and Great Britain. The Virginia House of Burgesses awarded him a sizable bonus of fifty pounds in appreciation of his difficult undertaking. Washington's prominence was on the rise.

Supported by the House of Burgesses, in the spring of 1754, Dinwiddie ordered a fort to be built at the forks of the Ohio River and a military force to protect it. As lieutenant colonel of the Virginia troops, Washington seized the opportunity to advance the interests of England, Virginia, and the Ohio Company, as well as to deal a blow to the hated French and advance his own station in life. The orders for the special commission called for his 159 ill-trained, ill-equipped, unmotivated group of men to act defensively and to deter any trespassers on British lands. If resistance ensued, he was to take prisoners or kill the intruders.

On May 28, 1754, Washington and his Indian allies surrounded a French scouting party and attacked. In the subsequent conflict, the French commander, Sieur de Jumonville, was killed. Washington had "heard the bullets whistle," he later told his half-brother, John, "and, believe me, there is something charming in the sound."[2] Perhaps realizing his good fortune, Washington sounded much more humble, just a few days later, as he gave thanks and made a special point to extol "Providence"—who had sent "a Trader from Ohio to our relief" and "whose flour" provided a much needed supply in camp.[3]

However, what first looked like an audacious and courageous act was soon viewed as a strategic mistake. The French party had been on a peaceful mission and carried documents demanding that the British leave their lands without bloodshed. When these documents became public, Washington rejected the insinuation that he and his men had acted rashly, insisting that a peaceful party would not have hidden themselves or sent thirty men to deliver a peaceful missive.[4]

The Virginian's hold on military greatness went downhill quickly thereafter. Angered by the treachery of the British raiding party, the French army quickly pursued and forced the surrender of the Virginia regiment at Fort Necessity on July 3, 1754. Washington's poor planning had put his men in a deplorable military position. To make matters worse, hidden in the capitulation language was the notation that the British raiding party bore full

2. Washington to John Augustine Washington, May 31, 1754, in Fitzpatrick, *Writings of Washington*, 1:70.

3. Washington to Robert Dinwiddie, June 10, 1754, in Abbot and Twohig, *Washington: Colonial Series*, 1:131.

4. Jones, *Washington*, 11.

responsibility for the "assassination" of Jumonville, the French commander. Washington's translator thought the wording meant "death" and not "assassination." By signing the agreement, Washington inadvertently admitted to the slaying, and the French later exploited the supposed confession when they issued a statement justifying war. When Washington returned to Virginia, he discovered that Dinwiddie had divided the regiments into companies. No officer would receive a rank higher than a captain. Refusing to accept a demotion, Washington resigned his commission.

Despite the poor execution and surrender at Fort Necessity, approbation of Washington's reputation grew. He had shown initiative and inflicted casualties on the hated French. Soldiers under his command praised his courage, daring, and self-assurance in combat.[5] They believed God had selected him for military leadership and noted his scrupulous devotion to duty as well as his religious faith. During their stay at Fort Necessity, they had participated in public worship and prayer together at their commander's insistence.[6]

In the summer of 1755, Major General Edward Braddock asked the ascendant Virginian to come along as a volunteer aid on his staff, and Washington eagerly agreed. The mission was to remove the French from Fort Duquesne and prohibit their advance into the Ohio Valley. Then, disaster struck.

The massacre at the Monongahela River, on July 9th, was one of the greatest British disasters of the eighteenth century. Two-thirds of all British officers involved were killed or wounded during the rout. Washington, however, had roused himself from the sickbed (he was suffering from dysentery) and performed valiantly under extreme duress during the one-sided battle. He rallied fleeing British troops, who were not accustomed to Indian fighting, and prevented a complete annihilation. He also carried the mortally wounded General Braddock off the field. During the battle, Washington had two or three horses shot out from under him (reports vary) and received four bullet holes in his clothes, one of which pierced his hat.[7] He had miraculously survived, while most of Braddock's army, and Braddock himself, did not.

---

5. Ferling, *First of Men*, 143–44.

6. M'Guire, *Religious Opinions*, 136.

7. Henriques, *Realistic Visionary*, 9–10.

Claude Regnier's lithograph of Junius Brutus Stearn's painting depicts the slaughter of the British army while also highlighting Washington's gallantry. Washington would officiate the funeral service of General Braddock who perished in the massacre. (Courtesy of the Mount Vernon Ladies' Association)

Before the British began their withdrawal, Washington assumed the role of chaplain in presiding over Braddock's funeral by torchlight. Reading prayers and Scripture passages, including references to John 11:25–26 and Job 19:25–27, from the Anglican *Book of Common Prayer*, Washington's spoken words highlighted the atonement found in Jesus's death and resurrection, the forgiveness of sins, and a believer's eternal reunion with God in Heaven.[8]

The military slaughter compelled Washington to reflect on God's divine will and intervention into earthly affairs, for events had not played out according to the odds. Rumored to be dead with many of the other officers in Braddock's command, he penned a reassuring letter to his brother one week after the horrific slaughter. He was thankful that "the all powerful dispensations of Providence" protected him "beyond all human probability and expectation; for I had 4 Bullets through my Coat, and two Horses shot under me yet escaped unhurt although death was leveling my companions on every side of me."[9] A week later he was still pondering the unexpected defeat: "It's true, we have been beaten—most shamefully beaten—by a handful of Men!" The French should not have won the battle, "but see the wondrous

8. Lillback and Newcombe, *Sacred Fire*, 43.

9. Washington to John Augustine Washington, July 18, 1755, in Abbot and Twohig, *Washington: Colonial Series*, 1:343.

works of Providence! the uncertainty of Human things! . . . contrary to all expectation & human probability and even to the common course of things, we were totally defeated . . . ."[10]

Reverend Samuel Davies, a clergyman in Hanover County, Virginia, preached a sermon a few weeks after the disaster in the wilderness entitled "Religion and Patriotism the Constituents of a Good Soldier." In his sermon, which was later reprinted in Philadelphia and London, Davies noted that the "heroic youth, Colonel Washington" had been "preserved" by "Providence" in "so signal a manner for some important service to his country."[11]

Washington had come to the same conclusion. God had spared him from bitterly cold temperatures on frontier wilderness journeys; when an Indian guide attempted to kill him from just fifteen paces away; when his makeshift raft capsized on the icy Allegheny River; and when he broke up friendly fire among his own troops (he rode in front of the line and hit muskets up with his sword to prevent soldiers from killing their own). He believed he had been preserved for a purpose. War on the frontier drove home the realization that he could not control everything in his life. The ways and interventions of Providence were mysterious, unpredictable, beyond human comprehension, but for one raised in the Anglican faith, they were also completely trustworthy and purposeful. As Washington told a Virginia neighbor, shortly after the debacle on the Monongahela, "the Hand of the Lord bringeth mighty Things to Pass."[12]

10. Washington to Robert Jackson, August 2, 1755, in ibid., 1:350.

11. Samuel Davies, Sermon: "Religion and Patriotism the Constituents of Good Soldier," August 17, 1755, in Fitzpatrick, *Writings of Washington*, 1:153.

12. Washington to Landon Carter, October 7, 1755, in Abbot and Twohig, *Washington: Colonial Series*, 2:82.

Charles Willson Peale's picture shows the only likeness of George Washington pre-Revolutionary War.
(Courtesy of the Mount Vernon Ladies' Association)

Emerging from defeat with his reputation enhanced yet again, the twenty-three year old Washington was appointed Colonel of the First Virginia Regiment, and he worked hard to rid his men of gambling, drinking, swearing, and other errant behavior. He would lead by example, inspire the men with "laudable" behavior, and "encourage the soldiers in the unerring exercise of their duty." The task was a difficult, he explained, because "the seeds of idleness" were "strongly ingrafted in their natures."[13] To the Speaker of the House of Burgesses, Washington pledged to rid his company of all "inordinate vices but especially of drunkenness and profanity!" He called on his "conscience, my God!" to guide him in the endeavor and help his men "distinguish between Good & Evil."[14]

The Colonel was serious about eliminating vice from his regiment. Profane and reprobate behavior was not tolerated. Any man who swore or used "an oath or execration" received "twenty-five lashes immediately." If there was a second offense, the perpetrator would be "more severely

13. Washington to Robert Dinwiddie, April 18, 1756, in ibid., 3:14.
14. Washington to John Robinson, April 18, 1756, in ibid., 3:15–17.

punished." Any soldier caught drinking or entering citizen homes, bars, "tippling houses and Ginn-shops" would receive fifty lashes.[15] Calling roll for each company twice a day for inspections and reports,[16] Washington also issued orders requiring his men to "attend Divine Services."[17]

In a letter to Governor Dinwiddie, he expressed gratitude for "the protection of Providence" over his "small company of irregulars." He also asked the Governor to commission a chaplain. Washington desperately wanted his men to "be reformed from those crimes and enormities we are so universally accused of."[18] A few years later, he would plead, yet again, with the House of Burgesses requesting a sober and serious chaplain for his regiment. "Common decency in a camp," he insisted, "calls for the service of a divine, and which ought not to be dispensed with, altho' the world should be so uncharitable as to think us void of religion, and incapable of good instructions."[19] In the meantime, without a suitable chaplain at his disposal, Washington took it upon himself to often administer the divine service for his regiment.[20]

Frustrated and disillusioned by military politics, British disdain for colonial regulars, and without hope for a well-deserved promotion, Washington resigned from the army in late 1758 after five years of military service. He planned to fully pursue the life of a Virginia gentleman and planter. With his military career shelved, he parlayed his popularity into a 1758 election to the Virginia House of Burgesses, a place he would serve until he became commander of the Continental Army during the Revolutionary War.

Washington absorbed many lessons during his frontier experience. He learned how lead, work with officers, and manage imperfect men who did not fulfill their duties, failed to execute orders, or simply performed poorly. The capacity of his mental toughness and doggedness increased. The hard knocks education on the frontier forced him to learn how to recover and bounce back from adversity, failure, and defeat. Being a commander of soldiers helped him better understand the feebleness of the human condition—his own and others—and steeled his resiliency in coping with imperfect people in a fallen world.

---

15. Washington, General Orders, July 6–8, August 5–9, 1756, in ibid., 3:240, 339.

16. Washington, General Orders, August 30–September 1, in ibid., 3:383.

17. Washington, General Orders, September 25, 1756, in Fitzpatrick, *Writings of Washington*, 1: 473.

18. Washington to Robert Dinwiddie, November 9, 1756, in ibid., 1:492–99.

19. Washington to John Blair, April 17, 1758, in ibid., 2:178.

20. M'Guire, *Religious Opinions*, 137–38.

This mental and internal maturation did not come easily for Washington. Indeed, during the French and Indian War, he resigned once, threatened to quit a half dozen times, and left his men for long periods of time. He acted obsessively in the pursuit of obtaining commissions and blamed others—governors, militias, the Virginia Assembly—instead of himself for failures.[21] He was far from perfect, and he knew it.

By the end of the war, however, Washington held a more rational and realistic attitude toward the reliability (or unreliability) of man. Having lived and endured the brutal realities of war on the frontier, he saw firsthand the fallacy of man's purported ability to improve upon one's own nature as Jefferson and other deists espoused. Recognizing his own imperfections, he emerged a more sagacious leader as he embraced and reckoned with the frailties and sinful nature of men. Since he was not immune to temptations, mistakes, and failure, Washington became a more sympathetic and discerning leader who accounted for the sinful condition in others.

This understanding of human infirmity reinforced the lessons he learned throughout his Anglican upbringing and through the teachings of his church. As an Anglican parishioner—who recites the *Book of Common Prayer* every worship service—Washington had always acknowledged mankind's unquestionable depravity and sinful nature. Perfection, though a virtuous pursuit, could never be attained. Things would go wrong, mistakes would be made, and sins would be committed. Only God, through his grace and mercy, could provide human beings with a certain nobility.[22] With God, one could persevere and build a mental stamina to endure the feebleness of the human condition.

The wondrous works and all-powerful dispensations of God that Washington wrote of during his frontier experiences increased his reliance on Christian faith. Although he could not foresee the path ahead, he believed Providence had spared him for a purpose and would continue to guide and protect him in the future.

21. Henriques, *Realistic Visionary*, 11.

22. Novak & Novak, *Washington's God*, 87.

3

The Anglican Way

Religion had always played a central role in Virginia and colonial America. As early as 1610, Virginia lived by the punitive Sunday Laws. The first time someone failed to attend church, the individual received a fine; the second infraction, a whipping; the third violation, death. Virginians were used to paying taxes to support the clergy. At the beginning of the American Revolution, over 99 percent of Americans claimed to be professing Christians.[1]

Religious passions, however, were intensifying in Virginia during the middle of the eighteenth century. Colonial America was in the middle of a religious debate between the more sober, reserved Christians and those who were being swept up in the rising evangelical use of emotion. Many New England Puritans, Anglicans, Unitarians, deists, and others expressed a profound distrust and scorn for emotionalism in worship. On the other hand, evangelicals embraced feelings, enthusiasm, and the vivid experience of being "born again" through a life-changing embrace of Jesus Christ as their Savior. Evangelicals were clear and outspoken on the certainty their faith, guaranteed by the blood of Jesus Christ, while traditional Christians, such as Anglicans, preferred a certain detachment and reserve in their religious piety.

Both sides of the cultural dispute had a certain dislike and mistrust of each other. Cool, rational, northeastern Christians exuded a sense of superiority while those of the warmer, more emotional style thought themselves the true believers of the faith. In central, southern, and western Virginia, Baptist and Methodist itinerant preachers stoked the fires of evangelicalism. Moreover, Baptist disdain for Unitarians, who did not accept the divinity

---

1. Hughes, *Washington,* 1:18–19; Lillback and Newcombe, *Sacred Fire,* 29.

of Jesus Christ, continued to fester. Anglicans felt Presbyterians were too severe, whereas Presbyterians thought Anglicans lax and too willing to relinquish conviction and doctrine for the sake of harmony. Unitarians scorned Trinitarians, and evangelical Christians were almost as disparaging of Anglicans as Roman Catholics. Many ascendant, evangelical Baptists and Methodists accused Latitudinarians of missing the main point or understating the crux of Christianity—salvation by faith through the blood of Jesus Christ.

Washington held a soft spot in his heart for religious toleration after witnessing the problems his brother, Lawrence, experienced with the Ohio Company. When German immigrants refused to buy Virginia land from Lawrence because of the law, which taxed all landowners for the support of Church of England, Washington agreed with his brother's petition to the Virginia Assembly. The petition sought to change the law and eliminate restrictions on people's consciences.[2]

Washington refrained from publicly articulating his specific religious beliefs because he already sensed the rising tide of anti-British, anti-Anglican sentiment in the colonies. British attempts to impose the Anglican/Episcopal system in the colonies certainly added to the mounting tensions between the mother country and her colonies. Washington intuitively understood the need to keep his creedal and personal beliefs on religion relatively silent and reserved.

Keenly aware of the religious turmoil unfolding in late eighteenth-century Virginia, Washington focused on what united various religious denominations as opposed to what divided them. As a well-traveled man, who had already met and served with men of many different Christian sects and denominations, he was careful and mindful not to offend or provoke citizens of various Christian perspectives. In addition to his embedded Latitudinarian mindset, there were good political and social reasons to avoid speaking or writing in a confessional way about God.

Nevertheless, Anglican Christians (named Episcopalians—essentially meaning "we have bishops"—after the American Revolution), held that Holy Scripture, and not the teachings of popes or church councils, was the final authority for Christian belief. Indeed, the Apostles, Nicene, and Athanasian Creeds—which stressed the Triune God and divine, redeeming Savior aspects of Christ—were emphasized as standards of faith precisely because Anglicans believed their teachings were true to Scripture. While churches could err in their doctrines and instruction because humans ran them, Holy Scripture remained inerrant and divinely inspired by God. Queen Elizabeth

---

2. Flexner, *Washington*, 1:48.

and her theologians attempted to position the Church of England as the prudent middle way—or *via media*—between Roman Catholicism and Calvinism. Catholics had added too much man-made doctrine, while Calvin took too much away that was important to Christianity.[3]

For his entire life, Washington lived, conspicuously and unapologetically, as a Christian according to the tenets of the Anglican Church. The Anglican way, or middle way, required the eschewing of enthusiasm and avoiding outward displays of piety in favor of understatement and reserve. Living the middle way meant that Anglicans practiced an aloof, commonsensical, practical way of putting things so as not to divide but to find common ground. Indeed, most Anglicans held three tenets sacred: First, give no offense. Second, keep the peace. Third, provide maximum common ground for unity and agreement. Anglicans were not to brazenly show their piety, be demonstrative, or boast of their faith. A truly devout man concealed his religious fervor and zeal.[4]

Outside of worship, Washington rarely mentioned Jesus just as his wife, Martha, and many other devout Anglican laypeople and ministers did not. He not only adhered to the Anglican way, but lived and followed the precepts of his church with great vigilance, devotedness, and dedication. A faithful church member his entire life, he never forced his particular religious views upon anyone or coerced anyone to believe or do anything contrary to one's conscience. In matters of faith, particularly as a Latitudinarian, actions always spoke louder than words.

After Washington's military service, during the French and Indian War, he became more active in his Anglican congregations. Certainly, one of the ways that he demonstrated and nurtured his Christian faith was through faithful church attendance at Pohick Church in Fairfax County and, in later years, Christ Church in Alexandria. As president of the United States, or when he visited New York City for governmental purposes, he regularly attended St. Paul's Chapel of Trinity Parish, and less frequently, Trinity Church on Wall Street. When the capital and political hub of the nation moved to Philadelphia, he habitually worshipped at Christ Church most often but also at St. Peter's Church. Washington would also worship at other churches of different denominations wherever the people's business brought him.

In addition to regular worship on Sundays, Washington gave much personal time and treasure to his home congregations. For Pohick parish, he donated a gold leaf for gilding the religious inscription on the altarpiece

---

3. Holmes, *Faiths*, 35.

4. Novak and Novak, *Washington's God*, 12.

and "Crimson Velvet with Gold Firing" for use on the pulpit and altar.[5] On his personal pew he had drawers made for the safekeeping of prayer books and papers and his monogram placed on the door.[6] Washington was quite disturbed, in 1773, when the vestry attempted to reclaim the pews on behalf of the parish. "As a Subscriber who meant to lay the foundation of a Family pew in the New Church," Washington asserted to one vestryman, "I shall think myself Injured" if the church would go through with the reclamation plans.[7] At Christ Church he generously and frequently donated money to repair and properly maintain the church.[8]

As a vestryman, Washington was required to sign an oath, or document, that specified one's conformity to the doctrine and discipline of the Church of England. The oath, more popularly known as "the Test," demonstrated one's rejection of the Catholic doctrine of transubstantiation (the teaching that bread and wine used in the communion service were actually transformed into the blood and body of Christ). Furthermore, the oath also proclaimed and affirmed the orthodox Christian view of the Trinity, the divinity of Jesus Christ, the sinfulness of mankind, and the efficacy and atonement on the cross. Washington attached his signature to this profession of faith and never expressed any regret in doing so.[9]

His commitment to the tasks and missions of his home congregations was impressive. He not only attended vestry meetings regularly, but also conducted meetings at his home when he could not report for duty. In one instance he surveyed a region of land extensively and drew construction plans for a new church building for Pohick parish. Washington argued that the new house of worship should be erected closer to the residencies of the members, and gently criticized George Mason's initial desire to construct the new church where the old one stood (and the accompanying cemetery). Churches were built, Washington insisted, for the living rather than the dead. He would donate a significant amount of money for the new building project.[10]

In addition to reviewing the new church construction, Washington, along with George William Fairfax, was assigned to handle collection by

---

5. Ibid., 170.

6. Freeman, *Washington*, 3:345; Holmes, *Faiths*, 60.

7. Washington to John Dalton, February 15, 1773, in Fitzpatrick, *Writings of Washington*, 3:113.

8. Ford, *Washington*, 77.

9. Thompson, *Good Providence*, 30–31; Eidsmoe, *Christianity and the Constitution*, 132.

10. Lossing, *Washington's Mount Vernon*, 86–95; M'Guire, *Religious Opinions*, 140; Meade, *Old Churches*, 227.

selling parish tobacco. These funds paid for the minister's salary and for the construction of a new place of prayer. Both men were responsible to auction the glebe and the plate of the old parish (Washington wrote "Warden" after his name in signing these accounts). Throughout the 1760s, 1770s, and 1780s, Washington spent a considerable amount of time raising funds for the construction of church facilities.[11]

Being a churchwarden meant that his leadership skills were especially renowned, coveted, and respected in the congregation. As a financial overseer and officer of the vestry, he retained the oversight and supervision of the church buildings and property. He was also in charge of administering relief and aid to the poor as well arranging for the moral training, education, and apprenticeship of orphans and other indigent children. Wardens were called to present persons of Sabbath-breaking, drunkenness, profane swearing, disturbing public worship, and other serious immoralities to the court or grand jury. They collected fines as assigned by the parish.[12]

Washington carried out his duties as a vestryman—the highest commitment an Anglican could provide his church short of being a minister—with great fidelity and diligence especially when compared to Jefferson's inactivity as a vestryman. While absent for the first four years of meetings as a town of Alexandria trustee, Washington missed only eight of his thirty-one vestry meetings from 1763 to 1774. Moreover, out of the eight missed, he was sick in bed for one, serving in the House of Burgesses during two, and out of the country for at least three, but probably five, times when a vestry meeting convened. Church affairs received a higher priority than other secular or government pursuits.[13]

However, even in matters of state, Washington's devotion to his Christian faith materialized in unique and opportune ways. In 1769, he was assigned to the newly created Committee on Religion in the House of Burgesses. The group's main purpose was to curb and refute the growing and troublesome theology of deism in Anglican Virginia. The committee occasionally produced and distributed sermons. One such sermon, later discovered in his library, "The Nature and Extent of Christ's Redemption," has Washington's signature across the top.[14]

As Washington's reputation ascended in Virginia, he became a much sought-after planter and neighbor. Many farmers and soldiers sought and

11. Ferling, *First of Men*, 75; Freeman, *Washington*, 3:177–78.

12. Johnson, *Washington: The Christian*, 52–53.

13. Lillback and Newcombe, *Sacred Fire*, 273. 2006; Novak and Novak, *Washington's God*, 97.

14. Lillback and Newcombe, *Sacred Fire*, 288, 290.

solicited his judgment even above the advice of lawyers. They looked to him as a counselor who would give advice on land purchases or be a judicious executor of their will and other legal functions.[15] These services rendered not only endeared him to neighbors and visitors alike, but also increased his understanding of human frailty and his sense of obligation to care for the needy.

One neighbor he took a special fancy to, for different reasons, was Martha Dandridge Custis. Shortly after Daniel Parke Custis died, Washington visited the enormous Custis estate to pay Martha his respects. He stayed for a day and a half. After one week, he returned to propose marriage. She accepted his proposal immediately.

Marrying Martha Dandridge Custis was the best decision Washington ever made. Complimenting each other in many ways, they also shared a devotedness to their Anglican, Christian faith. Picture by John C. McRae. (Courtesy of the Mount Vernon Ladies' Association)

Martha was short, plump, retiring in nature, and struck some people as dowdy. She was a good and constant soul who once described herself as "an old-fashioned housekeeper, steady as a clock, busy as a bee, and cheerful as a cricket."[16] Whether Washington was, at first, enticed with Martha's inherited estate—the estate was worth 23,000 pounds, approximately two million dollars today, and had 18,000 acres of land and 250 slaves—or her benevolent heart, warm personality, physical beauty, or all of these factors is hard to ascertain. Martha was known, however, for her affability, candor,

15. Freeman, *Washington,* 3:185.
16. Lewis, *King and Country,* 243.

and gentleness.[17] On January 6, 1759, a few months after they first met, Martha and George were married by Anglican minister Reverend David Mossom at Martha's home (ironically called the White House) in New Kent County, Virginia.

By all historical accounts, George and Martha had an extremely fulfilling and loving marriage. After the wedding, they moved into a one-and-a-half room farmhouse at Mount Vernon, a house that would be enlarged many times to accommodate their family during the next four decades. Each wore a painted miniature of the other around their neck.[18] During the Revolutionary War, Martha stunned her husband by announcing that she was undergoing a smallpox inoculation—a dangerous procedure involving the injection of the live virus and submission to what doctors, nurses, and patients could only pray would be a mild case of the deadly disease—so that she could be with him in camp. She knew she was putting herself at risk, but desired to be a healthy helpmate working alongside her husband.[19] When both were home together, she worked diligently to keep Mount Vernon a warm and uplifting sanctuary.

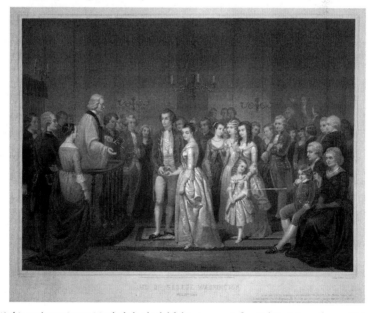

Washington's marriage to Martha helped solidify his rise as an influential Virginia gentleman. History laments the loss of most the correspondence between the two. Picture by Claude Regnier, after Junius Brutus Stearns. (Courtesy of the Mount Vernon Ladies' Association)

17. Unger, *Unexpected Washington,* 34.
18. Henriques, *Realistic Visionary,* 96.
19. Unger, *Unexpected Washington,* 112.

Martha's kind and winsome personality, along with the deference she showed her husband in public and private, provided great emotional support and solace for George. She loved her husband unconditionally, worked hard not to burden him in any way, and never gave him a reason to complain—even when his military or political duties took him away from Mount Vernon for long periods of time. She made sure that domestic life was peaceful, calm, and full of respite for her busy and in-demand husband. Martha became not only George's dearest companion, but also his most trusted advisor and confidante.[20]

Tender and sensitive to his "dear Patcy," Washington showed great care for her needs and earnest respect for her views. There is no historical evidence of a repressed or neglected spouse, but rather a happy, healthy, well-adjusted wife.[21] Together, Martha and George rode horseback, enjoyed late afternoon tea with neighbors and guests (the women to chat and men to play backgammon and cards), sang and danced, and enjoyed children's plays at night. Between 1768 and 1775, Martha and George entertained and had dinner with more than two thousand people. Twice in George's will, written carefully, thoughtfully, and in a tempered manner in 1799, he referred to Martha not as "my wife," or "my beloved wife," but my "dearly beloved wife." George's decision to marry Martha was the best of his life.[22]

Raised in the Anglican Church and in a devout family (her father was also a church vestryman), Martha was punctilious about attending church each Sunday and conducting her own private devotions. When her daughter from her first marriage, Patsy, died in 1773, Martha's religious sentiments deepened and become more manifest than ever. Her granddaughter, Nelly Custis, fondly recalled how Martha would retire to her room after breakfast each day to read the Bible and pray for over an hour. Later, she would sing hymns with her children and grandchildren at night. She performed these acts of devotion faithfully throughout the course of her entire life.[23]

Martha's religious devotion matched her husband's steadfastness in the faith. In one of the two surviving letters between the couple, written just after their engagement, George reassured Martha that his prayer was "that an all-powerful Providence may keep us both in safety . . . ."[24]

---

20. Chernow, *Washington,* 101.

21. Higginbotham, "Revolutionary Asceticism," 159.

22. Henriques, *Realistic Visionary,* 95; Unger, *Unexpected Washington,* 49; Johnson, *Washington: Founding Father,* 46.

23. Chernow, *Washington,* 82; Bryan, *Martha Washington,* 34–35; Smith, *Patriarch,* 13.

24. Washington to Martha Custis, July 20, 1758, in Fitzpatrick, *Writings of Washington,* 2:242.

Both George and Martha wanted to inculcate and pass on the Christian faith to their children. Although George was the stepfather, he dearly loved and showed great affection for Martha's children—John Parke Custis, known as Jackie, and Martha Parke Custis, known as Patsy. In 1761, shortly after they were married, George ordered Bibles, prayer books, and a volume of religious music from England for his two stepchildren when they were just eight and six years of age. That same year, George and Martha hired Scotsman, Walter Magowan, to tutor Jacky and Patsy on all the academic classics, the Anglican faith, and the church catechism. Magowan taught the children for six years before leaving in 1767 so that he could be ordained in England. The minister would stay in touch with the Washington family for life, returning to Mount Vernon often after becoming rector of St James Parish in Herring Bay, Maryland.[25]

After Magowan's departure, the Washingtons enrolled Jacky at a boys school run by the Reverend Jonathan Boucher (located a few miles out of Fredericksburg in his home) for the next five years. Regarded as one of the best preachers of his day, Boucher would later dedicate a sermon series in George Washington's name.[26] He also commended Washington's "exemplary" church attendance in his autobiography.[27] In 1772, George ordered a "Large Family Bible bound in Morrocco with Cuts, and Silver Clasps and a small and very neat Prayer Book with the new Version of Psalms and Comp'm to the Alter, with Silv'r Clasps" for all family members to use.[28]

Washington's stepchildren loved and adored him. More importantly, they knew he loved them. He was a man who cared for their spiritual and eternal well-being, insisting that they faithfully attend church as well as gather for sermon and Scripture recitations and family devotions on Sunday evenings. While they surely witnessed and endured his temper, they never expressed any fear of him.

Washington's reputation for being a loving family man later helped him become Commander in Chief. Delegates of the Continental Congress believed he would not only make the necessary sacrifices in leading the Continental Army, but he would also be eager to return to his harmonious domestic station after the war.[29] As the break from England and road to independence became more imminent and inevitable during the 1760s and

---

25. Thompson, *Good Providence,* 36–37.

26. Meade, *Old Churches,* 184; Thompson, *Good Providence,* 37.

27. Jonathan Boucher, Autobiography, in Fitzpatrick, *Writings of Washington,* 2:486–87.

28. Washington, Invoice of Goods, in ibid., 3:94.

29. Higginbotham, "Revolutionary Asceticism," 155.

early 1770s, Washington would rely and lean on his Christian faith more than ever in order to survive and inspire during the Revolutionary War.

PART II

Revolutionary War General

4

Road to Revolution

During the years of 1760 to 1774, Washington refocused on the management and production of his Mount Vernon estate and vast land holdings. Of course, as a Virginia gentleman, he found time to dine with friends, play cards, billiards, backgammon, dance at balls, attend horse races and theatre, fish, and hunt. He also carefully observed and conversed with others on the affairs and growing unease between England and her American colonies.

In the years following the French and Indian War, Washington became quite active in politics. He saved and alphabetized poll lists from each contested election he ran for and used Mount Vernon, ideally located between northern and southern states, to invite and entertain distinguished guests and travelers thereby cementing many close relationships with clergy, governors, and other gentlemen in this manner. He subscribed to and read ten newspapers daily. Having traveled to the colonial west, served in the French and Indian War, journeyed to the Atlantic seaboard, and met numerous people from all different ethnic, national, and religious backgrounds, Washington knew more about the interests of people from various states and regions, perhaps, than any other colonial leader at the time.[1]

1. Johnson, *Washington: Founding Father*, 90. Henriques, *Realistic Visionary*, 27; Fay, *Washington*, 163; Higginbotham, *Washington: Uniting a Nation*, 8.

Colonel George Washington
c. 1732 - 1799
Fischunter

Washington wanted to focus on farming and other pursuits as a Virginia grandee until problems escalated between mother England and her colonies. Picture by R.L. Boyer. (Courtesy of the Mount Vernon Ladies' Association)

As an Anglican, aristocratic grandee, Washington would, at first glance, appear to have little incentive or desire to separate from England. After all, he had served with distinction in the British army for decades, sought ascendency in a society that was shaped by English culture and tradition, and signed oaths of allegiance to the Church of England.

He had, however, grown disenchanted with the demeaning way English leaders treated American colonists as second-class citizens. He had experienced British disdain and condescension firsthand having been denied promotion primarily because he was a colonial. Moreover, his writings are filled with complaints of shortsighted and unfair British tax and trade policies (in particular when he received low prices for his tobacco but had to pay high prices for shoddy and outdated products). In 1775, when Lord Dunmore cancelled his rightful claim to thousands of acres of western land—apparently on the pretext that the Virginian was not qualified and properly licensed as a surveyor, Washington saw corruption and tyranny on the prowl.

He started reading political treatises, written by more ardent colonial rebels, and linked his own personal grievances to the emerging constitutional crisis between the colonies and the mother country.[2] A well-traveled man, Washington was also sensitive to perceptions—both real and perceived—that British dominance was interfering with the religious practices and political autonomy of many colonists and settlers on the frontier.[3]

After England passed the punitive Coercive Acts, in the spring of 1774, colonial political leaders rallied for nonimportation and called for a Continental Congress. As one of the representatives from Virginia, Washington was selected to attend because he was "an exceedingly honest man" and someone of "good private character." One observer to the assembly noted that Washington "never had . . . an open professed enemy in his life . . . His private character is amiable, he is much beloved and respected by all acquaintances."[4] Silas Deane, a merchant from Connecticut and delegate to the First Continental Congress, reported to his wife that Washington, on hearing of the retaliatory British actions in the Boston Port Bill, offered "to raise & Arm & lead One Thousand Men himself at his Own Expense for the defense of the Country were there Need of it." Deane praised the Virginian who had saved the remains of Braddock's army in 1755, and observed that Washington spoke "Modestly, & in cool but determined Style & Accent."[5]

The delegates of the First Continental Congress adopted a resolution calling for prayer at the opening of each daily session and designated an Anglican clergyman to act as chaplain. They also authorized a national day of humiliation, fasting, and prayer (July 20, 1775); made pay of chaplains equal to commanders; directed a minister to instruct Indians in Christian principles; recommended to the states that they encourage religion and suppress vice; endorsed an American edition of the Bible and recommended it to people as a careful and accurate work (and actually imported 20,000 of them); and later proclaimed the Treaty of Paris "in the name of the Most Holy and Undivided Trinity."[6] Much of the correspondence and paperwork of the First Continental Congress were filled with biblical phrases so that they would resemble Old Testament ecclesiastical documents. Members of

2. Henriques, *Realistic Visionary,* 31–32.

3. Draper, *Struggle for Power,* 42–43.

4. Hughes, *Washington,* 2:213.

5. Silas Dean to Elizabeth Dean, September 10, 1774, in Kaminski, *Founders,* 471.

6. Pfeffer, *Church, State,* 120.

Congress felt compelled to rely on religion because the government was still technically without definitive legislative authority. The Christian religion provided cover for these members and was thought of as a stabilizing force.[7]

As events continued to escalate between England and the American colonies, and war seemed inevitable, Washington came fully dressed in military uniform for the Second Continental Congress, which convened in the spring of 1775. The Virginian's position on the course of action the colonists should pursue was clear and unmistakable.

Congressional delegates selected Washington to be commander of the Continental Army because he was a vigorous man (at the age of 43) who already had a prominent military reputation, a Virginian (the largest and most populous colony), and one who impressively looked the part in uniform. Delegates admired him because he was a family man, a virtuous gentleman, and someone who had already demonstrated that he would sacrifice private interest for the public good. His past bravery in combat was only overshadowed by his modesty.[8] "He seems discrete & Virtuous, no harum Scarum ranting Swearing fellow, but Sober, steady, & Calm," wrote Eliphalet Dyer, a lawyer and delegate from Connecticut. His "modesty will Induce him I dare say to take & order every step with the best advice possible to be obtained in the Army."[9] John Adams recorded that there was "something charming to me in the conduct of Washington. A gentlemen of one of the first fortunes upon the continent, leaving his delicious retirement, his family and friends, sacrificing his ease, and hazarding all in the cause of his country!" The general was "noble and disinterested," and told the Congress "he would lay before us an exact account of his expenses, and not accept a shilling for pay."[10]

In a letter to the president of the Second Continental Congress, Washington explained that he was "truly sensible to the high Honour done me in this Appointment." Nevertheless, he confessed "great distress from a consciousness that my abilities and Military experience may not be equal to the extensive and important Trust." He would "enter upon the momentous duty, and exert every power I Possess In their Service for the Support of the glorious Cause." Yet, he begged everyone to remember that he did "not think my self equal to the Command I am honoured with."[11] He informed

7. Reichley, *American Public Life*, 98–99.

8. Henriques, *Realistic Visionary*, 38–39.

9. Eliphalet Dyer to Joseph Trumbull, June 17, 1775, in Kaminski, *Founders*, 471.

10. Adams to Elbridge Gerry, June 18, 1775, in ibid., 471–72.

11. Washington to President of Congress, June 16, 1775, in Fitzpatrick, *Writings of Washington*, 3:292.

Congress that he would not accept a salary as general of the Continental Army. Instead, he would set an example of self-sacrifice and hoped others would rise above their own self-interest and personal concerns for the cause of independence.[12]

On June 23, 1775, the day he was to leave to take control of the Continental Army, Washington worshipped at Christ Church in Philadelphia. "Religion and liberty must flourish or fall together in America," Reverend William Smith exhorted in his sermon. "We pray that both may be perpetual."[13]

Many colonists believed God favored the patriot cause. In Virginia, dissenting Baptists and Presbyterians had been severely oppressed and persecuted by British-backed, Anglican church officials for decades. If one denied the Trinity, one could be imprisoned and lose custody of his children. Baptist preachers were whipped, arrested, fined, and imprisoned on bread and water. In some areas of Virginia, the law requiring church attendance was strictly enforced. Anglican vestrymen levied tithes for ministers' salaries, upkeep of the church, and support of the poor. Moreover, vestrymen were to subscribe to the doctrine and discipline of the church by signing an oath of supremacy. Other states had similar religious disputes with the established Anglican Church. Many of these dissenters—Baptists and Presbyterians in particular—had no wish to establish compulsory support of any church, not even their own. Soon Virginia would pass legislation that eliminated the paying of tithes and protected other religious freedoms.[14] For many, freedom was the key to securing an opportunity to practice their faith as they pleased. This sentiment, of course, directly contributed to the patriot cause and Revolutionary fervor against England.

By the mid-1770s, religion and politics were deeply intertwined. In New England, the fusing of Whig ideology and vocabulary with American Protestantism had been coalescing for decades. Terms such as "virtue," "corruption," and "liberty" had resonance in both political and religious contexts. American Protestants, in particular, heralded republican government, stirred by a freedom-loving God and a righteous and God-fearing community on earth.[15]

Many clergymen and ministers believed the American Revolution was a religious movement long overdue and an opportunity to rekindle the Christian Church's focus on mission and outreach. America, much like the

---

12. Flexner, *Washington*, 3:111.
13. Meacham, *American Gospel*, 3.
14. Pfeffer, *Church, State*, 106–07.
15. Bloch, "Religion and Ideological Change," 50–51.

ancient Hebrews, had been divinely chosen for a special, Providential cause. Christian truth would flourish in a liberty-loving nation. The Revolution would, once again, place the church at the heart of American culture, communities, and society.[16] Where revolutionaries in France would interpret and employ the Enlightenment as a way to combat or suppress religious influence, revolutionaries in America saw the Christian religion, Bible, and Protestantism as inspiration to the republican revolution and light for a dark world. Numerous churches and congregations in America ardently embraced the cause of liberty.

The American Revolution would unleash a wave of evangelical Christianity and Christianize American society more than anything before or since—much to the chagrin and surprise of many liberal deists and enlightened leaders such as Jefferson.[17] The total number of church congregations doubled between 1770 and 1790, outpacing overall population growth in these years. Older, established, state churches which had dominated colonial society for a century and a half—Anglican, Congregational, and Presbyterian in particular—were supplanted by new religious denominations and sects. As late as 1760, the two primary religious establishments—the Church of England in the South and the Puritan churches in New England—accounted for more than 40 percent of all congregations in America. By 1790, however, the religious establishment dropped below 25 percent and looked to decline in the future.[18] No wonder Washington did not want to spotlight or make a public show of the Anglicanism of his Christian faith. His Latitudinarian sentiments buffered and navigated the times with pragmatic discernment.

Protestant ministers of all denominations—except many Anglicans—supported American independence for religious as well as political reasons. Americans were building a republican world of virtue and benevolence, and religion provided a crucial foundation in the construction. Clergy made sense of the Revolution and put it in meaningful context for their parishioners. While many founders and distinguished leaders of the Revolution were not outwardly emotional about their religion, most Americans were transparent in their religious faith and comprehended the world in religious terms.[19]

---

16. Hatch, *Sacred Cause*, 16.

17. Wood, *American Revolution*, 131–32; Hatch, "Democratization of Christianity," 97.

18. Wood, "Religion and the American Revolution," 186–87.

19. Wood, *American Revolution*, 131.

Keenly observant and aware of the religious ethos of the era, Washington understood that religion earnestly inspired many colonists to seek and fight for independence. Images of the biblical Exodus—Moses leading the Israelites out of slavery in Egypt—helped many Americans capture the essence, aims, and justifications of their break from England. Washington himself would eventually be viewed as the "new Moses" or "American Moses" of the Revolution.[20] *E Pluribus Unum*—"out of many, one" was put on the final seal of the new American Union. The back of the seal (it is the image to the left on the back of the one dollar bill today) depicted the "Eye of Providence" above the unfinished pyramid with the words of the second motto, *Annuit Coeptis*—"God (or Providence) has favored our undertakings." There was also a third Latin motto, *Novus Ordo Seclorum*—"a new order of the ages." Today, the United States's emblem is simpler—that of an eagle.[21]

Many colonial leaders—working collaboratively and individually—led and encouraged the colonies to declare independence and break away from England, but only one could serve as commander in chief of the Continental Army. During the War for Independence, Washington would endure his singular and daunting burden by trusting in God and relying upon a confidence that emanated from his Christian faith.

20. Hay, "American Moses," 143–51; Schwartz, "Heroic Leadership," 22, 24.
21. Meacham, *American Gospel*, 81.

5

Confident General

Washington formally took command of the Continental Army on Monday, July 3, 1775, the day that his first military campaign had ended in defeat at Fort Necessity twenty-one years prior. He had arrived at the Cambridge headquarters the day before, Sunday, with little fanfare and conducted no formal business adhering to the Sabbath.

WASHINGTON TAKING COMMAND OF THE AMERICAN ARMY,
At Cambridge, Mass. July 3ᵈ 1775.

Washington insisted on instilling discipline and moral rectitude in the Continental Army. He would require, among other things, divine worship attendance and prayers of thanksgiving from his officers and soldiers throughout the war. Picture by Currier and Ives. (Courtesy of the Mount Vernon Ladies' Association)

He inherited a miserable and deplorable army. Men lived in sprawling shantytowns; stench from open latrines filled the air; and incompetent officers were undifferentiated from their men in appearance, behavior, and decorum. Enlisted men were intemperate, undisciplined, and unrestrained. Training had largely been ignored. Idleness and lethargy infested almost all aspects of army life.

Washington confronted the army's dysfunction with intensity and intentionality. He created an elite and aloof officer corps that demanded more deference from soldiers and a culture of order and discipline. Before Washington arrived, enlisted men had come and gone as they pleased, called commanders by first name, were forced to work on their commanders' farms, and shaved and shined their shoes next to officers. Serious offenses such as cowardice, falling asleep on guard duty, or pillaging property of civilians went unpunished. Washington quickly established a barrier, an invisible line of respect, between commanders and their men.[1]

While a stern disciplinarian, the Commander in Chief was fair and truly loved his men. Often overlooked as one of his greatest accomplishments, Washington forged a republican army—the people's army—where men were not expected to serve and be disciplined as slaves but treated as free men. As general of the Continental Army, Washington had to develop a successful and republican approach in forming military habits, codes of conduct, and discipline procedures to maintain order and the republican virtues they were fighting for in earnest.[2]

Soldiers and officers soon learned that Washington possessed a reverent faith. From the very first days of training, he devoted a remarkable amount of attention to the religious life of his troops. Just as he had done in Virginia, during the French and Indian War, he requested and encouraged regimental commanders to procure chaplains, paid by the government, who were "persons of good Characters and exemplary lives." All officers and soldiers were to "pay them a suitable respect and attend carefully upon religious exercises." He wanted his men to know that "the blessing and protection of Heaven are at all times necessary but especially so in times of public distress and danger." He hoped that every man would live and act as a "Christian Soldier defending the dearest Rights and Liberties of his country."[3]

He issued numerous directives commanding his soldiers to fast, pray, observe days of thanksgiving, attend divine services, and respect the free

1. Palmer, *Washington and Benedict Arnold,* 110; Ferling, *First of Men,* 126–27.

2. Novak and Novak, *Washington's God,* 30, 78–82; Higginbotham, *American Military Tradition,* 16.

3. Washington, General Orders, July 9, 1776, in Fitzpatrick, *Writings of Washington,* 5:245.

exercise of religion for all citizens. Orders were read every morning only after prayers had been given.[4] Many soldiers saw the general himself partake in private and public prayer. Washington's faithful morning and evening worship attendance, as well as his fervent prayer life no matter how busy the days or events of army life, were conspicuous for all to observe.[5]

During the war, Washington not only required his men to attend divine worship, but also regarded the practice as a core component in the development and training of the army. His first General Order demanded punctual worship service attendance for all soldiers. At church they were to "take special care" and "appear clean and decent."[6] Vice and "Immorality of every kind" were discouraged.[7] Gambling, drunkenness, and blasphemy were abhorred and not tolerated. Soldiers and officers who breached these commands were considered "a disregard to decency, virtue and religion."[8] Men who practiced "profane cursing and swearing," "impiety," or "folly" would "have little hopes of the blessing of Heaven on our Arms." Cursing and swearing were "mean and low" vices "that every man of sense, and character, detests and despises."[9] The "unmeaning and abominable custom of *Swearing*," and especially the profaning the "Name of That Being, from whose bountiful goodness we are permitted to exist and enjoy the comforts of life" was "as wanton as it is shocking." He went on to insist that "for the sake therefore of religion, decency and order the general hopes and trusts that officers of every rank will use their influence and authority to check a vice, which is as unprofitable as it is wicked and shameful." Officers were to reprimand and punish soldiers for these offenses in hopes of reforming their manners and honoring God.[10]

In another General Order, Washington thought "it a duty to declare the regularity and decorum" of each Sunday worship service, and insisted that divine worship would "reflect great credit on the army in general" and "tend to improve morals." Faithful church attendance and virtuous, Christian behavior would "increase the happiness of the soldiery" and "afford the most pure and rational entertainment for every serious and well disposed

---

4. Flexner, *Washington,* 2:35.

5. Callahan, *Washington: Soldier and Man,* 187.

6. Washington, General Orders, April 12, 1777, in Fitzpatrick, *Writings of Washington,* 7:407.

7. Washington to William Smallwood, May 26, 1777, in ibid., 8:129.

8. Washington, General Orders, June 28, 1777, in ibid., 8:308.

9. Washington, General Orders, August 3, 1776, in ibid., 5:367.

10. Washington, General Orders, July 29, 1779, in ibid., 16:13.

mind." Therefore, he wanted "no fatigue except on extra occasions, nor general review or inspections to be permitted on the Sabbath day."[11]

Henry Melchior Muhlenberg, a German Lutheran pastor in Pennsylvania whose son served in the Continental Army at Valley Forge, recorded the general's conspicuous religious beliefs in his journal after visiting the troops in the spring of 1778: "General Washington rode around his army yesterday and admonished each and every one to fear God, to put away the wickedness that has set in and become so general, and to practice Christian virtues." Washington "respects God's Word, believes in the atonement through Christ, and bears himself in humility and gentleness." Muhlenberg was grateful that God preserved the general "from harm in the midst of countless perils, ambuscades, fatigues, etc., and has hitherto graciously held him in his hand as a chosen vessel."[12]

As much as Washington revered God and modeled his Christian faith, he never presented his religion in a coercive manner. As Commander in Chief, he allowed and protected each soldier's right to worship God in his own way. Keeping religious differences and friction at a minimum made sense for an army desperate to recruit, train, and retain any and every man for soldiery.

The makeup of the Continental Army was, in fact, diverse. The social background of the regiments assembled from the different regions of the emerging nation brought together Americans who had never interacted in social circles previously. More often than not, these soldiers, when they first met, had little in common and did not like each other.[13] The general did everything in his power to keep the army unified and focused.

Along with military necessity, however, Washington, as a Latitudinarian, believed in, and defended, the freedom of conscience. God could best be worshipped in spirit and in truth by individuals whose minds were free and not coerced. Human liberty as a gift from God made up an essential part of Washington's religious fabric.[14]

Early in the war, when Benedict Arnold's mission led his men to Catholic Quebec, the Commander in Chief warned Arnold to "avoid all Disrespect to or Contempt of the Religion of the Country and its Ceremonies." Instead, prudence "and a true Christian Spirit," he insisted to Arnold, "will lead us to look with Compassion upon their Errors without insulting them." Since

11. Washington, General Orders, March 22, 1783, in ibid., 26:250.

12. Muhlenberg, *Notebook*, 195.

13. Novak and Novak, *Washington's God*, 85; Boller, "Washington and Religious Liberty," 494–95.

14. Novak and Novak, *Washington's God*, 111, 134–35; Fitzpatrick, *Washington Himself*, 131.

Americans were "contending for our own Liberty, we should be very cautious of violating the Rights of Conscience in others, ever considering that God alone is the Judge of the Hearts of Men, and to him only in this Case, they are answerable." Washington did not want colonial regiments to "turn the Hearts of our brethren in Canada against us" with shameful, disgraceful acts of bigotry. "Good Behaviour" and "Prudance" might just "conciliate the Affections of the Canadians and Indians, to the great Interests of America, and convert those favorable Dispositions they have shewn into a lasting Union and Affection."[15] In another letter, Washington reemphasized that Arnold's army should refrain from displaying "Contempt of the Religion" of the people of Quebec nor should they ridicule "any of its Ceremonies" or affront "its Ministers or Votaries." Arnold was to "be particularly careful" to "restrain every Officer and Soldier from such Imprudence and Folly and to punish every Instance of it." In addition, he should "protect and support the free Exercise of the Religion of the Country and the undisturbed Enjoyment of the rights of Conscience in religious Matters" with utmost influence and authority.[16]

In an effort to curb anti-Catholic sentiment, Washington outlawed a favorite New England festivity known as "Pope's Day" or "Pope's Night." By direct order, he also ended the "ridiculous and childish custom of burning the Effigy of the pope." The general was dumbfounded that officers and soldiers would be "so void of common sense." America was trying to solicit "the friendship and alliance of Canada, whom we ought to consider as Brethren embarked in the same Cause." Therefore, the Continental Army should not fight for "the general Liberty of America" while "insulting . . . their Religion."[17]

The elimination of Pope's Day, the discouragement and banishment of anti-Catholic bigotry, coupled with the support for Catholic soldiers and commemoration of Saint Patrick's Day, won the profound gratitude and trust of American Catholics. An eighteenth-century legend would eventually emerge claiming that the general had joined the Catholic Church or was contemplating doing so shortly before he died.[18]

As a proponent of religious freedom and freedom of conscience, Washington prevented the establishment of an official religion in his army. Opposing a congressional plan to appoint chaplains at the brigade level, in

15. Washington to Benedict Arnold, September 4, 1775, in Fitzpatrick, *Writings of Washington*, 3:492.

16. Washington to Benedict Arnold, September, 1775, in ibid., 3:495–96.

17. Washington, General Orders, November 5, 1775, in ibid., 4:65.

18. Boller, "Washington and Religious Liberty," 493.

1777, he argued for the traditional, local-preference pattern that had grown up informally in regard to the appointment of chaplains.[19] Moreover, he upheld the right of John Murray, a founder of American Universalism, to officiate as chaplain in the Continental Army. Believing in universal salvation but not the existence of hell, Murray aroused bitter opposition among orthodox clergymen who felt Murray's beliefs undermined morality and led to atheism.[20] "Religious liberties were as essential as our Civil," Washington asserted to a Dutch Reformed congregation, and "my endeavors have never been wanting to encourage and promote the one, while I have been contending for the other." Realizing that many different denominations cherished his support of Christianity and religious toleration, he offered thanks and prayers to the Dutch congregation encouraging members to "hand down your Religion pure and undefiled to Posterity."[21]

For Washington, religious freedom and devotion to the Christian religion were key pillars of republican society. Freedom enhanced Christianity. Christianity enhanced freedom. A 1779 congressional proclamation gave praise and thanks for the "protection," "posterity," and "deliverance" of "Almighty God" and for "the wonders which his goodness has wrought in conducting our fore-fathers to this western world." The proclamation further expressed gratitude for "the glorious light of the gospel, whereby, through the merits of our gracious Redeemer, we may become the heirs of his eternal glory . . . ." The colonists should be thankful "to Almighty God for his mercies" and for "the continuance of his favor and protection of the United States." Americans were asked to pray that God would "grant to his church the plentiful effusions of divine grace, and pour out his holy spirit on all ministers of the gospel." For God "would bless and prosper the means of education and spread the light of Christian knowledge through the remotest corners of the earth" and "smile upon the labours of his people and cause the earth to bring forth her fruits in abundance." Almighty God would also "establish the independence of these United States upon the basis of religion and virtue, and support and protect them in the enjoyment of peace, liberty, and safety." Concurring with the congressional declaration, Washington ordered "a strict observance to be paid by the Army to this proclamation and the Chaplains are to prepare and deliver discourses suitable to it."[22]

19. Wills, *Cincinnatus,* 24.

20. Boller, "Washington and Religious Liberty," 493.

21. Washington to the Minister, Elders, and Deacons of the Reformed Protestant Dutch Church in Kingston, New York, November 16, 1782, in Fitzpatrick, *Writings of Washington,* 25:347.

22. Washington, General Orders, November 27, 1779, in ibid., 17:189–90.

As Washington prepared and trained his army for battle, the realities facing the patriots remained daunting. England had more arms, more professionally trained and better disciplined soldiers, established military practice and tradition, greater wealth, worldly prestige, more qualified and experienced officers, and the professional experience and prowess for war. Conversely, the Continental Army had limited and inadequate provisions, clothing, muskets, powder, shot, enlistments, and no bureaucratic and military systems of supply and assistance established.

Despite these insufficiencies and shortcomings, over the course of eight years (1775–1783), the undermanned and overmatched Continental Army would find a way to persevere and defeat the greatest military power the world had ever known. For Washington, the patriot victory would not be accidental. Only God's intervention and benevolence could grant the victory despite the considerable odds.

Washington was not shy about proclaiming and lauding God's generous intervention and protection throughout the war. When the colonists won the crucial battle at Saratoga, he publicly congratulated the troops "upon this signal victory" which was achieved by the gracious hand of "divine providence." Every soldier's face was to "brighten" and "every heart expand with grateful Joy and praise to the supreme disposer of all events" who had granted the colonists "this signal success."[23] Washington directed his men, following a strong showing at the Battle of Monmouth in June of 1778, to "publickly unite in thanksgiving to the supreme Disposer of human Events for the Victory which was obtained . . . over the Flower of the British Troops."[24] After the war-ending victory, at Yorktown in 1781, the Commander in Chief "earnestly" instructed soldiers to attend divine worship service with "that seriousness of Deportment and gratitude of Heart," and give thanks for the "reiterated and astonishing interpositions of Providence . . . ."[25]

The general often prayed and petitioned God for intervention during the war. He offered a "sincere and fervent prayer" for Benedict Arnold—that "the Almighty may preserve and prosper" him in an impending battle.[26] He reassured General Horatio Gates that the intervening "smiles of Providence" would provide "necessary Supplies of Medicines"[27] and "prevent Genl. Howe

23. Washington, General Orders, October 15 and October 18, 1777, in ibid., 9:377, 390–91.

24. Washington, General Orders, June 30, 1778, in ibid., 12:131.

25. Washington, General Orders, October 20, 1781, in ibid., 23:247.

26. Washington to Benedict Arnold, December 5, 1775, in ibid., 4:149.

27. Washington to Horatio Gates, August 14, 1776, in ibid., 5:433.

from executing his plans."[28] He told Major General Philip Schuyler that the "supreme Dispenser of every Good" would "bestow Health, Strength, and Spirit to you and your Army."[29] To Edmund Pendleton, a member of the Virginia legislature, he ardently prayed and hoped that "the God of Armies" would enable the patriots "to bring the present contest to a speedy and happy conclusion."[30] The "most fervent prayer of my Soul," he conveyed to Landon Carter, one of his wealthy neighbors, was to retire to "domestick Life." Hence, he prayed that "The God of Armies" would actively "Incline the Hearts of my American Brethren to support, and bestow sufficient abilities on me to bring the present contest to a speedy and happy conclusion."[31] When the colonists won an impressive, momentous battle at Saratoga, Washington expected Providence to "crown our Arms in the course of the Campaign, with one more fortunate stroke." He had complete confidence and "trust" that all would "be well in his good time."[32]

Even after terrible setbacks on the battlefield, Washington embraced and comprehended these events from the context and worldview of an intervening God. When "Thick Fog" stifled the army's promising position in an impending battle and took away what looked like a certain victory for the Continental Army, the general resigned himself to the notion that "Providence or some unaccountable something, disignd it" that way. Doing all he could "in his present situation," he recognized that "God only knows" who would ultimately "succeed."[33] Another time, Washington expressed frustration that "after two years Manoeuvring and undergoing the strangest vicissitudes that perhaps ever attended any one contest since the creation," both the British and Continental armies had been "brought back to the very point they set out from." For Washington, the "hand of Providence" remained "so conspicuous in all this." Perhaps when the war was over, he could "turn preacher" and ponder the mysteries of God's interventions. Until then, he would "add no more on the doctrine of Providence."[34]

God's frequent and benevolent interventions only reinforced Washington's belief that the War for American Independence was a Godly one. The "Cause of Virtue and Liberty is Confined to no Continent or Climate," he asserted early in the conflict. The "Violence and Rapacity" of the "tryannick

28. Washington to Horatio Gates, December 14, 1776, in ibid., 6:372.

29. Washington to Philip Schuyler, January 27, 1776, in ibid., 4:281.

30. Washington to Edmund Pendleton, April 12, 1777, in ibid., 7:394.

31. Washington to Landon Carter, April 15, 1777, in ibid., 7:414.

32. Washington to Israel Putnam, October 19, 1777, in ibid., 9:400–01.

33. Washington to John Augustine Washington, October 18, 1777, in ibid., 9:399.

34. Washington to Thomas Nelson, August 20, 1778, in ibid., 12:343.

Ministry" of England "forced Citizens of America . . . into Arms." However, the "wise disposer of all Events has hitherto smiled upon our virtuous efforts" by checking the "earliest Ravages" of England's "Mercenary Troops."[35] England had "formed a plan for enslaving America, and depriving her sons of their most sacred and invaluable privileges, against the clearest remonstrances of the constitution, of justice, and of truth." Therefore, as the struggle unfolded, the general expressed sincere gratitude for the "interpositions of that Providence, which has manifestly appeared in our behalf through the whole of this important struggle, as well as to the measures pursued for bringing about the happy event." He reiterated his certainty that God would continue to sanction the American cause:

> May that being, who is powerful to save, and in whose hands is the fate of nations, look down with an eye of tender pity and compassion upon the whole of the United Colonies; may He continue to smile upon their counsels and arms, and crown them with success, whilst employed in the cause of virtue and mankind. May this distressed colony and capital, and every part of this wide continent, through His divine favor, be restored to more than their former luster and once happy state, and have peace, liberty, and safety secured upon a solid, permanent, and lasting foundation.[36]

Washington continuously reminded his troops of the nobleness and justice of the American cause. After hearing of the courageous stand the patriots made at battle at Bunker Hill, Washington read Ps 101 to his troops[37]—a psalm which speaks primarily of a king's pledge to reign righteously. Justice, freedom, and liberty favored the American side. Reflecting on the twentieth anniversary of his escape on the Monongahela River, during the French and Indian War, Washington acknowledged how "the same Providence that protected us upon those occasions will, I hope, continue his Mercies, and make us happy Instruments in restoring Peace and liberty to the this once favour'd, but now distressed Country."[38]

Even before the army had taken the field, the Commander in Chief informed his soldiers that he was "confident" since God seemed to be "favouring the Cause of Freedom and America." If they showed "Gratitude to

---

35. Washington to the Inhabitants of the Island of Bermuda September 6, 1775, in ibid., 3:475–76.

36. Washington to the Massachusetts Legislature, March 28, 1776, in ibid., 4:441–42.

37. Lengel, *General Washington*, 105.

38. Washington to Adam Stephen, July 20, 1776, in Fitzpatrick, *Writings of Washington*, 5:313.

providence" and "thankfulness to God," and served with "zeal and persever-ance in this righteous Cause," they would "continue to deserve his future blessings."[39] On November 23, 1775, Washington, directed by Congress, ordered a day of "public thanksgiving to offer up our praises, and prayers to Almighty God, the Source and Benevolent Bestower of all good . . . that he would be pleased graciously" to "prosper the American Arms, preserve and strengthen the Harmony of the United Colonies, and avert the Calamities of a civil war."[40]

In many of his General Orders, troops were encouraged of the righ-teousness of their cause and reminded that they were under God's direc-tion and care. His men were to "devoutly" pray that "the Power which has hitherto sustained the Americans arms" continue to bless them "with his divine Protections."[41] Washington insisted that the "fate of unborn Millions will now depend, under God, on the Courage and Conduct of this army. . . ." Therefore officers and soldiers should "rely upon the goodness of the Cause, and the aid of the supreme Being, in whose hands Victory is, to animate and encourage us to great and noble Actions."[42]

When he had to chide or reprimand his men for their lack of discipline, cowardly inaction, poor execution, or inappropriate behavior, he reminded them that their destiny—freedom or slavery—was in the balance. "Next to the favour of divine providence, nothing is more essentially necessary to give this Army," one order read, "than Exactness of discipline, Altertness when on duty, and Cleanliness in their arms and persons."[43] Americans "have every reason to expect Heaven will crown" the Continental Army "with Success, so just a cause," he declared. Conversely, the British "Cause is bad; their men are conscious of it." Washington insisted that "the justice of the great cause" in which his men were engaged—"the necessity and impor-tance of defending this Country, preserving its Liberties, and warding off the destruction mediated against it"—would "inspire every man with Firm-ness and Resolution, in time of action." Only by the "blessing of Heaven, and the bravery of men," could the Revolution "be saved."[44]

Washington believed God favored the patriot side. "The Cause of our common Country, calls us both to an active and dangerous Duty," he wrote Governor Jonathan Trumbull of Connecticut early in the war. "Divine

---

39. Washington, General Orders, November 14, 1775, in ibid., 4:87.
40. Washington, General Orders, November 18, 1775, in ibid., 4:98.
41. Washington, General Orders, March 28, 1776, in ibid., 4:444.
42. Washington, General Orders, July 2, 1776, in ibid., 5:211.
43. Washington, General Orders, February 27, 1776, in ibid., 5:355.
44. Washington, General Orders, September 3, 1776, in ibid., 6:9.

Providence, which wisely orders the Affairs of Men," would grant Americans "Fidelity and Success."[45] The purity and justice of the American Revolution "appealed to that Being, in whose hands are all Human Events." So far, God had "hitherto smiled upon their virtuous Efforts." The "Hand of Tyranny has been arrested in its Ravages, and the British Arms, which have shone with so much Splendor in every part of the Globe, are now tarnished with disgrace and disappointment."[46]

Surviving and overcoming innumerable odds and obstacles reinforced the general's faith that God smiled upon the Revolutionaries. Contemplating an attack on British Redcoats stationed at Boston early in the war, Washington maintained that the "success of such an Enterprize" depended "upon the all wise disposer of Events, and is not within reach of human wisdom to foretell the Issue."[47] When a British storeship from London was captured, the Commander in Chief told a friend that "we must be thankful, as I truly am, for this instance of Divine favour; for nothing surely ever came more apropos."[48] He credited God for taking a "'band of undisciplined Husbandmen,'" as some had criticized the soldiers of the army, and molding them into brave men who paid great "attention to their duty."[49] If the American cause was just, as he "most religiously believed it to be," then that "same Providence which has in many Instances appear'd for us, will still go on to afford its aid."[50] Victory and success would come from God.

Washington assured officers and soldiers that God supported their mission and tasks. He told Brigadier General John Sullivan that conquest and victory would come "under the Direction of a gracious Providence . . . ."[51] He informed Major General Horatio Gates that he was "most devoutly" praying "that Providence may crown your Arms with abundant Success."[52] Writing the president of the Congress, Washington insisted that good policies, hard work, and determination were patriot responsibilities, "under the smiles of a Gracious and all kind Providence," in order to "promote our

---

45. Washington to Jonathan Trumbull, July 18, 1775, in ibid., 3:344.

46. Washington to the Inhabitants of Canada, September, 1775, in ibid., 3:478.

47. Washington to the Major and Brigadier Generals, September 8, 1775, in ibid., 3:483.

48. Washington to Joseph Reed, November 30, 1775, in ibid., 4:130.

49. Washington to President of Congress, April 18, 1776, in ibid., 4:489.

50. Washington to John Augustine Washington, March 31, 1776, in ibid., 5:92–93.

51. Washington to John Sullivan, June 13, 1776, in ibid., 5:133.

52. Washington to Horatio Gates, June 24, 1776, in ibid., 5:175.

happiness." Victory and independence would come to fruition because of "Divine Favor and our own Exertions . . . ."[53]

When France joined the American side, after the battle at Saratoga, Washington insisted the victory had "pleased the Almighty ruler of the Universe"—who had raised "up a powerful Friend among the Princes of the Earth to establish our liberty and Independence on lasting foundations . . . ." Therefore a special day should be set apart "for gratefully acknowledging the divine Goodness and celebrating the important Event which we owe to his benign Interposition."[54]

Even when the prospects of victory looked bleak or desperate, Washington remained confident insisting that Americans were fighting for a God-pleasing endeavor. He could lead and take the initiative since he had found reprieve in a "good Providence" who had "so remarkably aided us in all our difficulties" previously.[55]

After enduring a brutal winter, at Valley Forge, the Commander in Chief informed his men that Congress had set aside a day for "Fasting, Humiliation and Prayer." Americans should, "at one time and with one voice," acknowledge and implore "the righteous dispensations of Providence" and "His Goodness and Mercy toward us and our Arms . . . ." The general insisted "this day *also* shall be religiously observed in the army, that no work be done thereon and that the Chaplains prepare discourses suitable to the Occasion."[56]

After Benedict Arnold's betrayal, Washington conceded to his men that "Treason of the blackest dye" could have "given the American cause a deadly wound if not fatal stab." Instead, treason was "Happily" and "timely discovered to prevent the fatal misfortune." The "providential train of circumstances which led to it affords the most convincing proof that the Liberties of America are the object of divine Protection."[57]

When the French fleet, sent by "his most Christian Majesty," arrived off the shores of Yorktown, Virginia, late in the war, the general trusted that "the Author of all Blessings" would "aid our united Exertions in the Cause of Liberty" and grant "the particular Favor of Heaven."[58] After the victory at Yorktown, Washington acknowledged, with "particular Pleasure,"

53. Washington to President of Congress, July 10, 1776, in ibid., 5:247, 250.

54. Washington, General Orders, May 5, 1778, in ibid., 11:354.

55. Washington to Edmund Pendleton, November 1, 1779, ibid., 17:51.

56. Washington, General Orders, April 12, 1778, ibid., 11:252.

57. Washington, General Orders, September 26, 1780, ibid., 20:95.

58. Washington to the Citizens and Inhabitants of the Town of Baltimore, September 8, 1781, ibid., 23:108–09.

the "interposing Hand of Heaven in the various Instances of our extensive Preparations for this Operation" which had been "most conspicuous and remarkable."[59] He thanked French commanders and officers who aided the Continental Army, and anticipated that "divine Providence may shed its choicest blessings upon the King of France and his Royal Consorts, and favor them with a long, happy and glorious reign."[60]

After the war was won but the peace had yet been secured, Washington continued to rely on the steadfast "protection of divine Providence,"[61] and trusted that God would act and intervene in the future as he had in the past. "In a cause so just and righteous as ours," he insisted, "we have every reason to hope the divine Providence will still continue to crown our Arms with success, and finally compel our Enemies to grant us that Peace upon equitable terms, which we so ardently desire."[62]

Responding to a congratulatory letter on the American triumph, Washington contended "the praise is due to the *Grand Architect* of the Universe" who "did not see fit to Suffer his Superstructures, and justice, to be subjected to the ambition of the princes of this World, or to the rod of oppression, in the hands of any power on Earth."[63] He repeatedly referred to "the protection of a kind Providence"[64] and "the Smiles of a kind Providence"[65] when reflecting upon the Continental Army's good fortune as well as his own personal safety and success. The general and his army had frequently and "conspicuously" experienced "the Smiles of Heaven."[66]

As the war afforded both setbacks and triumphs, Washington's confidence—that God favored the American cause—remained steadfast. Even though soldiers and officers were sustaining "the fatigues of the Campaign," and in "some instances we unfortunately failed," he insisted that "upon the whole Heaven hath smiled on our Arms and crowned them with signal success." When Congress called for yet another day of "public Thanksgiving and Praise," soldiers were expected to convey their "grateful acknowledgements to God for the manifold blessings" granted. They were also instructed to

59. Washington to Thomas McKean, November 15, 1781, ibid., 23:343.

60. Washington to Chevalier De La Luzerne, June 5, 1782, in ibid., 24:314.

61. Washington to Secretary of War, March 21, 1782, in ibid., 24:83.

62. Washington to Magistrates and Military Officers of Schenectady, New York, June 30, 1782, in ibid., 24:390.

63. Washington to Elkanah Watson and Cassoul, August 10, 1782, in ibid., 24:497.

64. Washington to John Adams, April 15, 1776, in ibid., 4:484; Washington to Ben Franklin, May 20, 1776, in ibid., 5:65.

65. Washington to John Sullivan, June 16, 1776, in ibid., 5:151; Washington to Philip Schulyer, August 13, 1776, in ibid., 5:431.

66. Washington to Samuel Cooper, September 24, 1782, in ibid., 25:200.

remain in their quarters while chaplains performed divine services—worship that should be treated "with reverence the solemnities of the day."[67]

The general had never been naïve to the overwhelming challenges the Continental Army faced in War for Independence. "The day of Tryal, which will, in some measure decide the fate of America is near at hand," he confided to Colonel Thomas McKean. "If we should be beaten (our numbers among friends being unequal to those of the Enemy)," he wanted to deliver some "hard knocks" on the British. Ultimately, however, "that superintending Providence, which needs not the aid of numbers," he asserted, "will lead us I hope to a more fortunate Event."[68]

Trials and tribulations came in many forms during the war. Men who Washington cared about died in combat. Orders were not properly executed. Gunpowder was scarce, and government action and execution in supporting the war effort even scarcer. He lost battles, risked his reputation, and most especially missed his wife and the domestic life he treasured at Mount Vernon.

Through all the adversity and difficulties, however, Washington persevered and endured primarily because of his Christian faith. There was the bad news of war, but there was also the good news of God's grace, intervention, and protection. When New York was threatened early in the war by British artillery, he recommended the citizens evacuate the city. He trusted that "the blessing of Heaven upon the American arms" would allow these citizens to "return to it in perfect security" very soon.[69] In the spring of 1777, he pleaded for help from Congress, insisting that he was using every means in his power to "keep the Life and Soul of this Army together." Yet, the Commander in Chief, once again, asserted that "our cause is good and I hope Providence will support it."[70] When soldier discontent peaked near the end of the war over delinquent pay, lack of clothing, and a shortage of provisions, Washington had no doubt "that the same bountiful Providence which has relieved us in a variety of difficulties heretofore will enable us to emerge from them ultimately, and crown our struggles with success."[71] To Major General John Armstrong, he wondered if the affairs of the Continental Army would come to an "awful crisis" just so "the hand of Providence" would "be more conspicuous in our deliverance." For Washington, the "many remarkable interpositions of the divine governmt. in the hour of our

67. Washington, General Orders, December 17, 1777, in ibid., 10:167–68.

68. Washington to Thomas McKean, August 13, 1776, in ibid., 5:428.

69. Washington Proclamation, August 17, 1776, in ibid., 5:445.

70. Washington to Robert Morris, March 2, 1777, in ibid., 7:225.

71. Washington to Robert Livingston, January 31, 1781, in ibid., 21:163–64.

deepest distress and darkness, have been too luminous to suffer me to doubt the happy issue of the present contest."[72]

Military triumphs and successes verified and validated the general's belief that God supported the American cause. After one victory during the middle of the war, he celebrated the "glorious Success" insisting that "this singular favor of Providence is to be received with thankfulness and the happy moment which Heaven has pointed out for the firm establishment of American Liberty . . . ."[73] Claiming victory at the Battle of Monmouth, Washington explained that his men had been in "a Retreat," and that

> disorder arising from it would have proved fatal to the Army had not that bountiful Providence which has never failed us in the hour of distress, enabled me to form a Regiment or two (of those that were retreating) in the face of the Enemy, and under their fire, by which means a stand was made long enough.[74]

When an American and British fleet had to withdraw because of stormy weather, the general considered the event a "victory under the direction of a wise providence who no doubt directs them for the best purposes," and who brings "the greatest degree of happiness to the greatest number of his people."[75] After Benedict Arnold's capture as a traitor, Washington asserted to his close friend, Colonel John Laurens, that "in no instance since the commencement of the War has the interposition of Providence appeared more conspicuous than the rescue of the Post and Garrison of West point from Arnold's villainous perfidy."[76] While Arnold's conduct was "so villainously perfidious," God "remarkably interposed in our favor" and splendidly exposed the "horrid design of surrendering the Post and Garrison of West point into the hands of the enemy."[77]

When the British surrendered after the Battle of Yorktown in 1781, Washington gave thanks to God for the American victory. "I join in adoring that Supreme being to whom alone can be attributed the signal success of our Arms," he wrote to one Reformed Dutch congregation. He hoped that "same providence who has hitherto in so remarkable a manner Evinced the Justice of our Cause" would lead the colonists "to a speedy and honorable

---

72. Washington to John Armstrong, March 26, 1781, in ibid., 21:378.

73. Washington to James Potter, October 18, 1777, in ibid., 9:391.

74. Washington to John Augustine Washington, July 4, 1778, in ibid., 12:156–57.

75. Washington to Jonathan Trumbull, September 6, 1778, in ibid., 12:406.

76. Washington to John Laurens, October 13, 1780, in ibid., 20:173.

77. Washington to Joseph Reed, October 18, 1780, in ibid., 20:213.

peace."[78] Earlier in the war he avowed his "trust" in the "goodness of the cause and the exertions of the people living under divine protection." Washington believed "all the blessings" in war and peace "flow from piety and religion."[79] At times things had looked "gloomy indeed," but the "well-known firmness of my Countrymen," he explained, "and the expected aid of Heaven, supported me in the trying hour, and have finally reallised our most sanguine wishes."[80]

Washington faced overwhelming challenges as general of the Continental Army. His relationship with God and Christian faith nurtured and sustained his confidence. Picture by Charles Willson Peale. (Courtesy of the Mount Vernon Ladies' Association)

78. Washington to the Ministers, Elders, and Deacons of the Reformed Dutch Church of Schenectady, New York, June 30, 1782, in ibid., 24:390–91.

79. Washington to Minister, Elders, and Deacons of the Dutch Reformed Church at Raritan, New Jersey, June 2, 1779, in ibid., 15:210.

80. Washington to the Burgesses and Common Council of the Borough of Wilmington, Delaware, December 16, 1783, in ibid., 27:276.

That Washington led an inexperienced, ill-equipped, amateurish army to victory over the greatest empire and military fighting force the world had ever known cannot be overstated. The general commanded men who had little military training, one-year enlistments, little or no pay, and a constant shortage of supplies. No wonder so many officers and enlisted men saw him praying. Moreover, victory was achieved despite the unwillingness of many colonists to sacrifice for the war effort. Washington was especially disappointed when affluent citizens purchased and horded goods for money-making purposes at the expense of supplying the Continental Army. "The destruction of the army," he bemoaned to a friend early in the war, would come from "such a dearth of public spirit, and want of virtue, such stock jobbing, and fertility in all the low arts to obtain advantages of one kind or another." He "never saw before, and pray God I may never be witness to again" such selfish, sinful behavior. The "ultimate end of these manueavres is beyond my scan. I tremble at the prospect."[81] Throughout the war, he would continue to rail against the lack of virtue in America—"It really shocks me to think of it!" he lamented.[82]

As much as he abhorred a lack of virtue and patriotism, Washington's acute understanding and recognition of the infirmity and sinful nature of men turned out to be a leadership asset in disguise. He ordered his soldiers to "consecrate themselves to the service of their divine benefactor" with "sincere acknowledgements and offerings" that "they may join the penitent confession of their sins."[83] When Congress asked for a special day of fasting, humiliation, and prayer, he required his men to "acknowledge the gracious interpositions of *Providence*" and "to deprecate deserved punishment for our Sins and Ingratitude, to unitedly implore the Protection of Heaven."[84]

Knowing that orders would not be followed or executed properly, or that enlisted men would not always display the courage needed under fire, prepared and steeled Washington for inevitable adversity, disappointment, and failure. He knew all too well his own humanity and weaknesses. "I cannot doubt, nor do I wish my conduct to be exempted from reprehension farther than it may deserve," he admitted to Patrick Henry.[85]

A sinful, flawed, mistake-prone leader, Washington realized he was leading other sinful, flawed, mistake-prone soldiers. The experiences of war further impressed into his consciousness and psyche the biblical doctrine of

81. Washington to Joseph Reed, November 28, 1775, in ibid., 4:124.

82. Washington to Burwell Bassett, April 22, 1779, in ibid., 14:432.

83. Washington, General Orders, November 30, 1777, in ibid., 10:123.

84. Washington, General Orders, April 12, 1779, in ibid., 14:369.

85. Washington to Patrick Henry, March 28, 1778, in ibid., 11:160.

original sin. He better understood the selfishness inherent in human nature and, therefore, was not surprised by the failure, poor performance, or the depravity of his men. On the contrary, he endured these human flaws and learned to persevere in combat and civic duty with a pragmatism and realism that produced impressive results. He learned patience and resilience. He understood how he must lead and plan for the best while, at the same time, prepare for the worst.

When the Continental Army suffered defeat, he rallied his troops to press on and fight another day. Never rattled or surprised by mistakes, Washington believed that the finger of God was in all things and that he and his men could learn through their sufferings, humiliating defeats, and disasters. William Hooper, signer of the Declaration of Independence and member of the Continental Congress, representing North Carolina, noted that "misfortunes are the Element in which" Washington shined. "He rises superior to them all, they serve as foils to his fortitude, and as stimulants to bring into view those great qualities which in the serenity of life his great modesty keeps concealed."[86] Robert Morris, also serving in the Continental Congress on behalf of Pennsylvania, told the general, midway through the war, that "Heaven (no doubt for the Noblest purposes) has blessed you with a Firmness of mind, Steadiness of Countenance and patience in Sufferings that give You infinite advantage over other Men." The general, therefore, should not "depend on other People's exertions being equal to your own."[87]

Understanding the frailties of the human condition freed Washington to lead boldly and act courageously. Since Providence was "inscrutable"— his most frequent description of God—only Providence could know if a disaster was truly a bad occurrence for the short-term or an essential, unforeseen part of God's plans for the long-term.[88] Washington could take charge and press forward realizing the outcome of events were ultimately in God's hands, which is exactly what he did during the war.

Realizing men were motivated by pragmatic self-interest, Washington worked tirelessly to find different ways to motivate his troops. He used the term "interest" frequently throughout his writings calling it the "bonding cement" of his army. Soldiers might join the Continental Army, initially, for pay and promotion. Once they enlisted, however, he knew that men would need further incentive to fight the British.[89]

---

86. Hooper to Robert Morris, February 1, 1777, in Kaminski, *Founders,* 474–75.

87. Morris to George Washington, February 27, 1777, in ibid., 475.

88. Novak and Novak, *Washington's God,* 180.

89. Johnson, *Washington: Founding Father,* 12–13; Ellis, *His Excellency,* 209; Smith, *Patriarch,* 215.

One primary way he inspired his troops was by recruiting God's agents—chaplains, priests, and ministers—to play a significant role in the life of the Continental Army. Not only did Washington believe that chaplains could help instill a sense of discipline amongst the men, he also felt that clergy could "animate the Soldiery and Impress them with a knowledge of the important rights we are contending for."[90] Thus, he pleaded with Congress to fund one chaplain for every regiment instead of one chaplain for every two regiments as Congress desired.[91] By empowering the clergy and chaplains in the army, he allowed other influential voices to annunciate and reinforce the ideals and values that were truly important to him. Christian chaplains were vital to Washington's effectiveness and success as a leader, even beyond the Revolutionary War. As president, he would continue to appoint ordained ministers to serve in the US Army under the new Constitution.[92]

Unlike Jefferson, and many other deists who had a real disdain for the clergy,[93] Washington genuinely enjoyed the company of ministers. By the end of his life, his diaries and other records revealed that he knew some sixty pastors who were either personal friends or who were entertained at Mount Vernon. In addition, he regularly corresponded with over forty pastors across the country and prayed with clergymen, even at his own table.[94] Pastors and ministers were men of "Character and good conversation," individuals who would "influence the manners of the Corps both by precept and example."[95]

Ministers frequently and repeatedly dined at Mount Vernon and in Washington's army camps throughout the war.[96] Clergymen genuinely enjoyed being in the company and presence of the general who was an excellent listener. Moreover, the Commander in Chief worked hard to earn the respect and admiration of pastors and priests by cracking down on soldiers' bad manners, corrupt morals, vice, and other sinful behavior. Many clergy, when visiting the Continental Army's camp, noticed and appreciated how

90. Washington to Jonathan Trumbull, December 15, 1775, *Writings of Washington,* 4:164.

91. Washington to President of Congress, May 29, 1777, in ibid., 8:139.

92. Lillback and Newcombe, *Sacred Fire,* 185.

93. Gaustad, *Religious Biography,* 185, 205.

94. Lillback and Newcombe, *Sacred Fire,* 268.

95. Washington to George Baylor, May 23, 1777, *Writings of Washington,* 8:109.

96. Washington, *Diaries of Washington,* 4:200, 329.

clean, neat, moral, and disciplined Washington's army was compared to the British army.[97]

As a Latitudinarian Christian, the prayers and thoughtfulness of the army chaplains and ministers sincerely touched Washington. After reading, "with pleasure," one particularly meaningful sermon sent to him by Reverend Uzal Ogden, Rector of Trinity Church in Newark, New Jersey, he praised Ogden for the message "on practical religion" which could be "Inscribed to Christians of every denomination." He thanked the Reverend for "the favourable sentiment you have been pleased to express of me," but especially for "the good wishes and prayers you offer in my behalf."[98]

Through chaplain sermons and messages, as well as his own encouragement, Washington reminded his men that they had much to be thankful for even in the midst of a brutal Revolutionary conflict. He constantly implored his men to pray for divine intervention and the "blessings of heaven upon the means used for our safety and defence."[99] Days of fasting, prayer, and humiliation were initiated to "implore the Lord, and Giver of all victory, to pardon our manifold sins and wickedness's, and that it would please him to bless the Continental Arms, with his divine favor and protection." Officers and soldiers were to "pay all due reverence" and "attention" to the "Lord of hosts, for his mercies already received, and for those blessings, which our Holiness and Uprightness of life can alone encourage us to hope through his mercy to obtain."[100] In yet another General Order, Washington arranged for day of fasting, humiliation and prayer so that soldiers could humbly "supplicate the mercy of Almighty God" for the "pardon all our manifold sins and transgressions." In addition, they were to ask God "to prosper the Arms of the United Colonies, and finally, to establish peace and freedom of America, upon a solid and lasting foundation." The general wanted his soldiers to observe their religious duties in an "unfeigned" and "pious" manner so as to "incline the Lord, and Giver of Victory, to prosper our arms."[101] Showing gratitude for God's goodness was serious military business.

While fighting for independence and "zealously performing the duties of good Citizens and soldiers" were crucial, Washington insisted that the army "ought not to be inattentive to the higher duties of Religion." As important as it was to have a "distinguished Character of Patriot," the "highest Glory" was "to add the more distinguished Character of Christian."

---

97. Higginbotham, *American Military Tradition,* 76.

98. Washington to Uzal Ogden, August 5, 1779, *Writings of Washington,* 16:51.

99. Washington, General Orders, July 4, 1775, ibid., 3:309.

100. Washington, General Orders, March 6, 1776, in ibid., 4:369.

101. Washington, General Orders, May 15, 1776, in ibid., 5:43.

The general reminded his men that the "signal Instances of providential Goodness which we have experienced and which have now almost crowned our labours with complete Success, demand from us in a peculiar manner the warmest returns of Gratitude and Piety to the Supreme Author of all Good."[102]

Gratitude for the interventions and blessings of God was a major motivation in serving the patriot cause with enthusiasm and determination. When the British lost Montreal, in late 1776, Washington's order pronounced that "such frequent Favors from divine providence will animate every American to continue, to exert his utmost, in the defence and Liberties of his Country." To give anything less than one's maximum effort would demonstrate "the basest ingratitude to the Almighty."[103] The Commander in Chief explained, "we shall be loaded with a double share of Shame and Infamy, if we do not acquit ourselves with Courage, or a determined Resolution to conquer or die." Every soldier was to "pay the utmost attention to his Arms and Health," "Cleanliness and Care," to be "exact in their discipline, obedient to their Superiors and vigilant on duty." Only with "such preparation, and a suitable Spirit," and "by the blessing of Heaven," would the Continental Army "repel our cruel Invaders; preserve our Country, and gain the greatest Honor."[104] Officers and soldiers were to be disciplined, orderly, hard working, conditioned, and prepared to the best of their abilities. An unwavering attitude and disposition, and the "united efforts of the officers, of every Rank, and the Soldiers, with the smiles of providence," would "render a favourable account" to the country "whenever they chuse to make the appeal to the great Arbiter of the universe."[105]

Throughout the Revolutionary War, and his entire life, Washington emphasized that success and prosperity would not be granted if Americans were not faithful to God. He used the term "blessing" over 160 times in his writings. If the people of the United Colonies used the gifts—the blessings—bestowed on them in the pursuit of God-pleasing liberty, then God would generously give and shower down even more blessings upon his people. This is yet another reason why chaplains were so important: Washington knew they would provide divine inspiration as well as articulate the connection between God's blessings and the army's virtue, cause, and results.[106]

---

102. Washington, General Orders, May 2, 1778, in ibid., 11:342–43.
103. Washington, General Orders, November 28, 1776, in ibid., 4:119.
104. Washington, General Orders, July 21, 1776, in ibid., 5:315–316.
105. Washington, General Orders, August 12, 1776, in ibid., 5:423.
106. Lillback and Newcombe, *Sacred Fire*, 181.

Victory would only come to the patriots if the gifts God had bestowed were vigorously applied with great earnestness and purpose. As Washington explained to Major General Philip Schuyler, to defeat the British, the Continental Army's "utmost Exertions must be used" and they must receive the "Favour of divine Providence."[107] When Governor Trumbull sent reinforcements, Washington thanked him and noted "the Smiles of Providence upon our Arms and Vigorous Exertions." By "the kind Interpositions" of God and "Aid of our Friends," the American cause would prevail.[108] To the president of Congress, he asserted that "under the smiles of Providence" and "with our own exertions," the impending British attack could be repelled and "pleasing to every Friend of America and to the rights of Humanity."[109] For Washington, "the good of the cause depends, under God, upon our vigilance and readiness to oppose a Crafty and enterprising enemy."[110]

Complacency, lethargy, and unrealized potential were pitfalls for the Continental Army and the cause of American independence. "No time is to be lost," Washington wrote one general in the middle of the war, for "the exigency of our Affairs" has never been "more pressing, nor requiring more strenuous efforts at present." He was mortified by the "Languor and Supiness" exhibited by some regiments and soldiers during the war. "All agree our claims are righteous and must be supported," he declared. Too many, however, "withhold the means, as if Providence, who has already done much for us, would continue his gracious interposition and work miracles for our deliverance, without troubling ourselves about the matter."[111]

God would bless those who were good stewards of the cause of liberty and freedom. "Providence had done, and I am perswaded is disposed to do," insisted the general, "a great deal for" the Continental Army and American people only if "every Man (especially those in Office) should with one hand and one heart pull the same way and with their whole strength."[112]

Even when battle results disappointed or ended in tragedy, Washington believed that God would ultimately sanctify wise implementation and stewardship of God's gifts. Early in the war, after numerous setbacks and Light Horse Harry Lee's capture, the general remained resolute and trusted that, "under the Smiles of Providence and by our own exertions, we shall be

---

107. Washington to Philip Shuyler, July 11, 1776, *Writings of Washington,* 5:258.

108. Washington to Jonathan Trumbull, August 18, 1776, in ibid., 5:453.

109. Washington to President of Congress, August 22, 1776, in ibid., 5:475.

110. Washington to Fisher Gay, September 4, 1776, in ibid., 6:13.

111. Washington to Samuel Holden Parsons, April 23, 1777, in ibid., 7:456.

112. Washington to John Armstrong, May 18, 1779, in ibid., 15:96–99.

happy." The cause was "righteous, and must be Supported."[113] Having suffered "some unfortunate circumstances," he confidently assured the troops
that with "another Appeal to Heaven (with the blessings of providence,
which it becomes every officer and soldier humbly to supplicate), we shall
prove successful."[114] After suffering defeat at Germantown in the fall of
1777, Washington challenged Brigadier General Thomas Nelson to work
more diligently to "deserve better of Providence" whom he was persuaded
would "smile upon us."[115]

In the war's aftermath, the general repeatedly warned and encouraged
Americans to live up to their responsibilities and the blessings granted by
God. "The great Director of events has carried us thro' a variety of Scenes
during this long and bloody contest, " he contended. Yet while the "present
prospect is pleasing," the republic's future depended on "our own Improve-
ment" and a "vigorous prosecution of this Success." If Americans desired "an
establishment of Peace, liberty, and Independence," they could not afford
a "Relaxation of our Exertions" which would "be attended with the most
unhappy consequences."[116] Indeed, "under the favor of divine providence
the Freedom, Independence, and happiness of America will shortly be
established upon the surest foundation." Americans must continue "those
exertions which have already so greatly humbled the power of our inveter-
ate enemies."[117] Washington asserted, "Providence has done much for us
in this contest, but we must do something for ourselves, if we expect to go
triumphantly through with it."[118]

While Washington believed God favored the American cause, he also
felt personally blessed by God, too. The numerous references to God and his
Christian faith, as well as the *way* he spoke of his God throughout his war
correspondence, is impressive and striking especially considering the reticent personality and Latitudinarian worldview of the Commander in Chief.

Like gold being purified through fire, the Revolutionary War put
Washington's religious faith to the test. This personal crucible forged and
constructed a more intimate relationship between the general and his God.
Washington's Christian faith not only informed his biblical worldview and
shaped his character but also implanted a confidence that would manifest

113. Washington to Massachusetts Legislature, December 18, 1776, in ibid., 6:396.

114. Washington, General Orders, September 13, 1777, in ibid., 9:211.

115. Washington to Thomas Nelson, November 7, 1777, in ibid., 10:28.

116. Washington to William Ramsay, John Fitzgerald, Robert Hooe, and the Other
Inhabitants of Alexandria, November 19, 1781, in ibid., 37:356.

117. Washington to George Plater and Thomas Cockey Dey, November 23, 1782,
in ibid., 23:358.

118. Washington to James McHenry, July 18, 1782, in ibid., 24:432.

itself in his most impressive leadership traits—humility, audacity, persever-ance, resilience, and courage.

From the beginning of the conflict, Washington's faith provided an in-nate confidence and understanding that he was not alone at the top. In one of the two surviving letters written to his wife, he admitted, in June of 1775, that he was nervous about leading the Continental Army and filled "with inexpressible concern." Yet, his trust in God and God's plans gave him the confidence to lead. As he explained to Martha, Congress had determined that the

> whole army raised for the defence of the American cause shall be put under my care. You may believe me, my dear Patcy, when I assure you, in the most solemn manner that, so far from seek-ing this appointment, I have used every power to avoid it, not only from my unwillingness to part with you and the family, but from a consciousness of its being a trust too great for my capac-ity, and that I should enjoy more real happiness in one month with you at home, than I have the most distant prospect of find-ing abroad, if my stay were to be seven time seven years. But it has been a kind of destiny that has thrown me upon this service, I shall hope that my undertaking is designed to answer some good purpose. You might, and I suppose did perceive, from the tenor of my letters, that I was apprehensive I could not avoid this appointment, without exposing my character to such censures, as would have reflected dishonor upon myself, and given pain to my friends. This, I am sure, could not, ought not, to be pleas-ing to you, and must have lessened me considerably in my own esteem. I shall rely, confidently on that Providence, which has heretofore preserved and been bountiful to me, not doubting but that I shall return safe to you in the fall. I shall feel no pain for the toil or danger of the campaign . . . .[119]

During the Battle of Monmouth, in late June of 1778, retreating and disorderly Continental Army troops were rallied by the general to a higher ground where they made a fortified stand and counterstrike against the enemy. Alexander Hamilton, the general's talented aid-de-camp during the war, reported that he had never seen the Commander in Chief "to so much advantage." Washington's "coolness and firmness were admirable." The Continental Army inflicted over one thousand British casualties on the battlefield. "America owes a great deal to General Washington for this day's work," Hamilton insisted. "A general rout, dismay and disgrace would have attended the whole army in any other hands but his. By his own good sense

---

119. Washington to Martha Washington, June 18, 1775, in ibid., 3:293–94.

and fortitude he turned the fate of the day." The general was a "Master work-man," and had "brought order out of confusion . . . ."[120]

Contemporaries were not only impressed with Washington's courage and personal confidence in confronting overwhelming odds and dire cir-cumstances, but also for his dignity and resiliency in the face of such daily struggles.[121] David Humphreys, a friend, aide de camp, and biographer of Washington, praised the general's "active, indefatigable, persevering" char-acter and the "unbroken firmness of constitution & the unshaken resolution of soul with which nature seemed to have formed him to meet the shocks of adversity."[122] In April of 1778, Samuel Shaw, a doctor and later a representa-tive from the state of Vermont, told a pastor that Washington possessed a "steady, amiable character," and that his "fortitude, patience, and equanimity of soul," despite numerous setbacks in the war, "ought to endear him to his country" as it had done "exceedingly to the army." God had raised up the general "to show how high humanity" could soar.[123]

Of course he occasionally despaired internally and was transparent in reckoning with the grave realities and challenges of war. Yet Washington inspired soldiers with his perseverance, bravery, and steady optimism. He was certain the virtue of the Continental Army and the nobility of the cause would be rewarded by God.[124] One soldier noted:

> Our army love their general very much, but they have one thing against him, which is the little care he takes of himself in any action. His personal bravery, and the desire he has of animating his troops by example, make him fearless of danger. This occa-sions us much uneasiness. But Heaven, which has hitherto been his shield, I hope will still continue to guard so valuable a life.[125]

Washington's trust in God stirred him to act despite his personal fears and the daunting challenges. His mental toughness, grounded and bolstered by his religious faith, kept him balanced and levelheaded during setbacks and defeat as well as during triumphs and victories.

Few acts or interventions from Providence escaped his notice or reverence throughout the war. "I will not lament or repine at any act of Providence," he insisted, "because I am in great measure a convert . . . that

120. Hamilton to Elias Boudinot, July 5, 1778, in Kaminski, *Founders*, 479–80.

121. Tebbel, *Washington's America*, 203, 337.

122. Humphreys, *Life of Washington*, 7, 27.

123. Shaw to Reverend Mr. Eliot, April 12, 1778, Kaminski, *Founders*, 478.

124. Flexner, *Washington*, 2:542.

125. Fitzpatrick, *Writings of Washington*, 6:470.

whatever is, is right . . . ."[126] The many "signal Interpositions of Providence" inspire "every reflecting Mind with Confidence," he asserted to Reverend William Gordon. "No Man has a more perfect Reliance on the alwise, and powerful dispensations of the Supreme Being than I have nor thinks his aid more necessary." The "favourable Sentiments" expressed by the "Gentlemen of Providence," or clergy, were "exceedingly flattering," especially since he valued their "good opinion" almost as much as he did living with "conscious Integrity."[127] No doubt he wanted to "obtain the applause of deserving men," something which he said was his "highest wish." The general knew, however, that success and "approbation" meant he was to be used as "an instrument" in the "signal" interpositions of Providence.[128]

Washington's trust in God did not mean he always fully understood God's plans or interventions. The ways of Providence were "inscrutable." An inscrutable God was not easily understood, but mysterious, unfathomable, enigmatic. Just like the militia "who are here today and gone tomorrow," he contemplated, so *like the ways of Providence are, almost, inscrutable.*"[129]

Even if he did not immediately comprehend the plans and acts of God, the confidence derived from his faith kept him open to Providence's bidding and designs. The Bible he read regularly spoke of the depths of God's wisdom and knowledge and his unsearchable and inscrutable ways. Yet God's plans would not be harmful but prosperous, God-pleasing, and purposeful (Rom 11:33, Jer 29:11). Washington understood that human "actions, depending upon ourselves, may be controuled, while the powers of thinking originating in higher causes, cannot always be moulded to our wishes." One should not fear God's plans, however, since "the determinations of Providence are always wise" and "often inscrutable." God's "decrees appear to bear hard upon us at times," he acknowledged, but they were "nevertheless meant for gracious purposes."[130]

A personal, intimate trust and confidence in God permeates the general's war correspondence with striking regularity. In a letter to Reverend Israel Evans, while suffering in the cold at Valley Forge, Washington asserted that "the first wish" of his heart was to aid his friend's "pious endeavors to inculcate a due sense of the dependence we ought to place in that all wise and powerful Being on whom alone our success depends."[131] To a plantation

126. Washington to Joseph Reed, March 7, 1776, in ibid., 4:380.

127. Washington to William Gordon, May 13, 1776, in ibid., 37:526.

128. Washington to Josiah Quincy, March 24, 1776, in ibid., 4:422.

129. Washington to John Augustine Washington, February 24, 1777, in ibid., 7:198.

130. Washington to Bryan Fairfax, March 1, 1778, in ibid., 11:3.

131. Washington to Israel Evans, March 13, 1778, in ibid., 11:78.

friend who had congratulated him on his success so far in the war effort, the general instead gave credit to Providence's "protection and direction of me, through the many difficult and intricate scenes" of war. Moreover, he gave "humble and grateful thanks" for God's "constant interposition in our behalf, when the clouds were heaviest and seemed ready to burst upon us." Thanks be "to Heaven," the war seemed to be going in favor of the colonists.[132]

Washington's Christian faith certainly lifted his sprits and personally comforted him during the many stressful and gloomy moments of war. The fight for independence "is a kind of struggle designed I dare say by Providence to try the patience, fortitude, and virtue of Men." Those who placed their trust in God, however, would not "sink under difficulties, or be discouraged by hardships."[133] Christians were to submit to life's events with "the most perfect resignation and cheerfulness." He saw "every dispensation of Providence as designed to answer some valuable purpose, and hope I shall always possess a sufficient degree of fortitude to bear without murmuring any stroke which may happen, either to my person or estate."[134] He had "abundant reason to thank providence for its many favourable interpositions" during the war, especially since God had been "my only dependence" when "all other resources seemed to have fail'd us."[135] Knowing that he was under the "care of an indulgent Providence," Washington hoped for the "rapid increase and universal extension of knowledge virtue and true Religion" once a "speedy and honorable peace" was secured.[136]

As much as the Commander in Chief worried about the mental state of his soldiers, he too required psychological care and attention amidst all of the pressure, gloom, and daunting obstacles of war. Searching "the vast volumes of history" to find "a case similar" the plight of the Continental Army, he distressed over confronting the "flower of the British troops" for any duration which seemed futile and "too much too attempt." He had "scarcely immerged from one difficulty before I have been plunged into another." Through it all, however, he knew that "God in his goodness" would "direct" the outcome. "I am thankful for his protection to this time."[137] He lamented how much happier he would have been if, instead of accepting command under such circumstances, he "had taken my musket on my

132. Washington to Landon Carter, May 30, 1778, in ibid., 11:492–94.

133. Washington to Andrew Lewis, October 15, 1778, in ibid., 13:79.

134. Washington to Lund Washington, May 29, 1779, in ibid., 15:180.

135. Washington to William Gordon, March 9, 1781, in ibid., 21:332.

136. Washington to the Ministers, Elders, and Deacons of the Reformed Dutch Church at Albany, June 28, 1782, in ibid., 24:390.

137. Washington to Joseph Reed, January 4, 1776, in ibid., 4:211–12.

shoulder and entered the ranks" or "justified the measure to posterity and my own conscience" and "retired to the back country, and lived in a wig-wam." Nevertheless, while the "reflection on my situation, and that of this army, produces many an uneasy hour when all around me are wrapped in sleep," and "few people know the predicament we are in, on a thousand counts," Washington found comfort in his Christian faith: "If I shall be able to rise superior to these and many other difficulties . . . I shall most religiously believe, that the finger of Providence is in it . . . ."[138]

The hardships and tribulations of war compelled the general to find solace in his faith. Worried about the greenness and timidity of his soldiers, yet feeling the urgency to attack the British army at Boston before they could be reinforced in early 1776, Washington decided to act leaving the outcome to God. "Whether circumstances will admit of the trial, and if tried, what will be the event, the all-wise Disposer of them alone can tell," he disclosed.[139]

Later in 1776, as war difficulties mounted, he worried "almost to death with the retrograde Motions of things." Not even "a pecuniary reward of 20,000 pounds a year would not induce me to undergo what I do" in dealing with "such a variety of distressing Circumstances to conduct matters agreeable to public expectation." The general pined for a peaceable retirement to his own "Vine, and Fig Tree."[140] No officer "since the creation ever had such a variety of difficulties and perplexities to encounter as I have," he complained in the winter of 1777. He questioned how "we shall be able to rub along till the new army was raised." Once again, however, Washington turned to his faith and God—who "has heretofore saved us in a remarkable manner, and on this we must principally rely" for strength and comfort.[141]

As the burdens and stress of war increased and dragged on into the fall of 1777, so too did Washington's trust and dependence on God. "To Sum up the Whole," he explained to Richard Henry Lee, "I have been a Slave to the service . . . and undergone more than most Men are aware of, to harmonize so many discordant parts."[142] Yet, just when he thought he could not proceed or be of any more service to the cause, a "singular Instance of

138. Washington to Joseph Reed, January 14, 1776, in ibid., 4:243.

139. Washington to Joseph Reed, February 1, 1776, in ibid., 4:300.

140. Washington to John Augustine Washington, November 6, 1776, in ibid., 6:246–47.

141. Washington to John Park Custis, January 22, 1777, in ibid., 7:53.

142. Washington to Richard Henry Lee, October 17, 1777, in ibid., 9:389.

Providence" would demonstrate "that a Superintending Providence is ordering every thing for the best and that, in due time, all will end well."[143]

Throughout the conflict, Washington had the unenviable task of concealing the dire realities and condition of the Continental Army in order to maintain public and congressional support for the war effort. His Christian faith comforted him in the worst moments of the war. Valley Forge Picture by John McGoffin. (Courtesy of the Mount Vernon Ladies' Association)

During the winter campaign at Valley Forge (1777–78), the shortage of clothing, shoes, food, as well as the seemingly dim prospects for victory, significantly challenged the army's morale and Washington's. His distress— that "much more is expected of me than is possible to be performed"—was further complicated in that he was "obliged to conceal the true State of the Army from Public view and thereby expose myself to detraction and Calumny."[144]

Yet Washington's Christian faith helped him cope and overcome his despair. To his close friend, Marquis de Lafayette, he insisted that "we must not, in so great a contest, expect to meet with nothing but Sun shine . . . every thing happens so for the best," and "we shall triumph over all our misfortunes, and shall, in the end, be ultimately happy."[145] Even as supplies and monies for the Continental Army dwindled and war fatigue saturated the countryside and Congress, he never expected "that the path" to victory

143. Washington to Landon Carter, October 27, 1777, in ibid., 9:453–454.

144. Washington to the President of Congress, December 23, 1777, in ibid., 10:196.

145. Washington to Marquis de Lafayette, December 31, 1777, in ibid., 10:237.

would "be strewed wt. flowers." Instead, he pressed on knowing that the "great and Good Being who rules the Universe has disposed matters otherwise and for wise purposes I am perswaded."[146]

Washington expressed great disappointment and anger toward people "who seem to think the contest is at an end" and only demonstrated an interest in making money. Moreover, Congress did not appear to be serious about winning the war. "Friends and foes seem now to combine to pull down the goodly fabric we have hitherto been raising at the expence of so much time, blood, and treasure." Unless the "bodies politick will exert themselves to bring things back to first principles, correct abuses, and punish our internal foes, inevitable ruin must follow," he asserted. The general was frustrated that leaders like Thomas Jefferson and George Mason idly stood by during the country's great time of need. "Where are our Men of abilities? Why do they not come forth to save their Country?" he wrote in exasperation. Without their engagement "our hitherto noble struggle" would "end in ignominy."[147]

An irritated Washington reminded congressmen, who continued to carp at his generalship, that he never "assumed the Character of a Military genius and Officer of experience." Command was "forced upon me" and accepted with "the utmost diffidence from a consciousness that it required greater abilities and more experience than I possessed to conduct a great Military machine . . . ." For the past number of years, the Commander in Chief behaved as a "perfect Slave endeavouring under as many embarrassing circumstances as ever fell to one man's lott to encounter; and as pure motives as ever man was influenced by, to promote the cause, and Service I had imbarked in." Short and expiring terms of service of enlisted men, sickness, desertion, and lack of pay continued to take a toll on the army and, occasionally, his own psyche. Discouraging as these developments were, he held firm that the American cause would not fail since God had so often before "taken us up when bereft of every other hope."[148]

Confiding, late in the war, to his friend and compatriot, Baron von Steuben, Washington lamented that "the prospect" of victory was "gloomy and the storm thickens." Yet, he still remained hopeful. "I have been so inured to difficulties in the course of this contest," he reflected, "that I have learned to look upon them with more tranquility than formerly."[149]

146. Washington to Joseph Reed, November 27, 1778, in ibid., 13:348.
147. Washington to George Mason, March 27, 1779, in ibid., 14:298–301.
148. Washington to Joseph Reed, July 29, 1779, in ibid., 16:7–10.
149. Washington to Baron von Steuben, April 2, 1780, in ibid., 18:204.

"You ask how I am to be rewarded for all of this?" he wrote to his cousin and Mount Vernon overseer, Lund Washington, in the spring of 1780. Washington continued:

> There is one reward that nothing can deprive me of, and that is, the consciousness of having done my duty with the strictest rectitude, and most scrupulous exactness, and the certain knowledge, that if we should, ultimately, fail in the present contest, it is not owing to the want of exertion in me, or the application of every means that Congress and the United States . . . have put into my hands. Providence, to whom we are infinitely more indebted than we are to our own wisdom, or our own exertions, has always displayed its power and goodness, when clouds and thick darkness seemed ready to overwhelm us. The hour is now come when we stand much in need of another manifestation of its bounty however little we deserve it.[150]

Through all the hardship and suffering of war, Washington's religious faith not only comforted him, but also ingrained in him a hopeful perseverance.[151]

In December, 1781, John Jay, a member of the American delegation negotiating peace with England, spoke for many Americans when he told Henry Knox, the general's chief artillery officer in the army, that God had led Washington "with safety and success, through all the duties of his station" and carried the general "home with the blessings of all America on his head." Washington had exhibited the "the most singular instance of virtue, greatness, and good-fortune united which the history of mankind has hitherto recorded."[152]

Nearly eight years of war took a heavy toll on the tall and athletic Virginian. Poor teeth and sore gums plagued him and caused his face to swell often. His eyes, having read numerous military dispatches and correspondence, had weakened. He had only come home to Mount Vernon twice in eight years. His farms and plantations were not being meticulously cared for without his daily and vigilant supervision. As a general, he had lost many battles and witnessed thousands of his men die or be maimed in combat; he endured long marches and brutal winter encampments all while pressing on, despite a feeble, lethargic, and almost bankrupt government.[153] He was

---

150. Washington to Lund Washington, May 19, 1780, in ibid., 18:392.

151. Novak and Novak, *Washington's God,* 66.

152. Jay to Henry Knox, December 10, 1781, in Kaminski, *Founders,* 483.

153. Fowler, *American Crisis,* 163.

tired—mentally and physically. And yet, Washington somehow persevered and pressed on to win the war.

While so many other things had unraveled and weakened during the Revolutionary War, Washington's edifying and empowering, personal relationship with God had increased, intensified, and strengthened. Inspired by his Christian faith and intimacy with God, the general had led in an unshackled, confident manner that rubbed off on officers, soldiers, and anyone who came in contact with him. More than any other characteristic, Washington's most indomitable leadership attribute was an indispensable confidence, which emanated from his Christian faith and relationship with God. For even the American victory over the British, Washington believed, had unfolded exactly according to God's plan.

6

First Farewell and Legacy Address

After the British surrender at Yorktown, in October 1781, Washington kept the Continental Army battle-ready. The Treaty of Paris would eventually be signed on September 3, 1783. In the meantime, the general tried to calm outraged officers and soldiers who continued to resent congressional inaction on payment for services rendered.

As the army encamped near Newburgh, New York, conspiracy and mutinous tensions brewed. An anonymous letter from a "fellow soldier" circulated through the camp calling for action. (We know today that a young major named John Armstrong wrote the letter, but historians are still not sure if other senior officers had orchestrated that the letter be written and circulated). Officers openly talked about seizing control of the army and marching on Congress to demand pay at gunpoint. There were also whispers that Washington should assert himself as a patriot-king, take political control over the new government, and fulfill the government's pledge to remunerate the soldiers what they had been promised. Some congressmen wanted to use the military as a political weapon in an attempt to increase and expand their power over the states.[1]

While he certainly sympathized with the army's grievances and denounced Congress's broken promises, the Commander in Chief wanted nothing to do with a subversion of civilian authority. He would not allow the fledgling American republic to be overthrown by a military coup d'état.

On March 15, 1783 at New Windsor, New York (near Newburgh), Washington entered The Temple, a rough wooden hall only recently completed, and took the lectern with no great ceremony to address his men. The

---

1. Ellis, *His Excellency,* 141–42.

officers were astonished. Never before had the general come in person to formally to speak to such a gathering of officers. His appearance indicated the seriousness of the crisis at hand.

Normally restrained, cool, and deliberate in his communications, Washington's speech was personal and emotional. He rebutted the author of the anonymous letter who had questioned the Commander in Chief's support of the soldiers. Refuting the charge and reiterating his life-long loyalty to the army, he next read from a prepared statement telling his officers that he would personally make the case for justice before Congress. They should refrain from taking any action that might detract from their honorable and victorious service to the country. The room fell silent. Sensing that his message was not resonating, he took out and started to read a letter received from Congressman Joseph Jones—who indicated that Congress was indeed preparing to take action to rectify many of the army's grievances.

Struggling to read the first few sentences of the letter from the congressman, the normally composed and gallant looking general paused. He begged the indulgence of his congregated officers while he put on his reading glasses—which most officers had never seen before this moment. "Gentleman," he confided, "you must pardon me. I have grown gray in your service and now find myself growing blind."[2] The vulnerability displayed by their beloved leader at that moment—his aged face, weakened eyes, uncomfortable pause, and humble words—struck and touched an emotional chord with the men in attendance. They did not hear much of what was said afterward. Major Samuel Shaw insisted, "there was something so natural, so unaffected, in this appeal, as rendered it superior to the most studied oratory." Washington's earnest presentation and unpretentious words forced their way "to the heart" and "moistened every eye" in the room.[3] The show of humility, as well as their general's palpable loyalty to the nascent republic, indeed had left many soldiers in the audience in tears.

In a masterful exhibition from a man who loved theatre, Washington performed his finest hour. As soon as he left The Temple, officers of the Continental Army adopted a resolution expressing faith that Congress would make things right. The military coup was dead. Washington had saved the country from a hostile takeover and path to monarchy. The American republic would derive its power from the people and civilian government, not from the military.[4]

2. Fowler, *American Crisis,* 184–86.

3. Shaw to Reverend Mr. Eliot, April 1783, in Kaminski, *Founders,* 484–85.

4. Fowler, *American Crisis,* 186–87; Johnson, *Washington: Founding Father,* 77; Ellis, *His Excellency,* 142–44; Jones, *Washington,* 86.

GENERAL WASHINGTON.

The general's finest moments of public leadership came after the Revolutionary War was completed. In stifling a military takeover and resigning as commander of the Continental Army, Washington ensured and secured the republican ideals of the Revolution. Picture by Carington Bowles. (Courtesy of the Mount Vernon Ladies' Association)

With the Revolution won and the military takeover thwarted, Washington took great care in writing, in June of 1783, what he thought would be his final public discourse to the American people. Although the Circular to the States was sent to the thirteen governors of the United Colonies, the letter would be circulated and read by most Americans during the summer and fall of 1783.

The Circular was immediately labeled "Washington's Legacy" and highly acclaimed. One newspaper called the Circular the "finishing stroke" of Washington's "inimitable character." Other newspapers claimed it was "incomparable" and "dictated by the immediate spirit of God." After reading the Circular, one New Englander said he imagined himself "in the presence of the great general of the twelve United States of Israel."[5]

The Circular to the States reveals much about Washington's religious faith and thought. Over thirty spiritual and religious references are made in the document, including one to Holy Communion—"the cup of blessing." Some historians call the Circular "Washington's Confession of Faith" and note that the letter retains a strong pastoral tone—like a shepherd advises his flock.[6]

Washington certainly wanted his message to resonate with the American people. Having achieved victory over the British and independence for the new nation, he explained his desire to resign and "return to that domestic retirement, which, it is well known, I left with the greatest reluctance." Before departing from the public scene, however, he wanted to offer "sentiments respecting some important subjects, which appear to me to be intimately connected with the tranquility of the United States."

He had "spent the prime of my life" and countless "anxious days and watchful nights" fighting for the American people—who were "extremely dear" to him. The Circular was to be his last official communication. Thus, he wanted to "congratulate" Americans "on the glorious events which Heaven has been pleased to produce in our favor." They should be full of "gratitude and rejoicing" for the victory handed down from Heaven by an active, caring God. "Citizens of America" now possessed "absolute freedom and Independency" and were "to be considered as the Actors on the most conspicuous Theatre," he explained. The new nation, "peculiarly designated by Providence for the display of human greatness and felicity," was to be the shining example of republican virtue to the world. Each American had been blessed by God and "surrounded with every thing which can contribute to the completion of private and domestic enjoyment." Heaven had "crowned all its other blessings" on the young republic and provided "a fairer opportunity for political happiness" than "any other Nation has ever been favored with." The very "foundation of our Empire," he asserted, "was not laid in the gloomy age of Ignorance and Superstition," but "above all" from the "pure and benign light of Revelation." The "cup of blessing is thus reached out to us," affirmed Washington, and "happiness is ours, if we have a disposition to seize the occasion and make it our own."

Washington exhorted his fellow countrymen to understand that "this is the moment when the eyes of the whole World are turned upon them, this is the moment to establish or ruin" the American "national character

5. Freeman, *Washington,* 5:446.

6. Chernow, *Washington,* 443; Lillback and Newcombe, *Sacred Fire,* 213–14.

forever." While Americans could celebrate their victory over British tyranny, the Revolution was far from complete. The "Revolution must ultimately be considered as a blessing or a curse . . . not to the present age alone, for with our fate will the destiny of unborn Millions be involved." Therefore, even as he headed for the "shade of Retirement," he asserted that Americans should "implore divine benediction" for the support and sustenance of their new republican government.

In the concluding lines of the Circular, his "earnest prayer" was

> that God would have you, and the State over which your preside, in his holy protection, that he would incline the hearts of the Citizens to cultivate a spirit of subordination for obedience to Government, to entertain a brotherly affection and love for one another, for their fellow Citizens of the United States at large, and particularly for their brethren who have served in the Field, and finally, that he would most graciously be pleased to dispose us all, to do Justice, to love mercy, and to demean ourselves with that Charity, humility and pacific temper of mind, which were the Characteristicks of the Divine Author of our blessed Religion, and without an humble imitation of whose example in these things, we can never hope to be a happy Nation.[7]

Baring much of his religious soul and biblical worldview, the Circular to the States remains one of the most striking and significant statements of Washington's life. His call for the people "to do Justice" and "to love mercy" are words from the prophet Micah who asks, "What doth the Lord require of thee, but to do justly, and to love mercy, and to walk humbly with thy God?" (Mic 6:8 KJV). The explicit reference to Jesus Christ—"the Divine Author of our blessed Religion"—dominates the final sentences of his last will and testament to the nation and lifts up Jesus's Beatitudes of the Sermon on the Mount, which are the traits and characteristics that distinguish Jesus most among humanity.[8] Furthermore, Washington's devotion to the orthodox, Anglican teachings of the Christian faith are evident in the reference to a "Divine" Jesus and the "pure and benign light of Revelation"—the inspired and inerrant Bible.[9]

Like other biblical references and allusions he frequently used in his correspondence, the Circular injected Scripture into governance and the social fabric of society. Washington wanted Jesus's characteristics and

7. Washington, Circular to the States, June 8, 1783, *Writings of Washington,* 26:483–96.

8. Novak and Novak, *Washington's God,* 158.

9. Lillback and Newcombe, *Sacred Fire,* 213–14; Mapp, *Faith of Our Fathers,* 76.

teachings to be embraced and applied in the everyday lives of the American people. A humble, Christian, and thereby virtuous citizenry would be essential to the nation's well-being, security, and future prosperity.[10]

The Christ-like humility that Washington encouraged all Americans to live by was a characteristic which contemporaries lauded in him. Count Axel de Fersen, one of Rochambeau's aides during the war, said the general was "handsome and majestic," and at the same time, possessed a "mild and open countenance" which "perfectly reflects his moral qualities." Washington "looked the hero; he is very cold; speaks little, but is courteous and frank."[11] French staff officer Barbe-Marbois observed that the general "preserves in battle the character of humanity which makes him so dear to his soldiers in camp." Abigail Adams noted the Virginian's "dignity which forbids familiarity," but admired his "easy affability which creates love and reverence." Another contemporary found Washington's face "grave and serious" but "never stern" and "softened by the most gracious and amiable smile."[12]

During the downtimes of camp life throughout the war, Washington played wicket with the young men on his staff and took time to visit with and charm the loneliest of sentries. He trusted those who served around him and made himself vulnerable by expressing his own feelings and emotions which, in turn, empowered and gave people permission to be vulnerable and responsive to him. In this way, a tight bond formed between the general and his officers and soldiers.

Washington's humility made him an endearing and admirable figure throughout the entirety of his life. He did not speak about himself or any of his accomplishments. His adopted granddaughter, Nelly Custis, who lived with the general for twenty years, later recalled that her grandstepfather spoke very little in general. She never heard him share even one singular incident of his wartime exploits.[13]

Dr. Ashbel Green, a chaplain for the Congress during the early years of Washington's administration, commented, "there was more of the indefinable quality called *presence* in President Washington than any person I have ever known." He was "courteous and kind" and so well-mannered that Green could "never speak to him without feeling a degree of embarrassment such as I have ever felt in the presence of any other individual, man

---

10. Brookhiser, *Founding Father,* 148.

11. Tebbel, *Washington's America,* 96.

12. Flexner, *Washington,* 2:401, 541.

13. McDowell, *Apostle of Liberty,* 238–39.

or woman, with whom I was well acquainted."[14] One English visitor insisted that Washington had a great "deal of the milk of human kindness . . . and philanthropic turn of mind, which cannot be said of one in ten thousand of his countrymen." The general was meek and received people with "all of the complacency of a friend and with none of the disgusting *hauteur* of a superior." He listened to "persons of my humble sphere." Yet another visitor opined that when one gets to know a person of great fame, usually the individual's character does not hold up to scrutiny. Conversely, "Washington stands almost alone, a glorious exception to this general truth . . . Integrity and benevolence rusticate, domesticate, and ruralize with him . . . we view him a firm pillar of human virtue, the *Atlas* of the western continent."[15]

Elkanah Watson, a courier for Washington and for Benjamin Franklin in France during the war, one day fell ill with a bad cold and severe cough while traveling through Virginia. He stayed at Mount Vernon to recoup. Washington offered him several remedies for his cough and cold only to be politely declined by Watson. Later in the evening, when Watson was getting ready to retire, he was astonished to behold a persistent Washington at his bedside with a bowl of hot tea in his hand ready to serve. Watson left impressed with the general's compassion and private virtue.[16]

Humility enhanced Washington's effectiveness as a leader. A French officer remarked that Washington's greatest gift was "the art of making himself beloved." Colonial leaders, army officers, and soldiers alike recognized his refusal to take salary for his work as Commander in Chief, the shunning of lavish lifestyle, the private sacrifice for a public cause, the responsiveness to all men no matter their social status or rank, the submission to civilian authority, and the selflessness in serving the public interest with profound courage.[17] John Adams contended that the general's "gift of silence" was one of his greatest attributes.[18]

Washington's humility and humble submission to God emanated from his childlike faith and biblical worldview. He was convinced that America's success in the Revolutionary War bore testimony to a Heavenly Father who actively ruled the daily activities of men. Before he became Commander in Chief, he had lamented his lack of qualifications and called on God for help and guidance. This was not false modesty. Friends and colleagues knew he would lead deliberately but humbly, and this realization calmed and

14. Tebbel, *Washington's America,* 337.

15. Freeman, *Washington,* 7:267.

16. Ibid., 7:37.

17. Ferling, *First of Men,* 265; Flexner, *Washington,* 2:541.

18. Ellis, *His Excellency,* 194.

reassured many of his contemporaries in the anti-monarchical ethos of the American Revolution.[19]

As he wrote in the Circular to the States, God called everyone "to do Justice, to love mercy, and to demean ourselves with that Charity, humility and pacific temper of mind, which were the Characteristicks of the Divine Author of our blessed Religion." All Americans were to live in "humble imitation" of Jesus, otherwise "we can never hope to be a happy Nation."[20] Following Jesus's humble ways and characteristics could transform oneself, a society, a country, and even the world. This was the last message Washington desired to leave to his countrymen.

As Congress waited for the Treaty of Paris to be signed and ratified by England and France, Washington told a friend he was ready to

> bid a final adieu to a military life, and in the shade of retirement ruminate on the marvelous scenes that are passed . . . contemplating the wonderful workings of that Providence which has raised up so many instruments, and such powerful Engines . . . to over throw the British pride and power, by so great a revolution.[21]

When someone complimented him for his victorious and indomitable leadership during war, Washington humbly gave credit for "our glorious success . . . to the bravery of our Troops, the assistance of our Ally and the interposition of Providence."[22] Content that American independence been achieved, the general expressed the "most lively sentiments in gratitude to that divine Providence which has been graciously interposed for the protection of our Civil and Religious Liberties."[23] The American victory over the British, he insisted to Reverend John Rodgers, was due "to divine Providence" who should "be ascribed the Glory and Praise." Washington welcomed Rodgers's suggestion that each soldier in the army receive a Bible, something that "would have been particularly noticed by me, had it been suggested in Season." He lamented that many soldiers in the Continental

---

19. Connell, *Faith*, 74; West, "Religious Impulse," 270; Bowen, *Miracle*, 28; Fitzpatrick, *Washington Himself*, 440.

20. Washington, Circular to the States, June 8, 1783, in Fitzpatrick, *Writings of Washington*, 26:483–96.

21. Washington to Duc De Lauzen, October 15, 1783, in ibid., 27:193.

22. Washington to the Magistrates of the City and County of Philadelphia, December 13, 1783, in ibid., 27:267.

23. Washington to The Minister, Elders, and Deacons of the Two United Dutch Reformed Churches of Hackensack and Schalenburgh and the Inhabitants of Hackensack, November 10, 1783, in ibid., 27:239.

Army had already disbanded and would not, unfortunately, receive a copy of the sacred Scripture.[24]

Once the war had been won, Washington's thoughts turned to securing the future of the young republic. Religion would have to play a critical role in the development and stabilization of the country. "I attribute all glory to that Supreme Being," he wrote to members of Princeton College, who had "caused the several parts . . . in the production of the wonderful Events we now contemplate" and were realized "in the most perfect manner." God had employed the "humblest instruments as well as by the most powerful means to establish and secure the liberty and happiness of these United States." Washington's "earnest prayer to Heaven," was that every "divine blessing may be bestowed" on American citizens, and that Princeton would continue to promote and universally extend "the interests of Religion and Learning."[25]

To the American Philosophical Society, he conveyed "delightful" hope and joy that the society would encourage the "task of studying the works of the great Creator."[26] If God played the signal role in securing independence, then certainly the Christian religion must play a crucial part in stabilizing and enhancing republican virtue and a virtuous society.

Since God "so highly favoured"[27] the American cause, Washington believed he would not abandon the young republic as long as the government and citizenry remained firmly rooted in a biblical, Christian foundation. Therefore, everyone should pledge "grateful adoration to that divine Providence" which "hath rescued our Country from the brink of destruction" and "crowned our exertions with the fairest fruits of success." God had given America the "sweets of Peace and domestic happiness."[28] The fight and ultimate victory for American independence had been conducted on "purer principles" for "a higher and more efficient Cause." Indeed, since the struggle with England revolved around the "re-establishment of our once violated rights; for the confirmation of our Independence; for the protection of Virtue, Philosophy and Literature: for the present flourishing state of the Sciences, and for the enlarged prospect of human happiness," Washington

---

24. Washington to John Rodgers, June 11, 1783, in ibid., 27:1.

25. Washington to the Inhabitants of Princeton and Neighborhood, Together with the President and Faculty of the College, August 25, 1783, in ibid., 27:116.

26. Washington to the American Philosophical Society, December 13, 1783, in ibid., 27, 270.

27. Washington to John Gabriel Tegelaar, August 2, 1783, in ibid., 27:74.

28. Washington to the Magistrates and Inhabitants of the Borough of Elizabeth, August 21, 1783, in ibid., 27:113–14.

fervently asserted that "it is our common duty to pay the tribute of gratitude to the greatest and best of Beings."[29]

Responding to a congratulatory letter from the Massachusetts Senate and House of Representatives, Washington assured members that "through the many and complicated vicissitudes of an arduous Conflict," he had kept his eye "with a fixed Confidence on that superintendg. Providence which governs all Events." By relying and "dependg on the Guidance of the same Allwise Providence, I have performed my part in this great Revolution."[30]

Writing to a Reformed German congregation in New York, Washington insisted that "at every suitable opportunity," Americans should "acknowledge publicly our infinite obligations to the Supreme Ruler of the Universe for rescuing our Country back from the brink of destruction." No American should "fail at this time to ascribe all the honor of our late successes to the same glorious Being." Indeed, his own "humble exertions" were "subservient to the execution of the divine purposes, a contemplation of the benediction of Heaven on our righteous Cause." His "earnest wish and prayer" were that "the Citizens of the United States would make a wise and virtuous use of the blessings, placed before them." He hoped the congregation would be "conspicuous for their religious character" and "exemplary" in "support of our inestimable acquisitions."[31]

Washington gave "adoration to that all-wise and most gracious Providence which hath so conspicuously interposed in the direction of our public affairs and the establishment of our national Independence." Americans, as he explained to the New Jersey Legislature, could be comforted and confident in "a reliance on the aid of Heaven." Beyond "the divine Arm visibly outstretched for our deliverance," he was grateful that God had sustained him and used his "humble instrumentality in carrying the designs of Providence into effect." He wished the legislature the most "the indulgent care of Heaven."[32]

With his conscience and confidence grounded in his Christian faith, Washington led freely and boldly trusting in God's plans and divinely orchestrated outcomes. Officers, enlisted men, and political leaders were drawn to the general's humility and resilient, optimistic fortitude. Moreover,

29. Washington to the Learned Professions of Philadelphia, December 13, 1783, in ibid., 27:269.

30. Washington to Massachusetts Senate and House of Representatives, August 10, 1783, in ibid., 27:93–94.

31. Washington to the Ministers, Elders, Deacons, and Members of the Reformed German Congregation of New York, November 27, 1783, in ibid., 27:249–50.

32. Washington to the Legislature of New Jersey, December 6, 1783, in ibid., 27:261–62.

his confidence rubbed off on those around him. "If my conduct throughout
the War has merited the Confidence of my fellow Citizens, and has been
instrumental in obtaining for my Country the blessings of Peace and Freedom," he explained,

> I owe it to that Supreme being who guides the hearts of all; who
> has so signally interposed his aid in every Stage of the Contest
> and who has graciously been pleased to bestow on me the great-
> est of Earthly rewards: *the approbation and affections of a free
> people* . . . .

Just as his faith had shaped his confidence and character, Washington hoped "the Almighty" would "dispose the heart of every Citizen of the
United States to improve the great prospect of happiness before us."[33]

After the Treaty of Paris was finalized, Washington praised and expressed "his humble thanks to God" before Congress for all that had been
granted to the patriot cause.[34] Then, on November 2, 1783, he released his
Farewell Orders to the Armies of the United States. He acknowledged that
victory over "so formidable a power cannot but inspire us with astonishment
and gratitude." The "disadvantageous circumstances" the armies faced "can
never be forgotten." However, "the singular interpositions of Providence in
our feeble condition were such, as could scarcely escape the attention of
the most unobserving." The army had persevered "through almost every
possible suffering and discouragement for the space of eight long years," and
it was "little short of a miracle" that victory had been achieved. Honored
to command, he was grateful to "the God of Armies." Looking toward the
future, he hoped that "the choicest of heaven's favours . . . under devine
auspices" would secure "innumerable blessings for others."[35]

Washington's legacy as Commander in Chief is impressive. He led the
Continental Army to victory under perilous conditions and overwhelming
odds. He designed chevrons to be worn on the sleeves of soldiers to recognize their multiple enlistments. He ordered purple hearts, originally called
Badges of Merit, to be worn on the breast of any soldier who distinguished
himself by instances of gallantry in battle or extraordinary fidelity.[36] The
Purple Heart remains part of the American military tradition yet today.

---

33. Washington to the Mayer, Recorder, Aldermen, and Common Council of Annapolis, December 22, 1783, in ibid., 27:281.

34. Washington, Address to Congress, August 26, 1783, in ibid., 27:117.

35. Washington, Farewell Orders to the Armies of the United States, November 2,
1783, in ibid., 27:222–27.

36. Lillback and Newcombe, *Sacred Fire*, 205; Jones, *Washington*, 87.

A caring and thoughtful general, he often spent extra time seeking food and medicines for his men and was renowned for riding his horse full speed to help a fellow soldier or officer in need. Soldiers and officers witnessed, firsthand, an emotional man who felt deeply and loved his band of brothers in arms.[37] Moreover, having been directed to worship regularly and encouraged in their Christian decorum, the men of the Continental Army knew their leader cared for their spiritual well-being, too.

The Continental Army was Washington's army, and his men respected and loved their general. Emotions ran high at a goodbye banquet given in his honor at Fraunces Tavern, in Boston, Massachusetts, in the fall of 1783. Overwhelmed with gratitude, Washington sobbed and could not speak, eat, or drink. Eventually, he asked each man to simply give him a handshake, but could not bring himself to do so until Henry Knox embraced him. For several hours afterward, he stoically and silently hugged each of his officers and men in an extremely moving farewell.[38]

WASHINGTON'S FAREWELL TO HIS OFFICERS,
After the Evacuation of New York. Fraunces's Tavern, Corner Broad and Pearl, Sts New York. Dec. 4th 1783.

Washington was beloved by the men of the Continental Army. Many soldiers and officers witnessed and testified on their general's devout prayer and worship life during the war. His farewell to the army was an emotional moment. Picture by Thomas Phillibrown, after Alonzo Chappel. (Courtesy of the Mount Vernon Ladies' Association)

37. Flexner, *Washington,* 2:541.
38. Elkins and McKitrick, *Age of Federalism,* 42.

Before heading home for Christmas, the Commander in Chief appeared before Congress, in Annapolis, Maryland, to resign his commission on December 23, 1783. The night before, Congress hosted a magnificent dinner and ball in his honor with hundreds in attendance. After Washington tolerated the obligatory thirteen toasts at dinner, he proceeded to the dance floor. "The general danced every set," according to one observer, "that all the ladies might have the pleasure of dancing with him, or as it has since been handsomely expressed, *get a touch of him.*"[39]

Appearing before Congress, Washington measured what he presumed would be his last public words carefully. Stressing that he had been sustained by "a confidence in the rectitude of our Cause, the Supreme Power of the Union, and the patronage of Heaven," the general shared his deep and reverent "gratitude for the interposition of Providence." Looking to the future, and revealing the depth of his own Christian faith, he explained that it was

> an indispensable duty to close this last solemn act of my Official life, by commending the Interests of our dearest Country to the protection of Almighty God, and those who have the superintendence of them, to his holy keeping. Having now finished the work assigned to me, I retire from the great theatre of Action; bidding an Affectionate farewell to this August body under whose orders I have so long acted, I here offer my Commission, and take my leave of all the employments of public life.[40]

According to James McHenry, who witnessed the entire episode, the Commander in Chief's resignation was a most "solemn and affecting spectacle"—the likes of which history would never see again. Many spectators openly wept, "and there was hardly a member of Congress who did not drop tears." McHenry noticed Washington's hands trembling during his speech. When the general spoke of the officers who had composed his army family, "he was obliged to support the paper with both hands." But when "he commended the interests of his dearest country to Almighty God, and those who had the superintendence of them to his holy keeping, his voice faltered and sunk, and the whole house felt his agitations." Washington paused for several moments before he could read the last line of his address.[41] Having

---

39. James Tilton to Gunning Bedford Jr., December 25, 1783, in Kaminski, *Founders*, 489.

40. Washington, Address to Congress on Resigning His Commission, December 23, 1783, in Fitzpatrick, *Writings of Washington*, 27: 284–85.

41. McHenry to Margaret Caldwell, December 23, 1783, Kaminski et al., *Great and Good Man*, 28.

submitted to civilian and republican authority, he had also demonstrated a submission to God.

By denying the temptations of power, as few other men in history had done, he gained the reputation as the most extraordinary moral hero of his time.[42] Like the great Roman general and warrior Cincinnatus—who gave up power to return to his farm and plow, Washington had immortalized himself as he returned to his plantations and farms at Mount Vernon. When word reached England that the American Moses had laid down his sword to return to private farming, not as head of an army or head of state, King George III said that the act "placed him in a light most distinguished of any man living." Washington was "the greatest character of the age."[43]

At every juncture during his grand exit and resignation from the army—the Circular to the States, the goodbyes to soldiers and officers at Fraunces Tavern, the Farewell Orders to the Army, and the resignation as Commander in Chief before Congress—Washington highlighted and praised God's divine intervention and protection. God was on the side of freedom and liberty, and he had delivered for the American people. This was a personal and meaningful legacy that Washington desperately wanted passed on to the next generation. He hoped and prayed that the nation would listen and remember.

On December 24, 1783, the retired general arrived at Mount Vernon in time for a joyous Christmas Eve dinner. After dessert, Martha and George retreated to their parlor where they had coffee, rather than English tea.[44] He thought his public life of service was over.

42. Wills, *Certain Trumpets,* 152; Schwartz, "Whig Conception," 27; Flexner, *Washington,* 4:503.

43. Novak and Novak, *Washington's God,* 6.

44. Unger, *Unexpected Washington,* 153.

PART III

Hero in Transition

7

Accolades

The months of the latter half of 1783 and 1784 were some of the most gratifying of Washington's life. While Mount Vernon's deteriorating state— physically and financially due to his long war absence[1]—would require a great amount of attention and work, Washington cherished the daily company of family and numerous accolades received. His army had defeated the British, and he had triumphed over the temptations of monarchy. The exhilaration of success and accomplishment showed. "I had the happiness of seeing Genl. Washington the other day after an interval of 7 years," Jefferson wrote in November 1783. "He has more health in his countenance than I have ever saw in it before."[2]

He was the savior of his country and admired as a classical hero in his own lifetime. "At length then the military career of the greatest Man on earth is closed," John Marshall told James Monroe shortly after the war. "May happiness attend him wherever he goes. May he long enjoy those blessings he has secured to his country." Whenever Marshall thought of Washington—"that superior Man"—his heart overflowed "with gratitude."[3]

Beloved and venerated in America, the American Moses was as famous as any man in the Western world.[4] Ezra Stiles, president of Yale, declared Washington "the great ornament of humankind!" Poet Francis Hopkins praised the general as the "best and greatest man the world ever

1. Jones, *Washington*, 93.

2. Jefferson to Benjamin Harrison, November 11, 1783, in Kaminski, *Founders*, 487.

3. Marshall to James Monroe, January 3, 1784, in ibid., 489.

4. Henriques, *Realistic Visionary*, 45–46; Wood, *Revolutionary Characters*, 32–33; Higginbotham, *Uniting a Nation*, 15.

knew." The Virginian was living "in the lap of idolatry" and "worshipped as a god."[5]

The months after retirement from the army were some of the most gratifying of his life. General Washington's exploits were lauded across the globe. He was America's first national hero. Picture by Jean-Baptiste Le Paon. (Courtesy of the Mount Vernon Ladies' Association)

Congratulatory letters poured in acclaiming Washington's character and legacy. He was praised for his "disinterested virtue and patriotism" which "stamp'd a value on your character superior if possible to the laurels you have gained in the field, and the glorious independence you have established for your country."[6] Lafayette called him the "Savior of His Country, the Benefactor of Mankind, the Protecting Angel of liberty, the pride of America, and the Admiration of the two Hemispheres."[7] Another claimed that America owed its entire "political existence to your Courage and Virtues . . . ."[8] The "hero of our age, the man of all ages, the object of admiration of all Nations," one asserted that historians would properly refer to Wash-

5. Henriques, *Realistic Visionary,* 45–46.

6. Harrison to Washington, January 8, 1784, in Abbot and Twohig, *Washington, Confederation Series,* 1:22.

7. Lafayette to Washington, January 10, 1784, in ibid., 1:27.

8. Henry Pendleton to Washington, January 10, 1784, in ibid., 1:31.

ington in the same manner "in which we Address the Gods."[9] Others called him a "hero who is esteemed by All," a hero equaled among all "ancient or modern Ones,"[10] the "Grand Liberator of his Country," a man venerated "in the Eyes of the World above the most illustrious Monarchs,"[11] and a "Great Hero of the Western World."[12]

The South Carolina legislature praised the "distinguished" and "disinterested part" he played "during the course of a long, and arduous Contest, with the blessing of Heaven" on his labors. When "the Almighty Ruler of the Universe shall think fit to receive you to himself," the letter continued, "your illustrious name, and Character, will live in the Memories of our Countrymen, to the remotest period of time."[13] The citizens of Fredericksburg proclaimed their joy in observing God's "Divine Favor" and intervention on Washington's behalf. They implored "the great and Omnipotent Ruler of Human events" to continue "his favor and protection" through "the remainder of your life in the happy society of an Affectionate and grateful people."[14] The "immortal Washington" had "saved a whole nation."[15]

According to Reverend William Gordon, the general had secured his "public character" by "retiring to the private walk of domestick happiness, after having been in the hands of the Supreme Governor, a glorious instrument of establishing the rights of the American States." Gordon insisted that Washington's name would "be mentioned with honor by all historians, whether Whigs or Tories: but my prayer is, that it may be found written in the Lamb's book of life" and one day live "with answerable luster in the world of Spirits."[16]

Contemporaries lauded Washington's wartime service and rectitude. He was a servant leader "whose Dignity stands Recorded in the Warmest Corner of the Human Heart,"[17] "the Cincinnatus of America"—having "reduced himself to the condition of a private man."[18] Bestowed from Heaven with "happy and illustrious qualities," the general merited "the confidence

9. Marquise de La Rouerie to Washington, January 12, in ibid., 1:395.

10. Gerard Vogels to Washington, March 10, 1784, in ibid., 1:177.

11. Nicolas Simon and Lucretia Wilhemina van Winter to Washington, April 10, 1784, in ibid., 1:279–80.

12. Catharine Sawbridge Macaulay Graham to Washington, July 13, 1785, in ibid., 3:116

13. South Carolina Legislature to Washington, February 10, 1784, in ibid., 1:112.

14. Citizens of Fredericksburg to Washington, February, 14, 1784, in ibid., 1:121.

15. Marquis De Chastellux to Washington, March 6, 1784, in ibid., 1:175.

16. William Gordon to Washington, March 8, 1784, in ibid., 1:177.

17. John Harvie to Washington, April 14, 1784, in ibid., 1:286.

18. Maithe to Washington, May 19, 1784, in ibid., 1:399.

and the Love of all your Fellow Citizens" and "fully gratified their Hope." He was unique because most people "had never yet seen a Great Man Universally admired, commended, respected and enjoy his immortality whilst living," but Washington offered "this lovely and rare Instance to your Age."[19]

Not one to speak of himself, Washington repeatedly told his admirers that he was receiving too much credit for the victory over the British. Instead, God deserved his countrymen's gratitude. As he maintained to top government officials in New York City, victory was due to "the effect of divine wisdom" and "great exertion of her virtuous Citizens" rather than to "any merit of mine."[20]

Washington explained to his close friend and comrade, Henry Knox, that he "was just beginning to experience that ease, and freedom from public care" which would "take some time to realize . . . ." He was "no longer a public Man, or had anything to do with public transaction," but "a wearied Traveller" who, "after trading many a painful step, with a heavy burden on his shoulders, is eased of the latter, having reached the Goal to which all the former were directed." Like a man on a house top looking back "and tracing with a grateful eye the Meanders by which he escaped the quicksands and Mires which lay in his way," Washington was grateful for "the All-powerful guide, and great disposer of human Events" who "prevented his falling."[21]

Washington thanked Reverend John Rodgers, a Presbyterian minister in New York City, for sending him a sermon entitled, *The Divine Goodness Displayed in the American Revolution.* He had read the sermon with "much pleasure" and thanked Rodgers for "the favorable mention you have been pleased to make of me therein." The sermon text was based on Ps 126:3 (KJV): "The Lord hath done great things for us, whereof we are glad."[22] As Washington told his friend, David Humphreys, "neither the statesman or solder can determine" the course of a war. Only the "great governor of the Universe causes contingencies which baffle the wisdom of the first, and the foresight and valor of the Second."[23]

Just as it had throughout the Revolutionary War, Washington's confidence in God remained steadfast and palpable during the Confederation period. Reflecting upon "all the meanderings of our past labors, the difficulties

---

19. Joseph Madrillon to Washington, June 11, 1784, in ibid., 1:441.

20. Washington to the Mayor, Recorder, Aldermen, and Commonalty of the City of New York, April 10, 1785, in Fitzpatrick, *Writings of Washington,* 28:126.

21. Washington to Henry Knox, February 20, 1784, in ibid., 27:340–41.

22. Washington to John Rodgers, May 5, 1784, in Abbot and Twohig, *Washington, Confederation Series,* 1:371.

23. Washington to David Humphreys, February 7, 1785, in Fitzpatrick, *Writings of Washington,* 28:66.

through which we have waded, and the fortunate Haven to which the Ship has been brought!" he told his friend and Connecticut Governor, Jonathan Trumbull, "Will not the All Wise, and all powerful director of human events, preserve it?" The Virginian answered his own question presciently: "I think he will, he may however (for wise purposes not discoverable by finite minds) suffer our indiscretions and folly to place our national character low in the political Scale, and this unless more wisdom and less prejudice take the lead in our governments will most assuredly be the case."[24]

Even when his confidence began to wane in the Confederation government, Washington remained resolute that God would protect and guide the new nation in the future. At the height of Shays's Rebellion, in the fall of 1786 and winter of 1787, he revisited the Ohio and Pennsylvania lands where he had escaped death and the enemy several times during the French and Indian War. The recollections of God rescuing and delivering him and his soldiers at these moments of crisis reassured him that God was in control of all of life's events. He was confident that God would grant similar reprieve and deliverance to the young, fledgling republic during the Critical Period.[25]

Even before Shays's Rebellion, Washington exhorted his countrymen to secure and enhance the liberty and freedoms they inherited from God. He praised "the Smiles of Heaven" and "the exertions of my fellow Citizens of the Union—(not to superior talents of mine)" for acquiring "the blessings of that liberty, Independence, & Peace wch we are all now in the enjoyment." Since God had afforded Americans numerous blessings, it would "be our own fault indeed if we do not make them productive of a rich & plenteous harvest—and that of National honor & glory, which should be characteristic of a young & rising Empire."[26] He had been "an instrument in the hands of Providence," he insisted, used to secure "a revolution which is interesting to the general liberties of mankind." Now free and independent, the United States would be "an Asylum" to the world if "wise enough to pursue the paths wch. lead to virtue and happiness, to the oppressed and needy of the Earth."[27] The urgency to fortify and strengthen the American republic was due in large part to Washington's knowledge that other republics in history had floundered and eventually failed after birth. "In republican

---

24. Washington to Jonathan Trumbull, May 15, 1784, in ibid., 27:399.

25. Henriques, *Realistic Visionary,* 170.

26. Washington to Officials of the City of Richmond, November 15, 1784, in Abbot and Twohig, *Washington, Confederation Series,* 2:135.

27. Washington to Lucretia Wilhemina van Winter, March 30, 1785, in Fitzpatrick, *Writings of Washington,* 28:120.

Governments," he noted, "it too often happens that the people (not always seeing) must *feel* before they act."[28]

Before challenges and problems became more pronounced in the unraveling of the Confederation, a great religious debate took place in Virginia when Governor Patrick Henry proposed a tax to help pay the salaries of Protestant ministers. Even though Governor Henry declared that conscientious exemptions to the tax would be recognized and honored, fellow Virginians, Madison and Jefferson, adamantly opposed the proposal. They believed disestablishment was a necessary outcome of religious liberty and argued that government should have no say whatsoever on citizens' religious views.[29]

Washington, inevitably, was drawn into the political tussle. Like many of the founders, he maintained that government should encourage and endorse religious solemnity since sustainable republics depended on moral and virtuous citizens. He never wanted the government to be divorced from God or religion. Religion augmented and enhanced republican society. He agreed with Madison and Jefferson that the Episcopal Church, established by law in the Old Dominion and supported by public money, ought to be deprived of the special monetary advantage it held over other sects. At the same time, however, he also believed that all citizens of Virginia should pay taxes to support their particular church of preference. Virtue was best taught and uplifted by religion, particularly the Christian religion. Therefore, Washington insisted government should do anything possible to uphold and protect claims of conscience and religious expression. A Christian society was safe, secure, and prosperous one.[30]

When the Virginia Bill for Assessment came up for a vote before the Virginia Assembly after months of rancorous debate, Washington posted a letter to George Mason arguing that religious freedom *and* a religious citizenry were both necessary in a republican society. "Altho' no man's sentiments are more opposed to *any kind* of restraint upon religious principles than mine are," he was *not* "alarmed at the thoughts of making people pay towards the support of that which they profess," whether they were Christians, Jews, Muslims, or of another religious denomination. Nevertheless, after months of dispute, Washington hoped the polarizing and divisive bill would be withdrawn. Concerned with the vulnerabilities of the young

28. Washington to Edward Newenham , November 25, 1785, in Abbot and Twohig, *Washington, Confederation Series,* 3:387.

29. Novak and Novak, *Washington's God,* 112-13; Lambert, *Founding Fathers,* 270-72.

30. Novak and Novak, *Washington's God,* 112-13.

republic, he did not think the bill was worth fracturing or upsetting the harmony of Virginia or the nation.[31]

As a Latitudinarian, Washington was a strong proponent of religious freedom and disestablishment; at the same time, he was a transparent adherent of orthodox Christianity and devoted member of the Anglican Church. Jefferson, conversely, frequently accused the Christian Church of manipulating parishioners, rejected the Trinity, and blamed the apostle Paul for doctoring Jesus's words as they appeared in Scripture. Jefferson denounced and reviled priests and clergy as believers of superstition, enemies of individual freedom, and instruments of tyranny.[32] Washington, on the other hand, held that the Christian Church properly and orderly nurtured its citizens and virtuous republican government. He worshipped the Triune God and established close, life-long friendships with many ministers, priests, and clergymen.

Since Washington considered religion one of the most important elements in the stability and prosperity of American society, he favored the Virginia Bill of Assessment because he believed the utilitarian work of Christian churches benefited all, even non-Christians. Thus, all citizens should pay a tax to support Christian parishes or the church/religious house of their choosing.[33] While Jefferson and Madison wanted to sever all church and state ties, cooperation and harmony between church and state was Washington's *modus operandi*.[34]

The irony of Jefferson and Madison's quest for complete separation between state and church is that the Statute for Religious Freedom in Virginia, one of the three lifetime accomplishments that meant the most to Jefferson, was secured only with the help and vigorous support of dissident, orthodox Christians. These dissenter Christians—especially Baptists and Methodists—joined deists in the Virginia Assembly and intentionally requested that the words "Jesus Christ" not be included in any government legislation during the 1780s. The thought was that adding Jesus's name to an earthly creation, such as political legislation, would decrease reverence for the Son of God.[35]

As a Latitudinarian, Washington may have been reticent to specifically articulate Jesus's name more frequently in the public square and in

---

31. Washington to George Mason, October 3, 1785, in Fitzpatrick, *Writings of Washington,* 28:285.

32. Mapp, *Faith of Our Fathers,* 11.

33. Jones, *Washington,* 95.

34. Lillback and Newcombe, *Sacred Fire,* 297.

35. Noll, *One Nation.* 66–67.

his correspondence during case of the Virginia Bill for Assessment after noting the strong sentiments of orthodox Christians and others during the religious statute debate. He was well aware that religious controversies had divided other nations throughout history. Hence, as he told his close friend, Lafayette, in 1787, he would show "toleration in religious matters" and not be a bigot "to any mode of worship . . . ." He would "indulge the professors of Christianity in the church, that road to Heaven, which to them shall seem the most direct plainest easiest and least liable to exception."[36] Steering clear of denominational spats, Washington instead focused on securing religious freedom, which would liberate and encourage a religious citizenry.

Shortly after the Revolutionary War, the general listened to a sermon by Reverend William White in Christ Church, Virginia. Reverend White praised Washington's service and urged Americans, who "were now free in religion as well as politics, to make good use of these noble gifts."[37] Freedom *of* religion nurtured a freedom *for* religion. Indeed, Washington may have been the first person to use the phrase "free exercise of religion" which is now sacrosanct in the First Amendment.[38] In eighteenth-century America, however, many founders who promoted religious freedom were also ardent, religious men, like Washington, who felt strongly that religion was a positive influence on individual and societal behavior.[39]

In the winter of 1785, Washington received an interesting letter from his friend and fellow comrade-in-arms, John Armstrong. Armstrong had served with the general in the French and Indian War and as brigadier general in the Continental Army in 1776. His letter appears to be a continuation of a theological conversation he and Washington engaged often. Armstrong spoke of the "felicity" of the "world to which is to come," and reminded the general that the "heavenly road is to be fought inch by inch!" While "Corporeal Armour" could be "laid off," Armstrong insisted that "Spiritual Armour" was "every day more & more necessary." He warned Washington about the "seduction" of the Devil, "the inbred corruptions of the human heart and flesh," and "the allurements of the present World." To combat humanity's sinful nature, one must "employ the weapons prescribed by his word with fidelity and hope" since "the final event is not left to us, but secured by the Captain of our Salvation, to all who truly fight under his banner, in the use of such Spiritual means as he hath appointed & graciously proposed to

36. Washington to Marquis de Lafayette, August 15, 1787, in Fitzpatrick, *Writings of Washington*, 29:259.

37. William White, Sermon, March, 1784, in Abbot and Twohig, *Washington, Confederation Series*, 1:196.

38. Eidsmoe, *Christianity and the Constitution*, 123.

39. Rees, *Leadership Lessons*, 106.

bestow." Armstrong insisted that "many duties indeed are required of us far above our natural Strength to perform." Even though humankind had violated "the first Covenant with Adam," through the "Lord Christ, the Second Adam, the federal & Spiritual head of his Church . . . full provision is made, not only for the removal of the guilty, but also the qualification of all believers for glory . . . ." There was no "duty required of man" to attain salvation. Instead, a promise had been "made in consequence of the Covenant of grace with Christ, enabling all believers in the performance thereof." In Jesus, "all the promises center, and in order to be entitled to them, we must by faith receive, or accept him both for *righteousness & Strength*." Washington was encouraged to build a large library—one filled "particularly on theological Subjects, doctrinal, practical & Polemical" so "that some Orthodox & pious divine may minister to the Church in reach of your house." Armstrong also urged the general, "on the subject of Christianity," to read works of "the Divines of the last Century" rather than the works on "Deism of late." He suggested "*Dr. Leelands View of the Deistick writers*," a work which warned of the corrupting influence of deistic thought.[40]

By the end of his life, Washington would accumulate a library full of orthodox Christian works and sermons. Moreover, he did read and would possess sermons and other literature that criticized and ably refuted deistic thought and reasoning. And, of course, he did rely on God for his strength and righteousness. Armstrong and Washington would continue to correspond on religious matters for many years.

Robert Hunter Jr., sent to the United States to collect pre-Revolutionary War debts for his Scottish father, stayed at Mount Vernon, in late 1785, and recorded his observations of America's most popular man. Impressed with the general's gracious hospitality and physical makeup, Hunter also esteemed Washington's work ethic and studious habits. He "seldom makes his appearance before dinner, employing the morning to writing his letters" and overseeing his farms. Between tea and supper, the Virginian retired to his study to write and answer correspondence. "He is one of the most regular men in the world," Hunter declared noting Washington's habit of going to bed at nine o'clock and rising at the crack of dawn. "Though our greatest enemy, I admire him as superior even to the Roman heroes themselves."[41]

Washington's religious habits were quite conspicuous and observable to family members and contemporaries too. Sunday morning worship, sermon reading on Sunday afternoons or evenings, and daily Bible reading

---

40. Armstrong to Washington, January 25, 1785, in Abbot and Twohig, *Washington, Confederation Series*, 2:287–89.

41. Robert Hunter Jr., Travel Diary, in Kaminski, *Founders*, 495.

and prayers had always been routine throughout his life. And so was his charitable service.

A generous and active vestryman for decades in his church parishes, Washington religiously provided "temporary relief of the needy and distressed."[42] During the Revolutionary War, he had his cousin and overseer, Lund Washington, provide corn and other foodstuffs to any hungry person who made a request at Mount Vernon. A fishing station, on the Potomac River, was also made available for the poor and those enduring economic hardship.[43] After the Revolutionary War, he served as president-general of the Society of Cincinnati—a hereditary fraternity of former Continental army officers constituted "to establish a charitable fund for the relief of such of their compatriots, the Widows, and descendants of them, as were fit objects for their support; and for whom no provision had been made."[44]

Washington not only provided direct aid to those in need, but also financially supported institutions and organizations committed to helping the poor and downtrodden. In June of 1788, Washington sent a letter to Reverend John Lathrop applauding the newly founded "Humane Society," a "benevolent Institution" which provided "for the preservation of shipwrecked Marines." He asserted that "these works of charity and good-will towards men reflect great luster upon the authors and presage an era of still farther improvements." He noted "how pitiful, in the eye of reason and religion, is that false ambition which desolates the world with fire and sword for the purposes of conquest and fame." Instead, Washington hoped to make "our neighbors and our fellow men as happy as their frail conditions and perishable natures will permit *them to be!*"[45]

The Commander in Chief took particular interest in supporting families who lost fathers and husbands who had served with him in battle. Most of his charitable acts were done with little notoriety and public attention, although thousands of strangers would visit Mount Vernon having heard of Washington's compassionate generosity. Charity was simply a way of life and a fruit of his character.

The missionary zeal he exhibited for Native Americans was also impressive and generous. As early as September of 1775, he wrote the president of Congress praising the powerful impact and effect that Reverend

42. Washington to Daniel McCarty, February 22, 1784, in Fitzpatrick, *Writings of Washington,* 27:341.

43. M'Guire, *Religious Opinions,* 190.

44. Washington to James Madison, December 16, 1786, in Fitzpatrick, *Writings of Washington,* 29:113.

45. Washington to John Lathrop, June 2, 1788, in ibid., 30:5.

Kirkland's "Labour and Influence" was having on Native American tribes.[46] He asked Congress to continue funding Kirkland's missionary work. If religion was essential for upholding republican virtue, then it was important that Native Americans lived by the tenets and teachings of the Christian faith, too.

The desire to Christianize Native Americans, however, went beyond mere political considerations. Washington truly cared for their souls and held a lifelong interest in proselytizing indigenous tribes with government support.[47] He told the Delaware Chiefs that they would do well "to learn our arts and ways of life, and above all, the religion of Jesus Christ." These things, Washington insisted, "will make you greater and happier people than you are."[48] Efforts to "christianize" Native Americans were "benevolent."[49] In the spring of 1788, he sent a letter to Reverend John Ettewein along with a printed pamphlet containing the stated rules of "a Society for propagating the Gospel among the Heathen," founded in Bethlehem, Pennsylvania. Washington applauded the "laudable and arduous" undertaking of the society which focused on "converting the Indians to Christianity and consequently to civilization."[50] Moreover, he donated funds to The Society of United Brethren for Propagating the Gospel Among the Heathen in order "civilize and Christianize the Savages of the Wilderness."[51] The society had been created for profoundly religious reasons. The Brethren pamphlet he sent Ettewein stated that subscribers, full of "Christian zeal and godly concern," have "at all times endeavored to spread the saving knowledge of Jesus Christ, and to carry the same to the remotest Heathen nations . . . which has the salvation of men so near at heart." Unlike deists, who generally accepted the equivalence of all religions and felt no compulsion to proselytize, Washington genuinely desired to share Jesus and the teachings of the Christian faith with Native Americans.[52]

---

46. Washington to President of Congress, September 30, 1775, in ibid., 3:526.

47. Novak and Novak, *Washington's God,* 96.

48. Washington, Speech to Delaware Chiefs May 12, 1779, in Fitzpatrick, *Writings of Washington,* 15:55.

49. Washington to John Jay, January 25, 1785, in Abbot and Twohig, *Washington, Confederation Series,* 2:291–93.

50. Washington to John Ettewein, May 2, 1788, in Fitzpatrick, *Writings of Washington,* 29:489.

51. Washington to Directors of the Society of United Brethren for Propagating the Gospel Among the Heathen, Bethlehem, PA, Jun 10, 1789, in ibid., 30:355.

52. Lillback and Newcombe, *Sacred Fire,* 68–70.

8

Retirement Denied

After the Revolutionary War, Washington reasserted himself in domestic pursuits. Mount Vernon and the surrounding farming tracts demanded rejuvenation. Canals needed to be built to and from the Potomac River to encourage trade and westward expansion. Land and property which had been acquired—through war stipends and spoils throughout Virginia and the Ohio Territory—remained unsupervised, unsettled, and yet to be surveyed. He also looked forward to spending both quality and quantity time with his family. Free of his commander in chief responsibilities, Washington no longer felt the American experiment rested entirely on his shoulders. He was "gliding down the stream of life" hoping that his "remaining Days" would be "undisturbed and tranquil," he wrote a friend in June of 1785.[1]

During the 1780s, however, Washington's apprehension increased each passing day as he watched the republic flounder. Inevitably, he realized he would have to reengage and confront the political and social realities that threatened to unravel the new nation.

He dreaded reentry into public life for several reasons. Benjamin Franklin had jeopardized his renowned international reputation by reasserting himself into politics in Pennsylvania during the 1780s. Washington had no desire to see his reputation tarnished in the same manner. He had already begun to organize his vast correspondence and papers during the Confederation period and even considered building a storage facility for their preservation at Mount Vernon. He was content with his current legacy. A second reason he wished to stay away from the public scene was his deteriorating physical health. By the time of the Constitutional Convention, in

1. Washington to William Goddard, June 11, 1785, in Abbot and Twohig, *Washington, Confederation Series,* 3:50.

1787, only one tooth remained in his mouth. His arthritis had become so acute and debilitating, he had to partially immobilize one of his arms in a sling. A third reason was that he had promised Martha he would not leave Mount Vernon and the tranquil lifestyle they now both enjoyed.[2]

Nevertheless, he was concerned that the Confederation was in serious trouble and could not effectively govern. Tax collections were faltering to the point of nonexistence in some states. Interstate commerce conflicts were igniting state rivalries. States were refusing to send their best and brightest delegates to Congress, keeping them, instead, in their own legislatures. Foreign nations continued to ridicule the United States for a foreign policy conducted on a state-by-state basis. Rumors abounded that the viceroy of Canada was trying to lure eastern states into a British hegemony. In 1786, the country suffered a dramatic financial setback and the value of paper money depreciated to the extreme levels of the Revolutionary Continental. The Confederation government seemed powerless and lethargic on almost every political and economic front.

Moreover, American citizens were behaving selfishly and without any consideration of the collective interest. Republicanism itself appeared to be on trial, and few seemed willing and able to confront the challenges that enfeebled the young, fragile nation. "I confess that my opinion of public virtue is so far changed that I have my doubts whether any system without the means of coercion in the Sovereign, will enforce Obedience to the Ordinances of a Genl. Government" Washington lamented.[3] The ugly depravity and sinful nature of human beings were rearing their ugly heads yet again, and the state of the republic was suffering and unraveling because of it.

Nevertheless, Washington eventually reentered the political arena because he saw the void of leadership and desperately wanted to see the American experiment succeed and endure. Moreover, friends and comrades whom he respected—prominent individuals such as Madison, Hamilton, Knox, and others—begged and cajoled him to intervene, persuasively suggesting that his cherished reputation and fame would be damaged if he did nothing to bolster and secure the stability of the republic. Washington was indispensable to the republic, and he knew it. He simply could not ignore the warning signs and slippage in republican zeal. The seemingly self-centered character and wayward behavior of the first generation of citizens in the new republic's foundational years appalled him.[4]

2. Wood, *Revolutionary Characters*, 43; Unger, *Unexpected Washington*, 176; Higginbotham, "Revolutionary Asceticism," 158.

3. Washington to James Madison, March 31, 1787, in Fitzpatrick, *Writings of Washington*, 29:190.

4. Novak, "Influence of Judaism," 167; McDonald, *Presidency of Washington*, 25.

As Madison and Hamilton planned a national convention, in order to amend the Articles of Confederation, Washington believed God was calling, or recalling, him to lead and serve the American people during yet another crucial time for the young republic. Though he did not want to leave the domestic life he had reestablished, he eventually admitted, "Perhaps nothing can excite more perfect harmony in the soul than to have this string vibrate in unison with the internal consciousness of rectitude in our intentions." He would reenter public life and serve with the "humble hope of approbation from the supreme disposer of all things." He hoped "the good sense of my countrymen" would prevail and trusted "that a superintending Providence will disappoint the hopes of our Enemies."[5]

Bells chimed, artillery fired, soldiers saluted, and residents joyously gathered in the streets to celebrate their war hero's appearance in Philadelphia on May 13, 1787. Washington and the other "demigods," as Jefferson called them, prepared for what would turn out to be four months of arduous debate.

The man who was destined to be president of the Constitutional Convention arrived in Philadelphia concerned about the weaknesses of the Articles of Confederation as well as the decay of virtuous leadership in the new nation. Church membership had continued to decline precipitously during the Critical Period. Many Tory or Anglican ministers had fled the states during and after the Revolutionary War. Optimism in the republic waned as Americans had seemingly become apathetic about religion or, at the very least, church membership. Religious indifference allowed a languishing public spirit to emerge. Shays's Rebellion (1786–87) was a prominent and trenchant display of the fallen virtue of the republic. The Articles of Confederation would have to be reformed.[6]

Despite these downward trends, religion still remained an essential force in America. The Bible was read and quoted more than any other book. Most Americans, even deists, believed that the virtue required of a republican citizenry originated from religion.[7]

Along with significantly amending the Articles of Confederation or reforming the government, Washington believed the country could not survive without reasserting the critical importance of religion. Republicanism and Christianity complimented each other and formed a necessary, beneficial partnership. Republican government and virtuous, religious practice

---

5. Washington to Marquis De Chastellux, August 18, 1786, *Writings of Washington*, 28:523–24.

6. Bloch, *Visionary Republic*, 102–05, 109–111; Ahlstrom, *Religious History*, 365.

7. Schwartz, "Character of Washington," 214.

combined to create a prosperous country. Republican principles best expressed themselves in Christian values, and the Christian religion tempered and monitored the republican temptations of runaway power, especially the utopian impulse to perfect society.[8] Other prominent Virginian leaders, such as John Marshall and Patrick Henry, were convinced that a restoration of direct state support for religion was needed to strengthen and stabilize society and promote virtuous citizenry.[9]

Republics "can neither be so good nor so happy," asserted Reverend Jonathan Boucher to Washington, "if They are not so religious." He and Washington had been close friends and corresponded frequently, from 1768 to 1773, when Boucher was John Parke Custis's schoolmaster. Boucher, a practicing Anglican like Washington, reminded the general that if republics were "to secure national Felicity, some permanent national Religion" was "absolutely necessary." A religious society must be "espoused & patronized by a Person that is popular," and "no other Man can do it with such Advantage" as Washington could.[10]

The vast majority of the fifty-five delegates to the Constitutional Convention were devout, orthodox Christians—Episcopalians, Presbyterians, Congregationalists, Lutherans, Dutch Reformed, Methodists, and Roman Catholics. Three were deists.[11] While the Constitution did not mention God, the man-made document was expected to be carried out by Godly, religious men. Framers wanted to avoid the confusion and blending of religion and state that had prevailed in Europe and, to some extent, early colonial America. Church-state entanglement ultimately harmed religion and corrupted religious institutions, because authorities tended to abuse power and their proper authority over the people.[12]

William Pearce, a fellow delegate from Georgia, captured the context of Washington's celebratory return to political life at the beginning of the Philadelphia Convention. He noted that the Virginian wanted to construct "a Government to make the People happy." Like Gustavus Vasa—the sixteenth-century King of Sweden who liked to compare himself to Moses—Washington would be "the deliverer of his Country." And like Peter the Great, he would be "the States-man" of the nation. Washington was also Cincinnatus and would return to his farm "perfectly contented with being

8. Noll, *One Nation*, 41–43.

9. Reichley, *Religion in American Public Life*, 87.

10. Jonathan Boucher to Washington, May 25, 1784, Abbot and Twohig, *Washington, Confederation Series*, 1:405–07.

11. McDowell, *Apostle of Liberty*, 12.

12. Noll, *One Nation*, 69.

only a plain Citizen, after enjoying the highest honor of the Confederacy." All he wanted to do was seek "the approbation of his Country-men by being virtuous and useful."[13]

On May 25, 1787, the delegates unanimously elected Washington to be president of the Federal Convention (later known as the Constitutional Convention). Madison, who recorded the proceedings of the entire convention, documented that Washington, "in a very emphatic manner," thanked the delegates for the honor. Humbly, the general also "reminded them of the novelty of the scene of business in which he was to act, lamented his want of better qualifications, and claimed the indulgence of the House towards the involuntary errors which his inexperience might occasion."[14] Robert Yates, a delegate from New York, also observed Washington's humility and declaration that since "he never had been in such a situation, he felt himself embarrassed." The general "hoped his errors, as they would be unintentional, would be excused."[15]

For four laborious months the delegates debated, argued, and eventually constructed the Constitution. In addition to the complex political interests and monumental challenges associated with governance formation, the members conducted their business in cramped quarters, sweltering temperatures, and summer humidity. Sessions sometimes ended early due to the troublesome flies that would bite and cause irritation. Tempers flared and egos were easily bruised. Yet they persevered and the miracle of Philadelphia produced a brand new government.

Even though Washington did not speak much at the convention, his presence and influence were monumental. The hero of the American Revolution provided legitimacy to the proceedings—which were kept secret from the public. Delegates reported that his face showed approval or disapproval on almost every submission or recommendation. Near the end of the debate hearings, he was charged to keep all of the journal records of the convention safe and secure.[16]

---

13. William Pearce, Notes of Federal Convention, in Farrand, *Federal Convention,* 3:94.

14. Madison, *Notes of Debates,* 24.

15. Robert Yates on Washington, in Farrand, *Federal Convention,* 1:5–6.

16. Bowen, *Miracle,* 29.

While he did not speak much as president of the Federal Convention in Philadelphia, Washington's influence, political sentiments, and support for religion were felt and duly noted by those in attendance. Picture by John Rogers. (Courtesy of the Mount Vernon Ladies' Association)

The delegates created a fixed Constitution or supreme law where no civil or religious authority could transgress or contravene. Christianity, for example, would have no special privilege or place of authority in the new government. Hence, religious tests for political office were banned in the Constitution.[17]

Many founding fathers, including Washington, earnestly believed that religion would flourish in a society and government that promoted religious freedom. Madison, for example, regarded religion as a "natural right" that the governed should never surrender. Furthermore, he argued that "true" religion would triumph by its own merits if supporters were free to practice their religion without coercion.

The Constitution that Washington and other delegates constructed in no way threatened religion, but freed citizens to worship and practice their religious faith uninhibited and unencumbered. Even founders who were not overtly orthodox in their religious views believed that religion, particularly Protestant Christianity, was essential for a law-abiding nation. Most founding fathers and Revolutionary leaders correlated Christianity with good citizenship.[18] As long as freedom of religion was secured and pro-

17. Lambert, *Founding Fathers,* 4; Rakove, *Original Meanings,* 317.

18. Lambert, *Founding Fathers,* 4, 246–47.

tected, religion would not need governmental or constitutional help. Liberty and religion were mutually beneficial endeavors.

American history and tradition demonstrated that nearly all of the defenders and advocates of religious liberty—individuals such as Roger Williams, William Penn, Cecilius Calvert, and Isaac Backus—were devout Christians. Robust support for ending government subsidies to churches came primarily from Christian denominations—Baptists, Methodists, and Presbyterians in particular. These groups contended that tax support of churches corrupted true religion instead of promoting it. Some of Washington's most ardent statements favoring religious liberty were in response to members of Christian churches who were concerned that the new federal government might abuse its power and favor one church over another.[19]

Eventually ratified by the states, Washington strongly endorsed the Constitution, among other reasons, because he believed it would encourage and build up a more religious citizenry. The ideas embedded in the Constitution—limited power, the separation of powers, the rule of the people, checks and balances, and the need for amendment—were necessary because people were inherently sinful and would abuse and misuse power. The doctrine of human sinfulness or depravity, a basic Christian teaching, did not stop at the boundaries of the political arena.[20]

Although the temptation for sinful and corrupt men to abuse religion and use it as a divisive force remained, Washington never wavered in his belief that a prosperous republic required religious citizenry. A virtuous society would not only unite and cement the bonds between American people, but also prop up and strengthen the Constitution and republican principles in general. Only a God-fearing populace—one that both protected religious freedom and promoted the free exercise of conscience and religious practice—would unite the young republic.

During the intensely divisive representation debate between small states and big states at the Philadelphia Convention, Benjamin Franklin attempted to play peacemaker by proposing that every delegate take three days off to ponder compromise solutions to the impasse. Members were encouraged to listen to people who disagreed with their own positions and engage in fruitful discussions. When the delegates would gather after the social hiatus, Franklin hoped they would assemble "with a determination to form a constitution, if not such an one we can individually, and in all respects approve, yet the best, which under existing circumstances, can be obtained." After Franklin made these remarks, "the countenance of

19. West, "Religious Impulse," 282.
20. Lillback and Newcombe, *Sacred Fire*, 220.

Washington brightened, and a cheering ray seemed to break in upon the gloom" which had overtaken the convention.

Then Franklin made another suggestion: He wanted a chaplain appointed who would assemble the delegates and introduce the business of the day "by an *address to the Creator of the universe,* and the Governor of all nations." The chaplain would beseech God "to preside in our council, enlighten our minds with a portion of heavenly wisdom, influence our hearts with love of truth and justice, and crown our labors with complete and abundant success!" When Franklin finished speaking and sat down, a delegate recorded that he never observed "a countenance at once so *dignified* and *delighted* as that of Washington, at the close of this address!"

Alexander Hamilton objected to Franklin's proposal, insisting that the assembled delegates, wise as they were, did not need "foreign aid." Aghast, Washington "fixed his eye" on his former aid-de-camp "with a mixture of *surprise* and *indignation* . . . and then looked around to ascertain in what manner it affected others." Observing the president's palpable frustration with Hamilton's comment, the delegates quickly approved Franklin's suggestion.[21] The president wanted a chaplain, and a chaplain he got.

Washington's ardent support of religion was also evident behind the scenes. Most sessions of the Philadelphia Convention occurred during the day. At night, representatives assembled in taverns to converse on the great political issues of the day as well as other personal and social issues too. The majority of delegates had served with the general in war. They respected and admired him greatly, and looked to him for leadership and guidance. As a practicing Anglican who believed that Christianity provided the proper moral foundation for a republic, Washington explicitly and implicitly wielded his influence one founding father at a time.[22]

As delegates returned to their home states and prepared for a contentious ratification process, Washington acknowledged that the Constitution was "now a Child of fortune, to be fostered by some and buffeted by others." He did not know how the document would be received. "If it be good I suppose it will work its way good; if bad, it will recoil on the Framers," he opined to Lafayette.[23]

Many years later, during his eulogy on Washington, Gouverneur Morris praised his friend's confidence and faith that God would work all things out for good. Washington "was collected within himself. His countenance

21. William Steele to Jonathan Steele, September, 1825, in Farrand, *Federal Convention,* 3:469–72.

22. Unger, *Unexpected Washington,* 178; Lillback and Newcombe, *Sacred Fire,* 223.

23. Washington to Marquis de Lafayette, September 18, 1787, in Fitzpatrick, *Writings of Washington,* 29:277.

had more than usual solemnity—His eye was fixed, and seemed to look into futurity." Morris specifically recalled Washington's notion that the framers needed to work hard to "raise a standard" in their new Constitution. Ultimately, however, the American experiment "was in the hand of God." This was "the patriot voice of WASHINGTON" and "the constant tenor of his conduct."[24]

As the state ratifying conventions convened throughout 1788 and 1789, Washington's endorsement of the proposed Constitution was significant. The Revolution had been fought to rid the American colonies of a repressive, corrupt monarchy and Parliament—both of which had intervened intrusively and far too frequently in colonial affairs. The Articles of Confederation government had been created to lessen and dissipate the central government's power and potential overreach. The new Constitution, however, designed and constructed a more powerful federal government and a stronger national executive. Anti-Federalists feared the framers had overreacted to the shortcomings of the Articles of Confederation and created a new, more powerful central government.

Washington, however, believed the new Constitution would strengthen and stabilize the functionality and prosperity of the new nation. While he was "so wedded to a state of retirement" and found "the occupations of rural life so congenial," he realized that a "refusal to act, might, on my part, be construed as a total dereliction of my Country."[25]

For the next two years, he worked vigorously to secure the Constitution's ratification while expressing a divine confidence in America's fate. "The Omnipotent Being who has not yet deserted the cause of America in the hour of its extreme hazard," he wrote James McHenry in the summer of 1788, "will never yield so fair a heritage of freedom a prey to *Anarchy* or *Despotism*."[26] He could "never trace the concatenation of causes, which led to these events, without acknowledging the mystery and admiring goodness of Providence," he told another associate. "To that superintending Power alone is our retraction from the brink of ruin to be attributed."[27] No one could "look upon the events of the American Revolution without feeling the warmest gratitude towards the great Author of the Universe whose divine interposition was so frequently manifested on our behalf." Washington found solace and comfort in God's guiding hand and offered his "earnest

24. Gouverneur Morris, Eulogy on Washington, in Farrand, *Federal Convention*, 3:381–82.

25. Washington to John Armstrong, April 25, 1788, in Fitzpatrick, *Writings of Washington*, 29:464.

26. Washington to James McHenry, July 31, 1788, in ibid., 30:30.

27. Washington to Annis Boudinot Stockton, August 31, 1788, in ibid., 30:76.

prayer that we may so conduct ourselves as to merit a continuance of those blessings with which we have hitherto been favored."[28] The creation of the Constitution itself visibly demonstrated the "finger of Providence" as much as any event in America's history.[29]

Washington acknowledged the flaws in the Constitution that anti-Federalists—such as George Mason, Samuel Adams, and Patrick Henry—raised in spirited opposition to ratification. The "defects in the proposed system," he conceded, were "the lot of humanity." Despite the "malice" that had been directed at him during the Virginia ratification process, however, he rejoiced that he had been "shielded" by "a conscousness of having acted in conformity to what I believed my duty . . . ." Leaving the comfortable life of domesticity and retirement at Mount Vernon had not been easy. "At my age, and in my circumstances, what sinister object, or personal emolument had I to seek after, in this life?" Washington insisted "the great Searcher of human hearts is my witness, that I have no wish, which aspires beyond the humble and happy lot of living and dying a private citizen on my own farm."[30]

Nonetheless, Washington believed God had interrupted his retirement and used him as an instrument to ensure the stability and security of the republic. While Anti-Federalists worked diligently to defeat ratification, he would "trust in Providence, which has saved us in six troubles yea in seven, to rescue us again from any imminent, though unseen, dangers." With "Heaven" as his "witness," Washington expressed his "inextinguishable desire that the felicity of my country may be promoted . . . ."[31] By early September 1788, eleven out of the thirteen states had ratified the Constitution (only nine were needed). Moving forward with a new government, he remained confident that "the same Power, which hath hitherto kept us from Disunion and Anarchy, will not suffer us to be disappointed."[32]

Washington's presence was indispensable at the Constitutional Convention and the Virginia ratification convention. Both would never have passed or succeeded without his support. "Perhaps Washington is not to be compared to the most famous military leaders," said Brissot de Warville, who had spent three days with the general at Mount Vernon in 1788, "but he has all the qualities and all the virtues of the perfect republican . . . ."[33] James

---

28. Washington to Samuel Langdon, September 28, 1789, in ibid., 30:416.

29. Freeman, *Washington,* 6:135.

30. Washington to Charles Pettit, August 16, 1788, in Fitzpatrick, *Writings of Washington,* 30:42.

31. Washington to Benjamin Lincoln, August 28, 1788, in ibid., 30:63.

32. Washington to Thomas Ruston, August 31, 1788, in ibid., 30:79.

33. Brissot de Warville, New Travels in the United States of America, 1788, in Kaminski, *Founders,* 499.

Monroe, another Virginian of renown, told Jefferson that Washington had forsaken "the honorable retreat to which he so deservedly acquir'd . . . after so many and illustrious services, & at this stage of his life . . . Be assured his influence carried this Government."[34]

With ratification of the Constitution achieved, Washington implored Americans not to neglect or "depart from the road which Providence has pointed us to, so plainly . . . The great Governor of the Universe has led us too long and too far on the road to happiness and glory, to forsake us in the midst of it." Acknowledging humankind's frailty and sinful nature, he admitted that "by folly and improper conduct, proceeding from a variety of causes, we may now and then get bewildered." Nevertheless, he was hopeful and trusted "that there is good sense and virtue enough left to recover the right path before we shall be entirely lost."[35]

Ratification provided yet another opportunity for Washington, with a "kind and grateful and pious exaltation," to extol and praise the "finger of Providence" who "first induced the States to appoint a general Convention and then led them one after another . . . into an adoption of the system recommended by that general Convention." He trusted that, "in all human probability," the new Constitution would lay a "lasting foundation for tranquility and happiness." In the future, when "fear and misery" would confront the United States, Washington prayed that the "same good Providence may still continue to protect us and prevent us from dashing the cup of national felicity just as it has been lifted to our lips."[36]

When contemporaries insisted that he was to be—needed to be—the first president of the United States, Washington predictably demurred and reiterated his desire for retirement. Yet, one of the reasons Americans had approved the new Constitution was the understanding and expectation that their Revolutionary hero would become their first chief executive. Thus, Washington's friends and associates continued to pressure him to serve in the nation's highest public office.

Worried that assuming such a powerful position would damage his reputation, Washington explained that he was reluctant "to accept the office . . . after the Declarations I have made (and Heaven knows they were made in the sincerity of my heart)." Would not the world and posterity charge him with "inconsistency" as well as "rashness and ambition?" While the approbation of his countrymen was desirable, God's plans or calling was more

34. Monroe to Thomas Jefferson, July 12, 1788, in Hamilton, *Writings of Monroe*, 1:186.

35. Washington to Benjamin Lincoln, June 29, 1788, in Fitzpatrick, *Writings of Washington*, 30:11.

36. Washington to Jonathan Trumbull, July 20, 1788, in ibid., 30:22.

important. He would do "what my conscience informed me was right, as it respected my God, my Country, and myself . . . ."[37]

Confiding in his friend, Reverend William Gordon, Washington explained that his "heartfelt wishes" were to stay out of public life. Yet "circumstances seemed opposed to it." He did not want to "come again on the Stage of public affairs," especially "if the refusal can be made consistently with what I conceive to be the dictates of propriety and duty." God, the "great Searcher of human hearts," knew that "there is no wish of mine, beyond that of living and dying an honest man, on my own farm."[38]

As much as Washington pined for Mount Vernon, however, he knew the independent republic he had fought and sacrificed so much for needed him again. He was an indispensable leader and best suited to secure the ideals of the American Revolution and legitimize the new Constitution.

Knowing him to be a devout Christian, many of his closest associates and friends told him to think of the people's voice as the Lord's voice.[39] Their encouragement and compelling arguments, as well as his own belief that God was calling him again to ensure the solid foundation and footings of the new Constitution, propelled him forward to the next chapter of his life—president of the United States.

---

37. Washington to Henry Lee, September 22, 1788, in ibid., 30:97–99.
38. Washington to William Gordon, December 23, 1788, in ibid., 30:168–69.
39. Meacham, *American Gospel,* 100.

PART IV

His Excellency, Mr. President

9

Confident President

Thomas Jefferson, writing to his Virginia neighbor, Edward Carrington, in late May 1788, noted the eminent character and "confidence we all repose in the person whom we all look as our president." Jefferson, however, worried about presidential leadership beyond Washington. "After him, inferior characters may perhaps succeed and awaken us to the danger which his merit has led us into."[1] That concern would have to wait for another day.

On April 6, 1789, Congress officially recognized George Washington as the first president of the United States. The Chief Executive immediately went to work in the nation's capital in New York City. Elias Boudinot, a friend of Washington's who served as the Continental Congress's president in 1782 and 1783 and later in Congress, wrote his distinguished friend on that very day: "The importance of this transaction is so great in my estimation that I consider it, under Providence, as the key-Stone to our political Fabrick." Boudinot lamented that Washington "must again leave, all the sweets of domestic Felicity . . . ." Nevertheless, he told the president that "you have no choice in this great Business—Providence and your Country call, and there is no place for refusal—The Sacrifice is required & the Offering must be made."[2] Washington knew the sentiment all too well.

In becoming the nation's first president, Washington sacrificed family time and retirement and put his illustrious reputation on the line yet again. He publicly admitted the struggle he went through in deciding to serve. Yet "the unanimity of the choice, the opinion of friends," the "apparent wish of those" dissatisfied "with the Constitution in its present form, and an ardent

1. Jefferson to Edward Carrington, May 27, 1788, Kaminski, *Founders,* 498.

2. Boudinot to Washington, April 6, 1789, Abbot, *Washington, Presidential Series,* 2:24.

desire on my part, to be instrumental in conciliating the good will of my countrymen towards each other have induced an acceptance." While his "love of retirement" was great,

> no earthly consideration, short of a conviction of duty, could have prevailed upon me to depart from my resolution, *"never more to take any share in transactions of a public nature."* For, at my age, and in my circumstances, what possible advantages could I propose to myself, from embarking again on the tempestuous and uncertain ocean of public life?

Nevertheless, God had brought Washington and the American people together "after a long and distressing separation." He was confident, under the new Constitution and government, that "the same gracious Providence will again indulge us with the same heartfelt felicity."[3] Indeed, he would rely on God's guidance and intervening hand as president. Despite the "delicate nature of the duties," his own "incompetence" would be overcome with "the singular assistance of Providence." God would help him carry out his executive obligations "in a satisfactory manner." Having embraced the presidency "from a sense of duty, no fear of encountering difficulties and no dread of losing popularity" would "ever deter me from pursuing what I conceive to be the true interests of my Country."[4] Once again, he commended

> the Interposition of Providence, as it was visibly Manifested, in guiding us thro' the Revolution in preparing us for the Reception of a General Government, and in conciliating the Good will of the People of America, towards one another after its Adoption. I feel myself oppressed and almost overwhelmed with a sence of the Divine Munificense—I feel that nothing is due to my personal agency in all these complicated and wonderful Events, except what can simply be attributed to the exertions of an honest Zeal for the Good of my Country.[5]

Washington's humility and realization that he was a sinful, frail man propped up by an Almighty, benevolent God, once again, permeated his correspondence. He carried "distressing apprehensions" that he would "not be able to justify the too exalted expectations of my countrymen." His doubts and fears, however, were quelled "by a confidence that the most gracious

---

3. Washington to Mayor, Corporation, and Citizens of Alexandria, April 16, 1789, in Fitzpatrick, *Writings of Washington*, 30:286–87.

4. Washington to Citizens of Baltimore, April 17, 1789, in ibid., 30:288.

5. Washington to Mayor, Recorder, Alderman, and Common Council of Philadelphia, Abbot, *Washington, Presidential Series*, 2:83.

Being, who hath hitherto watched over the interests, and averted the perils, of the United States will never suffer so fair an inheritance to become a prey to anarchy, despotism, or any other species of oppression."[6]

Confident that God had prepared and equipped him for service and yet another task, Washington saw himself as an agent of Providence while serving as president. "Almighty God hath been pleased, in some sort, to make use of me as his instrument" and "awaken my deepest gratitude for his mercies in the time past." He would continue to put his trust "and humble reliance on them for the time to come."[7]

Just as Washington saw himself as an agent of God, so did the American people. Thomas McKean, writing on behalf of the president and faculty of the University of Pennsylvania, insisted that "the influence of sound learning on religion and manners, on government, liberty, and laws" was necessary for the fulfillment of a "civilized society." They were "devoutly" praying, to "the almighty Ruler of the Universe," that Washington "may long enjoy the felicity of that country, which you have rescued from tyranny, and established in the blessings of freedom and independence." He reminded the president of the Heavenly "reward which awaits good and faithful servants."[8]

Washington responded, "fully apprized of the influence which sound learning has on religion and manners, on government, liberty, and laws." Moreover, he expressed "hearty thanks" for McKean's "devout intercession at the Throne of Grace for my felicity both here and hereafter." He concluded his letter: "May you also, Gentlemen, after having been the happy instruments of diffusing the blessings of literature and the comforts of religion, receive the just compensation for your virtuous deeds."[9]

Many Americans prayed for God's continued guidance and blessings upon the president and sent their religious well wishes. Philadelphia businessman and Continental Army veteran, John Mitchell, prayed that "the Almighty ruller and Governor of the Universe" would grant Washington "long life, and every Happiness which this World, & blessings of the Grand Architect of Universe can give."[10] Philip Schuyler insisted that no one should "doubt that the divine hand," which "has so evidently interfered in favor of

---

6. Washington, Personal Note, April, 1789, in ibid., 2:84.

7. Washington to Judges of the Pennsylvania Supreme Court, April 20, 1789, in ibid., 2:85.

8. Thomas McKean, Address on behalf of the President and Faculty of the University of Pennsylvania, in ibid., 2:86–87.

9. Washington to Thomas McKean and The President and Faculty of the University of Pennsylvania, in ibid, 2:86–87.

10. John Mitchell to Washington, May 20, 1789, in ibid., 2:347.

America, and so remarkably assisted and conducted you in every stage of life, will continue to guide and direct you in your endeavors for the happiness of your country."[11]

Washington concurred with Schuyler's sentiments. "The invisible hand which has so often interposed to save our Country from impending destruction," he contended, "seems in no instance to have been more remarkably excited than in that of disposing the people of this extensive Continent to adopt, in a peaceable manner, a Constitution, which if well administered, bids fair to make America a happy nation."[12]

As he looked to the future, the president reassured the American people that he would continue to rely on "the kind of interpositions of Providence which has been so often manifested in the affairs of this Country." They were "to look up to that divine source for light and direction in this new and untried scene."[13]

Time and again, he encouraged other state and national leaders to put their trust and confidence in God. To the Governor and council of North Carolina, he "most earnestly implored the Divine benediction and guidance" upon their ratification process and governance.[14] To the Massachusetts Senate and House of Representatives, he asserted that he would be carrying out his duties "under the guidance of a superintending Providence." He thanked the legislators for "the Benedictions you have been pleased to implore the Parent of the Universe on my person and family." His most "ardent wish" was that "*all*" people, "by rectitude of conduct and a perfect reliance on his beneficience, draw the smiles of Heaven on ourselves and posterity to the latest generation."[15] In a letter to the Hebrew congregations of Philadelphia, New York, Charleston, and Richmond, he reminded members of many of the same themes he openly espoused to others—how "the power and goodness of the Almighty were strongly manifested in the events of our late glorious revolution"; God's "kind interposition in our behalf" which was "no less visible in the establishment of our present equal government";

---

11. Philip Schuyler to Washington, May 2, 1789, in ibid., 2:201.

12. Washington to Philip Schuyler, May 9, 1789, in Fitzpatrick, *Writings of Washington,* 30:317.

13. Washington to William Heath, May 9, 1789, in Abbot, *Washington, Presidential Series,* 2:238.

14. Washington to Governor and Council of North Carolina, June 19, 1789, in ibid., 3:48.

15. Washington to Massachusetts Senate and House of Representatives, July 9, 1789, in ibid., 3:165–66.

and how Providence "directed the sword and in peace he has ruled in our councils . . . ."[16]

Throughout his presidency, Washington publicly and repeatedly proclaimed his faith and trust in God, and exhorted Americans to do the same. He noted how "a recollection of past events and the happy termination of our glorious struggle . . . cannot fail to inspire every feeling heart with veneration and gratitude towards the great Ruler of events, who has so manifestly interposed in our behalf." Moreover, since "civilized Societies" and "the welfare of the State and happiness of the People are advanced or retarded in proportion" to "the morals and good education" of its citizenry, he desired an increase "of our Seminaries of Learning throughout this extensive country." The president "sincerely" prayed that "the great Author of the Universe" would smile upon the officials of Washington College, and other educational institutions, to be "an extensive blessing to this country."[17] Education, after all, enhanced one's ability to comprehend and learn more about God and Scripture.

A country devoted to God and the stewarding of liberty would be a secure and prosperous one. As he told to the Oneida Nation, "so long as our American nation pursue the paths of justice and virtue I trust the great Spirit will smile upon us."[18] He reiterated, to the General Assembly of Georgia, that the entire republic should "reflect on the unlimited gratitude which we owe, as a nation, to the supreme Arbiter of human events for his interposition in our favor."[19] Americans should not only "acknowledge a divine interposition in their affairs . . . so often manifested during our Revolution," but never forget "the omnipotence of that God who alone is able to protect them."[20]

Washington was confident that God would help shape and guide his decisions. Indeed, throughout his two presidential terms, he would display a certainty in his decision-making, a significant attribute considering the awareness that he would be setting enduring precedents as the nation's first chief executive. Strengthened by his Christian faith, Washington considered himself merely the humble agent of a benevolent and caring God.[21]

16. Washington to the Hebrew Congregations of Philadelphia, New York, Charleston, and Richmond, December, 1790, in Fitzpatrick, *Writings of Washington,* 31:185–86.

17. Washington to Officials of Washington College, July 11, 1789, Fitzpatrick, *Washington, Presidential Series,* 3:177–78.

18. Washington to Oneida Nation, October 12, 1789, in ibid., 3:544.

19. Washington to General Assembly of Georgia, December 22, 1789, Fitzpatrick, *Writings of Washington,* 30:481.

20. Washington to John Armstrong, March 11, 1792, in ibid., 32:2.

21. Nordham, *Age of Washington,* 246.

Desiring to retire to Mount Vernon as his first term expired, he once again placed his fate in God's hands. "Whatever my ultimate determination shall be," he wrote on August 26, 1792, "it may be for the best." Since the "allwise disposer of events has hitherto watched over my steps, I trust that in the important one I may soon be called upon to take, he will mark the course so plainly, as that I cannot mistake the way."[22]

Reelected for a second term, Washington was gratified and "impressed by so distinguished, and honorable testimony of public approbation and confidence." He did not "feel pleasure from the prospect of *commencing* another tour of duty"—such wishful thinking "would be a departure from the truth." The "opinion of the world" could not understand or "guess at my sentimts. as it never has been troubled with them." A few "confidential friends" knew that his decision to stand for a second term came "after a long and painful conflict in my own breast" as his ardent desire and "fixed determination" had been to "return to the walks of private life, at the end of my term."[23]

Throughout his second term, Washington's earnest appreciation for all of God's benevolence and abundance for the young republic continued to grow. "Let us unite our fervent prayers to the great ruler of the Universe," he told inhabitants of Richmond, "that the justice and moderation of all concerned may permit us to continue in the uninterrupted enjoyment of a blessing, which we so greatly prize."[24] He reminded the citizens of New London of "the calamities of war," and how "it must be the prayer of every good Citizen that it may long be averted from our land, and that the blessings which a kind providence has bestowed on us, may continue uninterrupted."[25] As he told James Madison, he placed his "entire confidence . . . under the protection of a kind providence," trusting in "a continuation of those blessings, which these States enjoy in a superior degree."[26] He insisted, "with such aid and support, under the direction of Divine Providence, I trust the flourishing condition and inestimable blessings now enjoyed, will be long continued for our Country."[27]

Washington believed freedom and liberty were God-pleasing pursuits everywhere in the world. Upon hearing the early successes of the French

22. Washington to Attorney General, August 26, 1792, in Fitzpatrick, *Writings of Washington*, 32:136–37.

23. Washington to Henry Lee, January 20, 1793, in ibid., 32:309–10.

24. Washington to Inhabitants of Richmond, August 28, 1793, in ibid., 33:72.

25. Washington to Inhabitant City of New London, September 2, 1793, in ibid., 33:80–81.

26. Washington to James Madison, September 23, 1793, in ibid., 33:97.

27. Washington to John Doughty, September 23, 1793, in ibid., 35:93.

Revolution, he told the French Minister that French citizens should "cordially join with me in purest wishes to the Supreme Being" and "soon enjoy in peace, that liberty which they have purchased at so great a price, and all the happiness which liberty can bestow."[28]

In public discourse and private correspondence, the president was not bashful in proclaiming gratitude for the bountiful gifts of God and encouraging republican stewardship. He hoped Americans would respond with sincere gratitude to God too. After reading a sermon sent to him by a pastor early in his presidency, Washington responded by insisting that no one could "look upon the events of the American Revolution without feeling the warmest gratification towards the great Author of the Universe whose divine interposition so frequently manifested on our behalf." The president's "earnest prayer," therefore, was "that we may so conduct ourselves as to merit a continuance of those blessings with which we have hitherto been favored."[29] To the general assembly of Presbyterian churches, he reiterated that the United States depended "upon Heaven as the source of all public and private blessings." While Americans were constitutionally protected to worship God according to "the dictates of their consciences; it is rationally to be expected from them in return . . . the beneficence of their action." No one "who is profligate in his morals, or a bad member of the civil community, can possibly be a true Christian, or a credit to his own religious society."[30] God had given generously to the American people—most of whom were Christian. God expected much in return.

Grateful and inspired by God and his blessings, Washington served the American republic with vigor and urgency. Providence had entrusted him, and the founding generation, with so much to steward and nurture. "I shall always strive," he insisted to members of the Methodist Episcopal Church in New York, "to prove a faithful and impartial Patron of genuine, vital religion."[31] He hoped for the same from the American people. Vital religion was a religion that put profession into practice. As he expounded to the Dutch Reformed Church, "'while just governments protects all in their religious rights,' true religion affords to government its surest support."[32]

Independence and republican government—dedicated to the protection of freedom and liberty—were gifts from God. Therefore Washington

28. Washington to French Minister, January 1, 1796, in ibid., 34:414.

29. Washington to Quakers, September 28, 1789, ibid., 30:416.

30. Washington to General Assembly of Presbyterian Churches in the United States, May, 1789, in ibid., 30:336.

31. Washington to the Methodist Episcopal Church, May 29, 1789, in ibid., 30:339.

32. Washington to the Dutch Reformed Church, October 9, 1789, in ibid., 30:432.

expected the American people to support the new government with vigilance and sincere gratitude. As he conveyed to New England congregations, the "path of true piety is so plain as to require but little political direction." He had not endorsed "any regulation, respecting religion," in the Constitution because this should be properly left up to "the guidance of the ministers of the gospel . . . ." A religious populace would take their inheritance and responsibilities seriously, "instruct the ignorant," and "reclaim the devious." The government's role was to "give every furtherance" to the "progress of morality and science" so that American citizens could "confidently expect the advancement of true religion, and the completion of our happiness."[33] Vital religion did not need governmental intervention, mandates, or even a written endorsement in the Constitution.[34] Government was only to guard the freedom of conscience so that vital religion could emerge unencumbered and uninhibited. In turn, a religious citizenry would encourage and empower the government by rigorously and robustly protecting liberty and freedom.

Washington turned sixty in 1792, as he contemplated running for another presidential term. He had lost all of his teeth, and his eyesight and memory were diminishing. He suffered from painful rheumatism in his fingers, knees, ankles, and back. Many of his older friends, and all but one of his brothers, had passed away. Having lived longer than most of his male ancestors, he wanted to retire to Mount Vernon to live and farm with the people he loved most.[35]

Nevertheless, when his closest personal friends, cabinet members, and congressional officials pleaded for him to serve a second term for the good and stability of the country, the president reluctantly agreed to stand for reelection and won unanimously. Once again, Washington's Christian faith and biblical worldview influenced his decision. "If it can be esteemed a happiness to live in an age productive of great and interesting events," he ruminated to his friend, David Humphreys, "we of the present age are very highly favored." The current events playing out in Europe and in America were "known only to the great ruler of events; and confiding in his wisdom and goodness, we may safely trust the issue to him, without perplexing ourselves to seek for that, which is beyond human ken." God-fearing

33. Washington to Congregations of New England, November, 1789, in ibid., 30:453.

34. Brookhiser, *What Would.* 62.

35. Unger, *Unexpected Washington,* 207.

individuals should take "care to perform the parts assigned to us, in a way that reason and our own consciences approve of."[36]

As he had in his first term, the president would focus on strengthening the foundations of United States in his second term. If the government, supported "by the virtuous Citizens of the United States," could "secure to our Country in the present crucial times, a continuance of peace and the enjoyment of its attendant blessings, which we have as it were but begun to taste," he would "feel amply compensated for the many anxious moments which I have lately experienced on account of our welfare, and we shall have fresh cause of gratitude to the Great ruler of events for his preserving goodness."[37]

Daunting challenges and growing political unrest would ensue and unfold during the second term. When Pennsylvania farmers rebelled against the federal government's whiskey excise tax in 1794, much of the country sympathized with the oppressed farmers—who gave the perception that they were the new anti-tax patriots. When the president called for lawful justice against the whiskey rebels, he did so "in perfect reliance on that gracious Providence which so signally displays its goodness towards this country, to reduce the refractory to a due subordination to the laws." He noted in the proclamation "that the people of the United States have been permitted, under the Divine favor, in perfect freedom, after solemn deliberation, in an enlightened age, to elect their own Government." Therefore the people's "gratitude for the inestimable blessing" could "best be distinguished by firm exertions to maintain the Constitution and the laws."[38]

Other trials and tribulations emerged for the administration. The rise of an opposition party—the Democratic-Republicans, growing animosity toward the Hamiltonian economic system, profound dispute over the French Revolution, and direct criticism of the Washington's leadership and policies—consumed the Federalist era. John Adams told his wife, Abigail, that he "pitied" the president. "With his Exertions, anxieties, Responsibilities, for twenty years without fee or reward or Children to enjoy his Renown, to be the Butt of the Insolence of Genets and Clubs is a Trial too great for human Nature to be exposed to. Like the Starling," Adams observed, Washington could not "get out of his Cage . . . he is very sick in it."[39]

Throughout these political and presidential ordeals, however, Washington found solace and encouragement in his Christian faith. Almost every

36. Washington to David Humphreys, March 23, 1793, in Fitzpatrick, *Writings of Washington,* 32:398.

37. Washington to Samuel Bishop, August 24, 1793, in ibid., 33:59.

38. Washington, Proclamation, September 25, 1794, in ibid., 33:508–09.

39. John Adams to Abigail Adams, December 30, 1794, in Kaminski, *Founders,* 506.

morning at five o'clock and every evening around nine o'clock, he went to his study to pray and read the Scriptures. Moreover, the president conspicuously and faithfully attended St. Paul's Chapel and Trinity Church in New York and Saint Peter's Church and Christ Church in Philadelphia when the capital moved to the city of brotherly love. Whether at Mount Vernon or the nation's capital, Sunday evenings were dedicated to sermon and Scripture reading with his family. Visitors in general, with the occasional exception of Speaker of the House, Jonathan Trumbull, were generally prohibited on the Lord's Day—a time for letter writing, family, worship, and rejuvenation.[40] As president, Washington carried a heavy leadership burden. Behind the hero and public image, however, was a religious faith, which sustained him daily.

40. M'Guire, *Religious Opinions*, 153–56, 168–75; Meade, *Old Churches*, 242–55; Chernow, *Washington*, 173, 585; Thompson, *Good Providence*, 52, 59 62, 71–74; Novak and Novak, *Washington's God*, 217; Lillback and Newcombe, *Sacred Fire*, 233–70, 639–62.

10

Providence in the Public Eye

While the vitality and influence of Christian churches waned during the Revolutionary period, the 1790s stirred up a renewal of vibrant Christianity. The concern over moral decay spurred the creation of reform societies as well as the spread of new congregations. By the turn of the century, a renewed zeal for the "Christianization" of American society and culture was ascendant.[1]

Religion was still the way most people made sense of the world around them. As the American republic became more democratic, it also became more evangelical. Many religious groups of the period pushed back and resisted the Enlightenment sentiment to separate church and state. Instead, they urged the country to recognize and acknowledge that America was founded and governed by Christian principles. Chaplains were placed in Congress, days of fasting and prayer were reestablished, and mail delivery was suspended on the Sabbath. Christianity—the prime and cohesive force that could unify and hold the nation together—had become "republicanized."[2]

Consistent with his life-long devotion to the Anglican way, Washington was careful not to coerce others to believe as he believed or denigrate those who practiced a religion different from his own. When many orthodox Christians asked him to boldly and publicly profess his faith in Jesus Christ and the Triune God, he politely ignored their requests as a Latitudinarian would. John Armstrong, for example, expressed concern that the Constitution and Bill of Rights made no mention of God. He wanted Washington to

1. Noll, *One Nation*, 70–71.

2. Wood, *Radicalism*, 330–32.

make "a Solemn acknowledgement of the One living & true God," an admission that was expected from "those to whom we commit the important trust of which I need not give a detail . . . ." Armstrong elaborated, "if God is the Ruler of the universe, the Author & patern of all order & good Government, it seems highly becoming in constituting a National Government, that notice should be taken of his cognizance, as well as of his patronage in the execution of it." American leadership should publicly recognize the Triune God. Failure to do so would "be displeasing to him, who requires us to acknowledge him in all our ways . . . ." Deists and nonbelievers, "who in this country are likely to do more injury to Christianity than any other sect we know," were against "all tests, Articles & Creeds, civil or Religious." Acknowledging the one true God would "be more respectable & give more Satisfaction to many of the Citizens, than the Constitution now stands."[3] Armstrong made a compelling argument for a public confession of Christ.

Six months after Armstrong's letter, Samuel Langdon also encouraged the president to do the same. Langdon was one of the nation's leading Congregational clergymen and president of Harvard from 1774–80. He had met Washington in Boston at military headquarters in 1775. The two had lived together at Cambridge and grew close as military comrades. One of Langdon's sermons was found in Washington's library after his death. Both men deeply respected one another. "I realize with pleasing astonishment & religious gratitude," Langdon wrote the general, "that the american States have been favored with such signal interpositions of Providence as fall little short of real miracles, & that the King of Heaven hath given them a great Charter of Liberty."

Langdon wanted to "take liberty in this private way to express the grateful & respectful sentiments of my heart." After meeting the general at Cambridge, "he was ready to look up to heaven, & say, 'Blessed by God; who hath given us a general who will not rashly throw away the lives of the Soldiers, or hazard the fate of his Country unnecessarily upon a single Battle, but will proceed with all wisdom & caution!'" Langdon would "never forget the high satisfaction I then enjoyed, in observing your religious as well as military character." Washington habitually relied on "the great Lord of the Universe, implored his help, acted as his servant, & found him present to support you under, & carry you through the most pressing & discouraging difficulties." God had "made good his word in your great Success & universal fame, 'Them that honour me I will honour.'"

3. John Armstrong to Washington, January 27, 1789, Abbot, *Washington, Presidential Series,* 1:253–55.

Americans loved and esteemed Washington "most of all," because he would "so constantly ascribe the glory of the great Events in America to him that rules over the kingdoms of the world, & orders all things for the accomplishment of his wise & holy purposes." Langdon applauded the Virginian for taking "every opportunity, in your public addresses, to pay your acknowledgments to the supreme Lord of heaven & earth for the great things he hath done for us." He told his friend not to be discouraged by the rise of deism and "the prevailing infidelity of the present degenerate times" which shunned "glory to the most High." The president's "conversation and Example" would have "great influence in your high Station," and Langdon encouraged him to "let all men know that you are not ashamed to be a disciple of the Lord Jesus Christ, & are seeking the honor of that kingdom which he has prepared for his faithful Servants." Langdon assured Washington that sharing Christ "will complete the satisfaction of your mind, to have the sure hope that when this World & all of its glory disappears, you shall receive an heavenly inheritance, & the crown of eternal Life." He hoped his friend would "condescend to accept this Letter as an unaffected testimony not only of the most honorable esteem, but likewise of the characteristic of christian love of your most obedient Servant."[4]

Having witnessed Washington's faith over many months during the Revolutionary War, Langdon's letter is striking for its intimacy and familiarity with the general. He knew Washington fretted over the rise of deism, relied on Providence during stressful times, promoted good stewardship of all that God provided, and was "not ashamed to be a disciple of the Lord Jesus Christ." Yet Langdon, like others, did not effectively compel or move Washington to use Jesus's name more frequently in correspondence or public speech.

Washington, however, let his own Christian faith speak for itself. The president's devotion to the Anglican way, which strongly encouraged the name of Jesus to be reserved for private and worship settings, was deeply earnest and sincere. A Latitudinarian and faithful member of Anglican congregations—which boldly professed and confessed the Triune God, resurrection of Jesus, forgiveness of sins, and inerrancy of God's Word—Washington chose to primarily let his actions, rather than words, exhibit his personal faith.

On April 30, 1789, he was inaugurated as the first president of the United States in New York City. As he stood in the balcony of the Senate chamber to take the oath, observers noticed the dark brown clothing he wore which was made from American manufacture and carried a steel-hilted sword. His hair

---

4. Samuel Langdon to Washington, July 8, 1789, in ibid., 3:149–51.

was powdered and drawn back in the fashion of the time. When he appeared in the chamber, a shout went up from the large crowd gathered beneath the balcony. In character, he bowed in silence to the people. As Chancellor Livingston administered the oath of office, Washington laid his hand on the Bible. (Whether or not Washington, after the oath, concluded with the words—"I swear, so help me God"—is a matter of historical debate. The comment was first reported sixty-five years after the fact. Yet it remains an established tradition to this day).[5] He then kissed the Bible, which had been intentionally opened to Gen 49—the chapter where Jacob, father of the sons of Israel, bestows his blessing upon them. Washington, for many years now, had already been called the Father of His Country.[6]

Over a third of Washington's Inaugural Address was dedicated to religious themes, and his very first public declaration was to thank Almighty God for the blessings and liberties given to the United States. Picture by Alonzo Chappel. (Courtesy of the Mount Vernon Ladies' Association)

5. Chernow, *Washington*, 568; Eidsmoe, *Christianity and the Constitution*, 117; Randall, *Washington*, 449.

6. Lillback and Newcombe, *Sacred Fire*, 224.

After the oath of office, the president gave the Inaugural Address—over a third of which was dedicated to religious themes. When completed he walked across the street to St. Paul's Chapel, accompanied by many contemporaries and elected government officials, to take part in a two-hour worship service and the singing of "Te Deum." He participated in Holy Communion with Mrs. Alexander Hamilton.[7]

From his very first public address as president to his final State of the Union speech, Washington consistently extolled God to the American people. The Inaugural Address is a revealing document in terms of its biblical worldview and the depth of its religious tone.[8] Attendees were struck by the president's grave and sincere delivery as well as his modesty. His body shook while he was speaking. Moreover, his barely audible voice, awkward stammering, nervous twitches, stage fright, and inability to properly enunciate the words of his prepared speech only endeared him to those in the Senate chamber. The nation's hero and the Father of His Country appeared vulnerable and poignantly human.[9]

Fisher Ames, who sat in the pew next to the president during the event, told a friend that he had "more veneration" for Washington "than for any other man." Even though time had "made havoc on his face," the president's speech was touching, grave, solemn, and "produced emotions of the most affecting kind upon the members." Ames became "entranced" by Washington's presentation, which seemed "an allegory in which virtue was personified, and addressing those whom she would make her votaries. Her power over the heart was never greater, and the illustration of her doctrine by her own example was never more perfect."[10]

Washington's very first public act as president was to pray on behalf of the nation. "It would be peculiarly improper to omit in this first official Act," he stated in his Inaugural Address, "my fervent supplications to that Almighty Being who rules over the Universe . . . and whose providential aids can supply every human defect, that his benediction may consecrate to the liberties and happiness of the People of the United States." The president assumed that "in tendering this homage to the Great Author of every public and private good," he was collectively expressing the American people's sentiments as well as his own. "No People can be bound to acknowledge and adore the invisible hand, which conducts the Affairs of men more than

7. Thompson, *Good Providence*, 79–84; Lillback and Newcombe, *Sacred Fire*, 224.

8. Flexner, *Washington*, 3:184.

9. Schwartz, *American Symbol*, 152–53; Hoffer, *Revolution and Regeneration*, 97; Freeman, *Washington*, 6:195.

10. Fisher Ames to George Richards Minot, May 3, 1789, in Kaminski, *Founders*, 500.

the People of the United States," he declared. "Every step" that advanced the "character of an independent nation" was "distinguished by some token of providential agency." Reflecting upon the Revolutionary War and the creation of the new Constitution, the president asked the people to return "pious gratitude along with a humble anticipation of the future blessings which the past seem to presage." Americans "ought to be no less persuaded that the propitious smiles of Heaven, can never be expected on a nation that disregards the eternal rules of order and right, which Heaven itself ordained."

As he continued his address, Washington asserted, once again, that it was Providence's active intervention and miraculous interpositions that bestowed American independence, liberty, and freedom. Americans, therefore, were to live a life of gratitude in God's honor and be good stewards of the republic. Furthermore, religion, or God's order of right, was to provide the essential moral fabric of the American republic.

If the country did not adhere to God's calling, Washington believed that the new nation, and the liberties granted to the United States, would suffer or even perish. Closing the address, he insisted that the "preservation of the sacred fire of liberty, and the destiny of the Republican model of Government, are justly considered as *deeply*, perhaps as *finally* staked, on the experiment entrusted to the hands of the American people." Preparing to assume the duties of office, he vowed to "once more" rely on

> the benign parent of the human race, in humble supplication that since he has been pleased to favour the American people, with opportunities for deliberating in perfect tranquility, and dispositions for deciding with unparalleled unanimity on a form of Government, for the security of their Union, and the advancement of their happiness; so his divine blessing may be equally *conspicuous* in the enlarged views, the temperate consultations, and the wise measures on which the success of this Government must depend.[11]

Throughout his many annual addresses to Congress—speeches that would later be termed State of the Union Addresses—Washington consistently and publicly proclaimed the nation's gratitude for God's care of the republic as well as the need to nurture a religious citizenry. In his First Annual Address to Congress, the president spoke of the "blessings which a Gracious Providence has placed within our reach" and called for "cool and deliberate exertion," as well as "patriotism, firmness, and wisdom," from the

---

11. Washington, Inaugural Address, April 30, 1789, in Fitzpatrick, *Writings of Washington,* 30:296.

American people.[12] In his Second Annual Address, he expressed thanksgiving for "the abundant fruits" God had bestowed upon the United States for yet another year.[13]

In his Third Annual Address to Congress, Washington lauded the numerous "Providential blessings which demand our grateful acknowledgements." In addition, he promoted a missionary outreach effort to Native Americans. While he frowned on any "coercion," he hoped that "an intimate intercourse may succeed; calculated to advance the happiness of the Indians, and to attach them firmly to the United States." He desired "a System corresponding with the mild principles of Religion and Philanthropy towards an unenlightened race of Men" that would be "honorable to the national character" and "conformable to the dictates of sound policy." Later in the address, Washington reminded his countrymen that the "safety of the United States" was "under Divine protection."[14]

After Native Americans attacked frontier setters, Washington encouraged members of Congress, in his Fourth Annual Address, on November 6, 1792, to take action to protect these westward settlers and to strengthen the people's attachments to their government "upon which, under Divine Providence, materially depend their Union, their safety and their happiness."[15] In his Fifth Annual Address, he "humbly implored that Being, on whose Will the fate of the nations depends, to crown with success our mutual endeavors for the general happiness."[16] The president opened his Sixth Annual Address to Congress reminding members of "the gracious indulgence of Heaven, by which the American people became a nation," and called on all Americans to "unite, therefore, in imploring the Supreme Ruler of nations, to spread his holy protection over these United States." By relying on Providence and using the gifts God had blessed America with—liberty, freedom, the pursuit of happiness—the United States could "turn the machinations of the wicked to the confirming of our constitution" and "enable us at all times to root out internal sedition." A religious citizenry, dedicated to a Christian worldview, would enjoy "prosperity, which his goodness has already conferred," and "verify the anticipations of this government being a safe guard to human

12. Washington, First Annual Address to Congress, January 8, 1790, in ibid., 30:491.

13. Washington, Second Annual Address to Congress, December 8, 1790, in ibid., 31:164.

14. Washington, Third Annual Address to Congress, October 25, 1791, in ibid., 31:396–404.

15. Washington, Fourth Annual Address to Congress, November 6, 1792, in ibid., 32:212.

16. Washington, Fifth Annual Address to Congress, December 3, 1793, in ibid., 33:164.

rights."[17] In his Seventh Annual Address, Washington invited members of Congress "to join with me, in profound gratitude to the Author of all good, for the numerous, and extraordinary blessings we enjoy."[18]

These annual addresses to Congress were the most public pronouncements the president could make. His words were printed in newspapers and read by most Americans. In almost every address, the president revealed his confidence in the divine care, protection, and benevolence of the same Triune God he worshipped almost every Sunday. He urged Americans to acknowledge and give thanks for the many bountiful blessings of God and to be good stewards of everything that God had provided the country. Washington was intentional, consistent, and clear in expressing a biblical worldview and a vision essential for the long-term prosperity of the American republic.

With the same intentionality he deployed in his public words, Washington's decisions and actions were also calculated and purposeful. Cognizant of the power and significance of precedents, the president spent a great deal of time deliberating and reflecting upon the legacies and practices he wanted, or did not want, to establish as America's highest elected official. As soon as he was informed of his election as president in 1789, for example, he refused the $25,000 salary compensation (approximately $500,000 in today's money) set by Congress. Instead, he simply asked for out-of-pocket expenses to be paid, though Congress rejected his generous offer. He would spend a good portion of his own salary on presidential entertainment.[19]

He intentionally worked to establish legitimacy, pomp, and prestige to the presidency and new Constitution while being careful not to give the impression that the government would drift back to a monarchical framework. He posed for portraits to raise the perception and status of the presidency both in domestic and international circles. He rode around the capital in a carriage pulled by six, cream-colored horses. Desiring to make the executive branch respectable and esteemed, Washington successfully transformed his popularity into respect for the office and the Constitution. To avoid a fragmentation of the newly created government, he implemented a variety of initiatives that would establish and secure a strong executive and sound economic policies.[20]

17. Washington, Sixth Annual Address to Congress, November 19, 1794, in ibid., 34:28–37.

18. Washington, Seventh Annual Address to Congress, December 8, 1795, in ibid., 34:386.

19. Rees, *Washington's Leadership Lessons*, 58.

20. Burns and Dunn, *Washington*, 156–57; Landy and Milkis, *Presidential Greatness*, 23; Freeman, *Washington*, 6:226.

One prominent way Washington built respect for the office of the presidency was by hosting levees. Levees or social dinners—where the president invited congressional officials, American citizens, and important dignitaries—were employed to build trust, relationships, and communication avenues as well as to increase the validity and influence of the new government. The president intuitively and shrewdly understood the importance of pomp as most Americans approved a bit of ceremony from their head of state.[21]

During presidential levees, George and Martha welcomed and greeted guests at the door. Washington did not shake hands; he would only bow to guests. These levees exhibited none of the bonhomie entertainment at Mount Vernon, or the jocular relaxations and interactions in army camps, but were often stiff, dull, and stately. The dinners were large, frequent, and elaborate. The spectacle was heightened by the presence in the halls of powdered lackeys; food was consumed in prodigious quantities; orders for wine ran to twenty-six dozen claret and like volume of champagne. Just as the Anglican way had nurtured and informed Washington's reserve and moderation in expressing his religiosity, presidential levees entertained in a balanced way—enough so that cries of monarchy could be made but not too little so as to incur the ridicule from the more traditional upper class of English gentry.[22]

Another precedent or legacy Washington established was that of an energetic executive who preserved and promoted constitutional republicanism. Elaborate levees and triumphal processionals to occasions of state were balanced by deferential responses to lawmakers. Reserved in most formal settings, the president deliberately focused on strengthening the relationship between the people and their newly drafted government. Aristocratic by nature but republican by choice, Washington embraced an energetic government as the only means of protecting the American republic from its own self-destruction. The president should be vigorous and ready to lead, but also one who would listen to the people and demonstrate executive restraint.[23]

Washington conscientiously and intentionally also set many precedents in regard to religion. One contemporary remarked that the president "was a firm believer in the Christian religion" which was evident "at his first entrance on his civil administration." As one who honored the Sabbath, Washington insisted "that no secular business could be transacted with him,

---

21. Johnson, *Washington: Founding Father,* 98.

22. Flexner, *Washington,* 3:197; Freeman, *Washington,* 6:384; Smith, *Patriarch,* 87; Fay, *Republican Aristocrat,* 254

23. Landy and Milkis, *Presidential Greatness,* 13.

on the day set apart by Christians for worship of the Deity."[24] Moreover, many of Chief Executive's associates observed him praying and giving blessings, especially at mealtimes, which were no small gestures considering the attention the president garnered for every little precedent and action.[25]

By faithfully attending worship services on the Sabbath, American citizens realized that if they wanted to see their president in person, they could most easily find him at church. Washington's own diaries note, for example, that he often "went to Crouded Churches in the Morning & afternoon" on Sundays.[26] The president asked colleagues, congressional members, guests, and friends to join him at church or inquired if he could accompany them at their church. He once asked John Jay for a ride to worship after his carriage had broken down.[27] Samuel Nasson, who served in the American Revolution as quartermaster, captain, and later as a Massachusetts delegate to the Constitution Convention, shared with a fellow delegate how "almost all the Revd. Clergy in this Country" praise the president "for all his Virtues but none more than for his attendance to Public Worship."[28]

During his presidency, Washington worshipped in churches of various denominations in numerous states. He recorded some, but not all, of these experiences in his diary. For example, he attended the Moravian Church, in Salem, Georgia, with Governor Alexander Martin and heard members "Sing, & perform on a variety of instruments."[29] In York, Pennsylvania, "being no Episcopal Minister present," he worshipped at the Dutch Reformed Church. Not able to understand the language, the president humorously insisted he was "in no danger of becoming a proselyte to its religion by the eloquence of the Preacher."[30] He attended First Presbyterian Church, in Carlisle, Pennsylvania, and "heard Doctr. Davidson Preach a political Sermon" praising "order & good government; and the excellence of that of the United States."[31] When Washington proclaimed a Thanksgiving Day, on February 19, 1795, he worshipped at Christ Church in Philadelphia, a church he regularly attended during the Revolutionary War and his presidency. Reverend William White preached on "the connection between religion and civil

---

24. J.M. Sewall, Eulogy on Washington, December 1799, in Schroeder, *Maxims of Washington*, 297.

25. Grizzard, *Ways of Providence*, 3.

26 Jackson and Twohig, *Diaries of Washington*, 6:133.

27. Freeman, *Washington*, 6:246.

28. Samuel Nasson to George Thatcher, July 9, 1789, in Kaminski, *Founders*, 502.

29. Jackson and Twohig, *Diaries of Washington*, 6:153.

30. Ibid., 6:168.

31. Ibid., 6:182.

happiness." White later recalled that Washington's worship behavior was faithful, "serious and attentive."[32]

During his presidency, Washington went to church more often than any other time in his life. In the capital cities of New York and Philadelphia, churches were located only a few blocks from his residency. His most frequent places of worship were St. Paul's Chapel and Trinity Church in New York City, and Christ Church and St. Peter's Church in Philadelphia. His faithful and regular church attendance was highly visible to the public, and he was admired as a model, God-fearing, Christian leader of the people.

On October 3, 1789, the president issued the nation's first thanksgiving proclamation. "Whereas it is the duty of all Nations to acknowledge the providence of Almighty God, to obey his will, to be grateful for his benefits, and humbly implore his protection and favor," Washington recommended a day of "public thanks-giving and prayer to be observed by acknowledging with grateful hearts the many signal favors of Almighty God, especially by affording them an opportunity peaceably to establish a form of government for their safety and happiness." Echoing Heb 13:8—which stated that Jesus Christ is "the same yesterday and today and forever"—the president insisted that Thursday, November 26, 1789 would be set aside to honor "the service of that great and glorious Being, who is the beneficent Author of all the good that was, that is, or that will be."

Washington's thanksgiving proclamation encouraged a humble spirit in the American people. He believed the country should "unite in rendering unto him"—the Divine Author—

> our sincere and humble thanks for his kind care and protection of the People of this country previous to their becoming a Nation, for the signal and manifold mercies, and the favorable interpositions of his providence, which we experienced in the course and conclusion of the late war, for the great degree of tranquility, union, and plenty, which we have since enjoyed, for the peaceable and rational manner in which we have been enabled to establish constitutions of government for our safety and happiness, and particularly the national One now lately instituted, for the civil and religious liberty which we are blessed, and the means we have of acquiring and diffusing useful knowledge and in general for all the great and various favors which he hath been pleased to confer upon us. And also that we may then unite in most humbly offering our prayers and supplications to the great Lord and Ruler of Nations and beseech him to pardon our national and other transgressions, to enable us all,

32. Tebbel, *Washington's America*, 357.

whether in public or private stations, to perform our several and relative duties properly and punctually, to render our national government wise, just and constitutional laws, discreetly and faithfully executed and obeyed . . . To promote the knowledge and practice of true religion and virtue, and the encrease of science among them and Us, and generally grant unto all Mankind such a degree of temporal prosperity as he alone knows best.[33]

The Day of Thanksgiving Proclamation repeated many of the religious themes Washington had expressed and exhibited throughout his life. He not only recognized that good government's inspiration came from God and that Americans should acknowledge, thank, obey, and pray to God, but he also implored the the nation—collectively and individually—to seek forgiveness for their transgressions. By humbly thanking and appealing to God for protection, favor, and forgiveness, the president revealed his orthodox Christian worldview and understanding of Scripture. For a deist, of course, there would be no reason to pray, because the Deity does not keep track of sins or intervene to wipe away one's sins. A deist God performs no miracles and plays no favorites.[34] Continuous prayer and expressions of thanksgiving were precedents and religious legacies Washington would leave with the American people.

Washington heeded Jesus's teaching—"Ask and it shall be given unto you" (Matt 7:7; Luke 11:9, John 16:24)—and frequently urged Americans to implore the Almighty for continued blessings. Unlike Jefferson, who declined to proclaim national days of solemn humiliation, fasting, or prayer, Washington consistently called for days of remembrance, prayer, fasting, and thanksgiving throughout his administration. Many Americans hid their Bibles during Jefferson's presidency believing that he intended to lawfully confiscate the Scriptures and replace them with his own edited version. When Washington was president, however, no one concealed their Bibles or worried about confiscation by the government. Most Americans deemed The Father of His Country to be a humble, Christian man.[35]

In mid-June of 1789, the ministers and elders of the German Reformed congregations told Washington that they were praying for him, his family, and the government "with all temporal and spiritual blessings in Christ Jesus." The president responded happily with "the sentiments and gratitude

33. Washington, Day of Thanksgiving Proclamation, October 3, 1789, in Fitzpatrick, *Writings of Washington*, 30:428.

34. Novak and Novak, *Washington's God*, 146–50; Eidsmoe, *Christianity and the Constitution*, 118.

35. Novak and Novak, *Washington's God*, 155; Gaustad, *Faith of Our Fathers*, 98; Woodward, *Image and the Man*, 144.

and piety towards Almighty-God, which are expressed with such fervency of devotion in your address." He also praised them for seeing "the necessity of uniting reverence to such a government and obedience to its laws with the duties and exercise of Religion." Promising the German Reformed congregations that he would continue to follow "the dictates of my conscience," Washington trusted that their own "devotions before the Throne of Grace" would "be prevalent in calling down the blessings of Heaven" for their congregations and country.[36]

Writing to the Pennsylvania House of Representatives near the end of his presidency, Washington held on to the hope that "my fellow Citizens" would choose "wise and virtuous men who will successively administer every branch of the Government in such manner, as under divine providence, to enforce the general happiness."[37] A religious citizenry was essential for the future stability and prosperity of the nation. The government, therefore, had a civil duty to augment and support religion as long as it also protected the free exercise of religion.[38]

At the end of his second term, Washington sent a touching letter to the rector, churchwardens, and vestrymen of the United Episcopal Churches (Christ Church and St. Peter's Church in Philadelphia). Having worshipped frequently at these orthodox Christian churches during his presidency, Washington thanked them for their "affection" and "prayers" during his tenure in office.

> It is with peculiar satisfaction I can say, that, prompted by a high sense of duty in my attendance on public worship, I have been gratified, during my residence among you, by the liberal and interesting discourses which have been delivered in your Churches. Believing that Government alone can be approved by Heaven, which promotes peace and secures the protection to its Citizens in every thing that is dear and interesting to them, it has been the great object of my administration to insure those invaluable ends; and when, to a consciousness of the purity of intentions, is added to the approbation of my fellow Citizens, I shall experience in my retirement that heartfelt satisfaction which can only be exceeded by the hope of future happiness.[39]

36. Washington to German Reformed Congregations, June 10, 1789, in Abbot, *Washington, Presidential Series*, 3:92–93.

37. Washington to Pennsylvania House of Representatives, February 17, 1797, *Writings of Washington*, 35:393.

38. Grizzard, *Ways of Providence*, 10; Eidsmoe, *Christianity and the Constitution*, 124; Woodward, *Image and the Man*, 142–43.

39. Washington to Rector, Church Wardens, and Vestrymen of the United Episcopal

Indeed, for eight years the president had faithfully attended divine worship as president. Moreover, he intentionally and deliberately had constructed a legacy that both the government and citizenry needed to be propped up, shaped, and nurtured by a loving God and the Christian religion. "*Religion* and *Morality*" are "the essential pillars of Civil society," he insisted to the clergy of different denominations residing near Philadelphia. Consequently, he took "unspeakable pleasure" in the "harmony and brotherly love which characterizes the Clergy of different denominations" throughout the United States. The world would see, by the United States's example, "a new and interesting spectacle, at once the pride of our Country and the surest basis of universal Harmony." He praised the clergy and prayed that their "labours for the good of Mankind may be crowned with success . . . and that the future reward of good and faithful Servants" would be theirs according to "the Divine Author of life and felicity."[40]

In addition to promoting of religion and morality as critical pillars of American society, Washington also established the expectation that a man of faith would occupy the president's office. Indeed, his moral integrity and rectitude had inspired trust and confidence in the chief executive position and government. Thus, even when he made an unpopular decision—such as endorsing Jay's Treaty in 1795—the Senate eventually complied with his wish and ratified the treaty. The president was trustworthy, and members of Congress believed he would never dupe them on an issue of great importance, especially considering how much he had sacrificed to establish the American republic in the first place.[41] Christian character and confidence mattered, and the Washington provided both to the American people. Furthermore, congressmen and citizens alike found great comfort in the realization that their nation's leader submitted and humbled himself before God and abided by the Scriptures—a higher rule of law. Washington was their hero and American Moses, but he was not God or a divine king.[42]

As ardently as he worshipped and believed in the Christian God, and as earnestly as he encouraged a religious citizenry, Washington did not want to coerce or legalistically impose a particular religion in a republican society. Religious freedom, after all, allowed for the development of a religious, moral nation.

Churches of Christ Church and St. Peter's, March 2, 1797, *Writings of Washington*, 35:410–11.

40. Washington to the Clergy of Different Denominations Residing in and near the city of Philadelphia, March 3, 1797, in ibid., 35:416–17.

41. Phelps, *American Constitutionalism*, 17.

42. Bailey, *Presidential Greatness*, 268.

The president cherished and promoted the right of religious free exercise. He wanted people to worship and practice their faith uninhibited. "If I could have entertained the slightest apprehension, that the constitution framed at the convention, where I had the honor to preside, might possibly endanger the religious rights of any ecclesiastical society," he asserted to the United Baptist Churches of Virginia, "certainly I would have never placed my signature to it." Moreover, if the country ever drifted and moved "to render the liberty of conscience insecure, I beg you will be persuaded, that no one would be more zealous than myself to establish effectual barriers against the horrors of spiritual tyranny, and every species of religious persecution." Each man was "accountable to God alone for his religious opinions" and "ought to be protected in worshipping the Deity according to the dictates of his own conscience."[43] As he told a group of Quakers, "Government" was "instituted to protect the persons and consciences of men from oppression . . . ." The liberty enjoyed by Americans "worshipping Almighty God agreeably to their consciences, is not only among the choicest of their *blessings*, but also of their *rights*." Humankind was "responsible only to their Maker for the religion, or modes of faith, which they may prefer or profess."[44] To the Society of Free Quakers, Washington insisted that "the conscientious scruples of religious belief" rested "entirely with the sects that profess, or the individuals who entertain them."[45]

The president's support for religious freedom made him a popular figure with many different religious groups and sects. Responding to a Roman Catholic address, the president expressed his appreciation for the "extraordinary candor of my fellow-citizens of all denominations." He wanted Catholics—"animated alone by the pure spirit of Christianity, and still conducting themselves as the faithful subjects of our free government"—to know that they should "enjoy every temporal and spiritual felicity."[46] As he explained to the Hebrew congregations at Newport, Rhode Island, "the government of the United States . . . gives to bigotry no sanction, to persecution no assistance." Repeating Mic 4:4 yet again, Washington insisted that every American should be able to "sit safely under his own vine and fig-tree" where "there shall be none to make him afraid." He was "inexpressibly happy that by the smiles of divine Providence, my weak but honest endeavors to serve my country have hitherto been crowned with so much success." God

43. Washington to United Baptist Churches in Virginia, May 10, 1789, in Fitzpatrick, *Writings of Washington,* 30:321.

44. Washington to Quakers, September, 1789, in ibid., 30:416.

45. Washington to Society of Free Quakers, March, 1790, in ibid., 31:16.

46. Washington to Roman Catholic Committee, March, 1790, in ibid., 31:22.

had equipped and strengthened him throughout his life to be "useful to this numerous and free People over whom I am called to preside."[47]

Washington deemed religious freedom a God-given right and unifying force for the nation. Since "human happiness and moral duty" were "inseparably connected," he found it edifying "to see Christians of different denominations dwell together in more charity, and conduct themselves in respect to each other with a more christian-like spirit than ever they have done in any former age, or in any other Nation."[48] Having "now attained the desirable object of uniting under one general Government all those States which were originally confederated," he wrote in shortly after ratification, "we have a right to expect, with the blessing of a divine providence, that our Country will afford us all those domestic enjoyments of which a free people can only boast."[49] Religious freedom allowed for a harmonious religious society to flourish.

The president was well aware of the religious turmoil and conflicts that had embroiled other nations. He lamented, for example, the "disputes between the Protestants and Roman Catholics" in Ireland. Exhibiting his Latitudinarian worldview, he noted, "religious controversies are always productive of more acrimony and irreconcilable hatred than those which spring from any other cause." He hoped that "the enlightened and liberal policy of the present age would have put an effectual stop to contentions of this kind."[50] Christians, "of every denomination so far," should never "see their religious disputes carried to such a pitch as to endanger the peace of Society."[51]

For Washington, religious freedom provided a platform for the development and emergence of a religious and, thus, a prosperous nation. As he told members of the New Church in Baltimore, "the manifest interposition of an over-ruling Providence" and the "patriotic exertions of united america" had given "a respectable rank among the nations of the Earth." The American people had "abundant reason to rejoice that in this Land the light of truth and reason has triumphed over the power of bigotry and superstition, and that every person here may worship God according to the dictates of his own heart." Never, "in this enlightened Age and in the Land of equal liberty," would a "man's religious tenants . . . forfeit the protection of

47. Washington to Hebrew Congregations at Newport, August, 1790, in ibid., 31:93–94.

48. Washington to Convention of Protestant Episcopal Church, August, 1789, in ibid., 30:383.

49. Washington to Arthur Fenner, June 4, 1790, in ibid., 31:48.

50. Washington to Edward Newenham, June 22, 1792, in ibid., 32:73.

51. Washington to Edward Newenham, October 20, in ibid., 32:190.

the Laws, nor deprive him of the right of attaining and holding the highest Offices that are known in the United States." He expected members of the New Church to "taste those blessings, which a gracious God bestows upon the Righteous."[52]

The president's commitment to religious freedom, however, was anything but a desire to be free from religion. Such an interpretation would have exasperated Washington. The freedom to exercise religion gave permission and assurance to Christian churches and organizations, as well as other religious sects, to practice and flourish uninhibited by the government. Of course, he did not believe that the federal government should endorse or favor a national church or any one denomination over the other. Nevertheless, Washington's apprehension to reveal his own particular faith in any official or governmental capacity led some to incorrectly cast him or misconstrue him as one who was ambivalent to the Christian faith.[53]

Thomas Jefferson is one of the few contemporaries who asserted that Washington "had never on any occasion said a word to the public which shewed a belief in the Xn religion." In a conversation between Benjamin Rush and Ashbel Green, Jefferson heard that the Philadelphia clergy thought they could force the president "at length to declare publicly whether he was a Christian or not." Jefferson claimed, however, that "the old fox was too cunning for them," as Washington "answered every article of their address particularly except that, which he passed over without notice." Jefferson also recorded that Gouverneur Morris, a deist, had "often told me that Genl. Washington believed no more of that system than he himself did."[54]

By 1796, however, Washington was estranged from Morris and Jefferson.[55] The rupture in the Jefferson-Washington relationship was so bitter that no correspondence was exchanged between the two for the last three years of Washington's life. Jefferson would not even attend the general's funeral, fearing Martha's wrath. Moreover, Ashbel Green later refuted the notion that the Philadelphia clergy had tried to force a public confession and also disputed Jefferson's religious caricature of the man. Indeed, Morris and Jefferson's assessment of Washington's personal faith—something the president was reluctant to share even with closer political associates and friends—should be noted with considerable reservation.

52. Washington to Members of New Church in Baltimore, January 27, 1793, in ibid., 32:314–15.

53. Johnson, *Washington: Founding Father*, 102–03.

54. Jefferson, Notes on a Conversation with Benjamin Rush, February 1, 1800, in Boyd, *Papers of Jefferson*, 31:352–53.

55. Henriques, *Realistic Visionary*, 117–23.

Washington's alleged silence or restraint in expressing his personal views on religion was due both to his reserved nature and Latitudinarian worldview. As general and as president, he spoke for all Americans and did not want doctrinal differences to fracture the nation. His public and private correspondence reveals a man who intentionally avoided any revelation or manipulation of his religious affiliation even as most contemporaries and peers knew he was lifelong member of the Anglican Church. Nonetheless, his refusal to publicly endorse or favor a specific denomination enticed various Christian denominations, as well as nonbelievers and future historians, to claim the Father of His Country, and his religion, as their own.

Washington wanted religion to be a unifying force rather than a divisive one. He received many letters and addresses from Presbyterian, Baptist, and Methodist congregations as well as from Jewish synagogues. All of these groups, and more, sought assurance from the president that their religious rights would be honored and protected. Washington did not disappoint. He responded to each letter contending that religion and churches were essential for good citizenship, republican virtue, and a moral foundation for good government.

A committed nationalist, Washington did everything he could to keep the fragile, young republic closely knit together. He envisioned a government above party and faction.[56] When he sat for innumerable portraits, delivered numerous proclamations, and exchanged salutations with all sorts of government and religious groups, he not only hoped to increase the visibility of America's chief executive, but also used these opportunities to unite the country around the ideals Americans fought for and secured during the American Revolution and at the Constitutional Constitution.[57]

The president desired a national university to improve the bonds of union, adopted plans and measures from ideological opposites—Jefferson and Hamilton in particular—in his cabinet, and sought advice and counsel from almost anyone. He promoted and invested in the building of canals, roads, and post offices—anything that would bring different states and regions of the country together. He read ten newspapers daily as well as numerous pamphlets. When he considered federal appointments, he looked for the best man available but also deliberated on how he could build local support throughout the country with his selections. He regularly inquired of other people's thoughts and ideas, and demonstrated a sincere desire to learn more about the citizens he was leading. Hamilton admired the president's modesty and how he "consulted much, pondered much, resolved

---

56. Elkins and McKitrick, *Age of Federalism*, 292.

57. Henriques, *Realistic Visionary*, 50–52.

slowly, resolved surely."[58] The president used any piece of information, advantage, or policy to keep the United States whole.

Many years after Washington's death, Timothy Pickering—who served as Secretary of State during the administration's second term—hailed the "correct judgments" of the president and how they were "scrupulously directed to the promotion of the public welfare."[59] Even in their personal lives, George and Martha sought harmony and unity as matchmakers who arranged over sixteen marriages including that between Dolley Paine and James Madison.[60]

The president was the nation's most compelling unifying force. Traveling farther than any non-preacher and touring every state in the Union during his first term, he asked questions and listened to American citizens everywhere he went. These tours brought the government to the people and earned the loyalty and confidence of many who had never seen the Father of His Country.[61] Washington went on these tours to "render" the new government "more popular."[62]

Out of respect for the Sabbath, however, he rarely traveled on Sundays. Instead, he often went to church twice on Sunday—once in the morning and evening.[63] On his southern tour in 1791, the president went to more worship services than there were days of travel. Binding religious people to the republic and promoting Christianity as the surest means of ensuring the moral health of the country were prime objectives.[64] Moreover, his travels across the different states exposed him to the rich religious and cultural diversity of the people of the United States. He took the opportunity to support and delight in the free exercise of religion among Baptists, Catholics, Jews, and other denominations alike.[65]

During the 1790s, the president's image was everywhere—in printings, prints, lockets, on coins, silverware, plates, and household bric-a-brac. A popular toast in America proclaimed Washington as "the man who unites

58. Hamilton, Concerning the Public Conduct and Character of John Adams, Esq. President of the United States, October 1800, in Syrett, *Papers of Hamilton*, 25:214.

59. Timothy Pickering to John Marshall, January 2, 1827, in Hobson, *Papers of Marshall*, 11:67–68.

60. Wood, *Revolutionary Characters*, 59–60.

61. Johnson, *Washington: Founding Father*, 98–99.

62. Kaminski et al., *Great and Good Man*, 145–51.

63. Smith, *Patriarch*, 31.

64. Novak and Novak, *Washington's God*, 170.

65. Grizzard, *Ways of Providence*, 11–12.

all hearts." He was the Unifier, American Zeus, Moses, and Cincinnatus all at once.[66]

A devout Anglican and Latitudinarian, Washington strove to be proactive in minimizing differences between denominations and religious faith. He highlighted commonalities and beliefs that united various Christian denominations and lifted up people of all faith by promoting liberty and the free exercise of religion. As general and president, he exchanged salutations with numerous religious, mostly Christian, groups including: the Dutch Reformed, Protestant Dutch, German Lutheran, Catholic, United Baptist, Presbyterian, Methodist, German Reformed, Episcopal, Congregational, Swedenborgian, Quakers, United Brethren, Universalist, and Jewish synagogues. Themes like the "Throne of Grace" and "pure spirit of Christianity" demonstrated his verbal and written attempts to focus on what unified different Christian sects and denominations. Moreover, he insisted that government should protect its citizens in everything that was dear to them, most especially their religion. Furthermore, he wanted the government to cooperate with religious groups in order to spread Christianity among the Native Americans. He attended mostly Episcopal churches, but also Presbyterian, Dutch Reformed, Lutheran, and German Reformed parishes.[67]

Most religious groups delighted in Washington's unifying efforts, outreach, and promotion of religion, and did not purport or assume that he was indifferent to his own Christian faith. Instead, they saw the president protecting not only his own right to practice his Anglican faith but the religious faiths of all people.

Baptists and Catholics praised Washington when he promised to zealously protect them from religious persecution. Quakers rejoiced when he lauded their exemplary citizenship despite their pacifism and refusal to aid the United Colonies during the Revolutionary War. Jews loved the friendship and toleration he expressed and defended. Universalists, disdained by the pious for their liberal religious views, were congratulated for their strong vocational performances and contributions to society, especially in politics. In short, under Washington's leadership, deep-rooted fears and persecution in regard to religious practice and worship dissipated and subsided. The president made religious freedom, union, and liberty an appealing code of the country.[68]

The religious groups most vocal and supportive of president's leadership and elevation of religion in the public sphere came primarily from

---

66. Ellis, *Founding Brothers*, 121; Higginbotham, "Revolutionary Asceticism," 141.

67. Eidsmoe, *Christianity and the Constitution*, 121.

68. Schwartz, *Washington: American Symbol*, 85–86.

Christian denominations—especially dissenter Christian groups. Out of the thirty or so addresses he received from religious groups, the vast majority came from Christian organizations and congregations. No deistic or atheistic group ever contacted Washington. Most contemporaries knew he was an orthodox Anglican Christian who sincerely desired to provide the proper moral guidance and inspiration for the country. Washington had placed God and a Christian worldview at the forefront of the new nation.

11

A Private and Charitable President

Washington's Christian faith was evident in both his public and private life. He spoke publicly of the importance of religion and morality for the nation's well-being, and he embraced the responsibility and role as the spiritual leader of the nation.

His allegiance to the Christian faith, however, was not only a public act. Indeed, in the private and domestic sphere of life, Washington lived his religious faith unswervingly. He possessed great affection for family members and endearing concern for their spiritual well-being. Washington reminded his nephew, George Steptoe Washington, that if he wanted to make an impact in the world or became a "figure on the Stage . . . you should take the first steps right." Therefore education, the "habit of industry," making friends with good company, "economy & frugality," "decency & cleanliness," were character attributes to be emulated and embraced. In addition, his nephew was to "always keep some clothes to wear to Church, or on particular occasions, which should not be worne every day." Men of integrity pay "due attention to moral virtues."[1] Several months later he offered more advice, insisting, "good moral character is the first essential in a man, and that habits contracted at your age are generally indelible, and your conduct here may stamp your character through life." He wanted his nephew to understand that it was "highly important . . . to be learned but virtuous."[2]

Washington did not hesitate to share spiritual wisdom with his obstinate and indolent stepgrandson, George Washington Parke Custis, who

1. Washington to George Steptoe Washington, March 23, 1789, in Fitzpatrick, *Writings of Washington*, 30:246–47.

2. Washington to George Steptoe Washington, December 5, 1790, in ibid., 31:163.

enrolled at Princeton in 1796. In addition to the ten dollars he sent for his stepgrandson to purchase an academic gown, the president referenced the biblical story of the widow's mite hoping Custis would be inspired with a generous heart and disposition.[3]

A generous and munificent character was exhibited throughout Washington's entire life. When a Native American guide—who led the young Colonel through the forest during his militia days—tried to kill him with a rifle shot at point blank range, Washington eventually freed the betrayer. When he provoked an argument with William Payne, at the Fairfax Courthouse, over the merits of the different candidates for the Virginia Assembly, Payne violently pushed Washington to the ground. Friends encouraged him to punish Payne, but he demurred and apologized to Payne. During the Revolutionary War, the general treated British prisoners humanely and immediately released General Cornwallis and his soldiers after their surrender at Yorktown. Compassionate, merciful, and forgiving, Washington embraced and lived the core teachings of Christianity.[4]

He could occasionally be stingy with his money, especially in his youth. When he handed Commander Van Braam over to the French in a hostage exchange at Fort Necessity, he sold the French commander a dress uniform, which he might otherwise have found a nuisance to carry away with him anyway.

As the years passed, however, the Virginian's compassion and generosity grew and matured. By the time of his retirement, he lent money frequently, privately, and without being asked—even when he knew there was little guarantee of remuneration.[5]

Whether he was at Mount Vernon or away on military or civic duty, Washington's generosity was preeminent in his life. Contemporaries frequently mentioned his compassion and philanthropy toward the indigent.[6] Washington told Lund Washington—his cousin and superintendent of Mount Vernon's farms from 1775 to 1785—that "the Hospitality of the House, with respect to the poor, be kept up." No one was to "go away hungry. If any of these kind of People should be in want of Corn," he instructed, "supply their necessities, provided it does not encourage them in idleness." He had "no objection to your giving my Money in Charity, to the Amount of forty or fifty Pounds a year, when you think it well bestowed."

3. Smith, *Patriarch*, 291.

4. Schwartz, *American Symbol*, 170.

5. Cunliffe, *Man and Monument*, 45.

6. Chernow, *Washington*, 133.

By having no objection, he meant, "it is my desire that it should be done."[7]
He gave old army comrades large interest-free loans he never expected
to be repaid. Cash entries in his personal account books carry succinct
but meaningful notations—"To an old soldier"; "To a wounded soldier";
"To a Virginia Soldier." He provided his weaver a loan to bring his wife
and children from England fully anticipating the man would probably
never be able to repay him (which he never did). He quietly paid for the
schooling and education of cash needy relatives, neighbors, friends, and
the sons of several of his friends.[8] Nearby farmers, widows, and others in
need increasingly called on him for advice and assistance over the years,
and he gave his personal time willingly. He served as executor of many
estates of his deceased neighbors. Moreover, Washington donated money
for twenty-two nieces and nephews for college; designated 1,000 pounds
to an academy in Alexandria; and anonymously gave several hundred dollars to the poor virtually every Christmas.[9]

No charitable event or issue was too little for his attention or benevolence. When General Sir William Howe's little pet dog strayed from
the British commander into no-man's land during the Revolutionary
War, Washington had it returned to the British general.[10] When the Reverend James Caldwell passed away, he gave money to support the pastor's
children.[11]

From youth to adulthood, Washington's charitable giving increased in
frequency and means. Entries of small charities grew more frequent and
common in his ledger. When individuals asked for help, he rarely refused
his services or charity. He provided money, food, seed, or business advice
to his neighbors. Chance travelers were given free meals and had purses of
money slipped into their pockets as they departed. He offered William Ramsay annual funding to help him pay his son's college tuition on condition
that it not be mentioned or regarded as an obligation. He even took on all
of Captain Thomas Posey's debts after reckless behavior and his subsequent
warnings went unheeded (they became friends during the Revolutionary
War). Washington also paid for the education of Posey's son.[12]

7. Washington to Lund Washington, November 26, 1775, in Fitzpatrick, *Writings
of Washington,* 4:115.

8. Randall, *Washington,* 256; Flexner, *Washington,* 1:251–52.

9. Parry et al., *Real Washington,* 92, 599.

10. Mayo, *Myths and Men,* 45.

11. Washington to Elias Boudinot, December 14, 1782, in Fitzpatrick, *Writings of
Washington,* 25:427.

12. Flexner, *Washington,* 3:61; Freeman, *Washington,* 7:148, 394.

Some of the fruits of Washington's Christian faith were his service, generosity, and compassion for others. Many would come to Mount Vernon seeking his aid and advice. Picture by Thomas Oldham Barlow, after Thomas Pritchard Rossiter and Louis Remy Mignot. (Courtesy of the Mount Vernon Ladies' Association)

Compassion and financial generosity were natural fruits and outcomes of his Christian worldview and faith. He gave money to "be applied towards relieving the poor of the Presbyterian Churches."[13] He donated funds to the Dutch Reformed Church, in New York City, for the charity school.[14] He included a deposit to the Society of New York "for the relief of distressed Debtors confined in Prison."[15] He sent a letter offering to help a woman find shelter explaining that he was "feeling for her situation" and "desirous of affording relief."[16] When he read a newspaper account about citizens suffering from inclement weather and disaster, he sent a deposit of money.[17] He sent annual payments "for the support of the poor-School in the Alexandria Academy."[18] Shortly after his second inaugural address, he gave $150 to the

13. Washington to John Rodgers, November 28, 1789, in Fitzpatrick, *Writings of Washington,* 30:467.

14. Washington to John Henry Livingston, December 24, 1789, in ibid., 30:467.

15. Washington to John Rodgers, August 30, 1790, in ibid., 31:109.

16. Washington to Battaile Muse and Elizabeth Haynie, December 27, 1790, in ibid., 31:178.

17. Tobias Lear to John Field, January 7, 1791, in ibid., 31:191.

18. Washington to William McWhir, February 7, 1793, in ibid., 32:345.

Guardians of the Poor in Philadelphia. The monies were to be distributed to distressed "persons of every denomination not participating in the benefits" of the Philadelphia Almshouse and House of Employment.[19] After asking Bishop William White, of Philadelphia, if he could anonymously contribute to the relief of widows and orphans, a $250 gift was sent. He gave $300 to residents of Charlestown, South Carolina after a terrible fire.[20] To the manager of his distant western lands, Washington demanded that his tenants be treated fairly. No family was to be denied land who had no other claim.[21] In addition to his annual contribution to the charity school at the Academy in Alexandria, he also annually donated "ten pounds to the Revd. Mr. Davis (incumbent of the Episcopal Church in Alexandria)."[22]

No matter how busy Washington remained as the nation's chief executive, he took time to reach out and help people and did so in a compassionate and detailed manner. When a family associate, Mrs. Haney, passed away, he promised to "receive her daughter the moment I get settled at this place" (Washington had returned to the capital in Philadelphia). "Such necessities as she needs in the meantime, may, however, be furnished here at my expence." He would make sure Mrs. Haney's daughter was suitably boarded "in some respectable family, where her morals and good behavior will be attended to; at my expence also." The young girl should "want for nothing that is decent and proper."[23]

Washington's attention to the poor and downtrodden was fatherly and heartfelt. He saw the problem of poverty—how it was created and how it could be alleviated—not in class but in individual terms. Even when he had to borrow money to pay his own bills, he forbade the collection of any debts that would cause suffering to widows and the fatherless. When he offered to pay for the education of George Washington Greene—son of his deceased war comrade and friend, Nathanael Greene, he did so at a particularly lean and financially challenging time in his own life.[24]

As his Christian charity and philanthropy became more renowned, Washington struggled to keep up with those seeking help and support. In the spring of 1793, he lamented that he was asked "for aids beyond my means, for in truth I escape few contributions to anything of this sort, or to

19. Tobias Lear, Note, March 4, 1793, in ibid., 32:375.

20. Freeman, *Washington*, 7:148, 394.

21. Flexner, *Washington*, 3:61.

22. Washington to William Pearce, November 19, 1794, in Fitzpatrick, *Writings of Washington*, 34:38.

23. Washington to Robert Lewis, June 26, 1796, in ibid., 35:100.

24. Alden, *Washington*, 217; Flexner, *Washington*, 4:481.

public buildings, such as Colleges, Churches, &ca.&ca that are undertaken *by Subscription* within a circle of considerable extent around me."[25]

Nevertheless, even as he struggled to meet all of the needs of individuals and organizations, Washington continued to provide and give generously—often mentioning the biblical reference of the widow's "mite" in the his correspondence. Wanting to make sure his donation did not benefit the bureaucracy or individual members of the Philosophical Society, the president would "add my mite to the means of encouraging" the society in its goals. They could count on him for "respectable sums which may be Subscribed."[26] When the citizens of Charleston, South Carolina suffered destruction from "unfortunate fires," he offered "my mite towards their relief without any desire of having my name mentioned."[27] He reminded his stepgrandson, George Washington Parke Custis, to "never let an individual person ask, without receiving *something*, if you have the means; always recollecting in what light the widow's mite was viewed."[28]

Washington's benevolence and charity increased as he aged. As one local newspaper in Connecticut put it so succinctly and rhetorically in June, 1791: "Many a private man might make a great president; but will there ever be a president who will make so great a man as Washington?"[29] A good number of Americans saw and experienced the man's generosity and Christian charity firsthand. Numerous others simply heard about his good works and benevolent deeds. The lesson was not lost: In both public *and* private life, Washington lived and served as a Christian leader.

---

25. Washington to Samuel Hanson, April 7, 1793, *Writings of Washington,* 32:409–10.

26. Washington to Secretary of State, January 22, 1793, ibid., 32:310–311.

27. Washington to Charles Cotesworth Pinckney, July 8, 1796, in ibid., 35:131.

28. Washington to George Washington Parke Custis, November 15, 1796, in ibid., 35:282–83.

29. Kaminski, *Founders,* 505.

12

The Grand and Godly Farewell

The "all-time master of exists,"[1] Washington carefully prepared and crafted his Farewell Address—the last public statement he thought he would ever share with the American people—as his second term drew to a close. Although he had much help from Hamilton in writing the document, the Farewell Address was distinctly his work. Much like the Circular to the States at the end of the Revolutionary War, the Farewell Address revealed his religious faith and captured his hopes and desires for the future of his beloved country.

Issued on September 19, 1796, the Farewell Address demonstrated, once again, Washington's humility and understanding of humankind's sinful nature. He had decided not to serve a third term, thereby setting yet another historical precedent for the young nation. "I will only say, that I have, with good intentions," he maintained, "contributed towards the Organization and Administration of the government, the best of exertions of which a very fallible judgment was capable." Well aware of the "inferiority of my qualifications" when he began his presidency, "the encreasing weight of years admonished me more and more, that the shade of retirement is as necessary to me as it will be welcome."

After thanking the citizens of the United States for entrusting him as their leader, Washington immediately drew attention to the blessings that God had bestowed on the country. "I shall carry it with me to my grave, as a strong incitement to unceasing vows," he asserted, "that Heaven may continue to you the choicest tokens of its beneficence." He hoped "that your Union and brotherly affection may be perpetual; that the free constitution

1. Ellis, *His Excellency,* 147.

. . . may be sacredly maintained; that its Administration in every department may be stamped with wisdom and Virtue." The happiness of the American people "under the auspices of liberty," could only be made complete "by so careful a preservation and so prudent a use of this blessing."

Having worked for decades on the long-term security of the Union, and as the first advocate of American exceptionalism,[2] Washington insisted the "name of AMERICAN . . . must always exalt the just pride of Patriotism, more than any other appellation derived from local recriminations." While acknowledging "slight shades of difference," most Americans subscribed to "the same Religion, Manners, Habits, and political Principles." They had "fought and triumphed together," and the independence and liberty now enjoyed was "the work of joint councils, and joint efforts; of common dangers, sufferings, and success."

The president asserted that of "all the dispositions and habits which lead to political prosperity, Religion and morality are indispensable supports." A patriot would never "subvert these great Pillars of human happiness, these firmest props of the duties of Men and citizens." Politicians and pious men alike "ought to respect and to cherish them," for religion and morality, as demonstrated by history, led directly to "private and public felicity." Without religion and morality, the "security for property, for reputation, for life" would cease to exist in a republic.

He warned his countrymen not to "indulge the supposition, that morality can be maintained without religion." Taking a subtle dig at the "refined education" of deists and rationalists—who believed that man's reason alone could guide and inspire virtuous behavior, he insisted that "reason and experience both forbid us to expect that National morality can prevail in exclusion of religious principle." He viewed religion as a crucial pillar to republican society rather than a force to be walled off as Jefferson would later assert.[3]

Education would benefit the United States only if it lifted up and enhanced American morality as well as religious understanding and practice. "Tis substantially true," he insisted, "that virtue or morality is a necessary spring of popular government." Americans should "promote then as an object of primary importance, Institutions for the general diffusion of knowledge." Since the "structure of government gives force to public opinion, it is essential that public opinion should be enlightened" by religion and morality. Virtue was essential for the maintenance of republican government and

2. Johnson, *Washington: Founding Father,* 109.

3. Novak and Novak, *Washington's God,* 43; Brookhiser, *Founding Father,* 145; Reichley, *American Public Life,* 103;

the natural fruit of religion. Enlightened education was important, but only if religiously enlightened and inspired. Morality sprung from religion.[4]

Washington concluded his thoughts in the address with typical humility and conviction. "Though in reviewing the incidents of my Administration I am unconscious of intentional error, I am nevertheless too sensible in my defects not to think it probable that I may have committed many errors," he confessed. "Whatever they may be I fervently beseech the Almighty to avert or mitigate the evils to which they may tend." He hoped "that my Country will never cease to view them with indulgence." He then reflected upon his public life referencing a passage on Heaven in John 14:2: "After forty five years of my life dedicated to its Service, with an upright zeal, the faults and incompetent abilities will be consigned to oblivion, as myself must soon be to the Mansions of rest."[5]

Far more public and outspoken in his declarations of faith compared to presidents who would succeed him, contemporaries noted the conspicuous religious depth of their American Moses.[6] The Farewell Address, one of his greatest legacies, recapped Washington's conviction that religion was a crucial matter of national policy and essential to the republic. Only those republics and populaces that lived and embraced a biblical worldview and morality would experience happiness, security, and prosperity.

Washington's presidency was not without challenge or criticism. As war and rivalry between Great Britain and France intensified, the relationship between the United States and France deteriorated. Republicans, led by Madison and Jefferson, repeatedly repudiated the administration's policies and, indirectly, the president's leadership. Partisanship, once considered anathema in republics, grew more intense and pervasive as the 1790s progressed. An emerging Federalist, Washington was no longer universally beloved, especially among Republicans. Instead, he was frequently criticized for being a dupe of the Treasury Secretary and partisan advocate.[7]

Nevertheless, the vast majority of historians consider Washington's presidency a resounding success. The nation's financial crises, once stifling, had been resolved through a strong dose of Hamiltonian economic reform, and commerce thrived. The Bill of Rights had been passed, and the Whiskey Rebellion crushed. The Ohio country had been secured and protected against Native American counter-intrusions. Washington had injected life

4. Landy and Milkis, *Presidential Greatness*, 36; West, "Religious Impulse," 275.

5. Washington, Farewell Address, September 19, 1796, in Fitzpatrick, *Writings of Washington*, 35:214–38.

6. Novak and Novak, *Washington's God*, 220; Schwartz, *American Symbol*, 197; Carroll, *Eulogy*, 21; Woodward, *Image and Man*, 143

7. Henriques, *Realistic Visionary*, 64.

and vitality in the paper document that was the new Constitution. The establishment of the Cabinet and collegial relations with Congress, use of annual messages and appointment powers, executive vetoes on constitutional and practical grounds, proclamations (which included ordering days of thanksgiving), treaties and declaring neutrality, and claims of executive privilege were all important precedents and achievements that would shape the executive branch for decades to come. He had strengthened and legitimized the republican experiment and, at the same time, honorably conducted the affairs of the presidential office.[8]

Many historians consider Washington—along with Lincoln and FDR—one of the United States's greatest presidents. As president, he repeatedly thanked God for his blessings upon the country. In his Farewell Address, he reiterated his belief that religion was essential for national prosperity and republican virtue. Engraving by G. Petit after Lansdowne portrait by Gilbert Stuart. (Courtesy of Ladies' Association of Mount Vernon)

8. Henriques, *Realistic Visionary,* 65; Ferling, *First of Men,* 480.

Throughout the ups and downs of the presidency, Washington's Christian faith nurtured and sustained his character and confidence. His biblical understanding of the world was ballast in tumultuous and triumphant times. Looking back, in 1811, John Jay insisted that the Washington Administration "raised the nation out of confusion into order, out of degradation and distress into reputation and prosperity. It found us withering—it left us flourishing."[9] The president had the trust and confidence of the American people. As long as he had been in charge of the government, the people followed. Indeed, he had transformed "the improbable into the inevitable."[10] The bar was set high for the president's successors.

After John Adams's inauguration, on March 4, 1797, Washington returned to his Philadelphia residence and put his papers and belongings in order. He then walked to Francis Hotel, where President Adams was staying, to pay his respects. On the way over to the hotel, he was almost mobbed by citizens who wanted to get one last glimpse the nation's first ex-president. The mood, however, was somber and quiet as they walked. At the door of the hotel, Washington turned and looked back at the people who had followed, his cheeks wet with tears. "No man ever saw him so moved," declared one eyewitness. For a long moment, the Father of His Country stood face-to-face with the onlookers in solemn silence. Then he turned, and when the door closed behind him, a "great smothered sigh went through the crowd, something between a sob and a groan."[11] Americans grieved as they said goodbye to their national hero, president, and Christian leader.

9. John Jay to Richard Peters, March 29, 1811, in Kaminski, *Founders*, 517.

10. Ellis, *His Excellency*, 188–89.

11. Henriques, *Realistic Visionary*, 64.

PART V

Twilight Testimonials

13

Under His Vine and Fig Tree

About a year after Washington left the presidency and returned to Mount Vernon, he penned a reflective letter and sent it to Sally Fairfax—widow of George William Fairfax, former neighbor, and romantic interest from his youth—who now resided in England. He was "worn out" by "the toils of my past labour," but was now happily "again seated under my Vine & Fig tree." Though he worried about America's foreign affairs, he continued to place his trust in a merciful, benevolent God—"that faithful expositor of all things." He hoped "to spend the remainder of my days (which cannot be many) in rural amusements—free from those cares which public responsibility is never exempt."[1]

Washington's most often used biblical reference, "under his vine and under his fig tree," is found in Mic 4:4, 1 Kings 4:25, and Zech 3:10. Revealing and significant, he used or made reference to the vine and fig tree phrase almost fifty times throughout his correspondence, particularly later in his life. The Mic 4:1–5 (KJV) passage speaks of how nations and individuals should learn the ways of the God of Jacob and "walk in his paths"—sentiments Washington echoed faithfully in his public and private life. The reference of swords being beaten into plowshares must have also appealed to the general-turned-farmer again. Most poignantly, everyone who sat "under his vine and under his fig tree" should not be afraid, "for the mouth of the Lord of hosts has spoken." Confident in their fate and relationship with God, Christian followers would "walk in the name of the Lord our God forever and ever." This was the religion of the Bible-reading and Bible-believing Washington.

1. Washington to Sarah Cary Fairfax, May 16, 1798, in Abbot and Twohig, *Washington, Retirement Series*, 2:272.

Washington was finally able to retire to Mount Vernon and rest under his vine and fig tree in the spring of 1797. Although he still worried about the state of his country's foreign affairs, he had "walked on a straight line" with God's help and felt secure in his legacy and Christian faith. Picture by Adolf Ulrik Wertmuller. (Courtesy of the Mount Vernon Ladies' Association)

As much as he was relieved to be home with his family and farms, retirement challenged Washington. For most of his life, he had been a public servant—completely engrossed in the pursuit of independence, liberty, freedom, and republican stability. He now found himself politically detached from citizens. "I am alone *at present*, and shall be glad to see you this evening," he told his personal secretary, Tobias Lear, in the first summer of retirement. "Unless some one pops in, unexpectedly, Mrs. Washington and myself will do what I believe has not been done with the last twenty years by us, that is to set down to dinner by ourselves."[2]

In the spring of 1797, Washington was sixty-four years old and had lived a full life. He did not believe he would live much longer, and his

---

2. Washington to Tobias Lear, July 31, 1797, in ibid., 1:281.

family's health history confirmed his intuition. More than once, he pointed out that both his grandfather, Lawrence, and father, Augustine, died at relatively young ages—37 and 49 respectively. His half-brother, Lawrence passed away at the age of 34. None of his natural siblings lived to sixty-five.[3]

Even though he no longer officially served the public interest, Washington did live with a great sense of personal fulfillment and peace in his twilight years. He was comfortable with himself, his legacy, and his God. Fulfilled and content, the eventual reckoning with death did not induce anxiousness nor concern.[4]

During his last few years, he oversaw the administration of Mount Vernon, embraced his newfound family time, stayed informed of world events, and lived a "quiet and regular life." He "gets up at 5 o'clock in the morning, reads or writes until seven," noted a visitor who stayed at Mount Vernon for a few weeks in May and June of 1798. "He breakfasts on tea and cakes made from maize; because of his teeth he makes slices spread with butter and honey." Soon after he "goes on horseback to see the work in the fields" and "returns at two o'clock, dresses, goes to dinner." If guests were present, he conversed with them "after dinner with a glass of Madeira in his hand. After dinner he diligently reads the newspapers, of which he receives about ten different kinds." In addition to answering letters, the president had "tea at 7 o'clock" and "chats until nine, and then he goes to bed."[5]

During his retirement, Washington had ample opportunity to reflect on his service to his country. "If it has pleased the supreme architect of the Universe to make me a humble instrument to promote the welfare and happiness of my fellow men," he explained to the Alexandria, Virginia masons, "my exertions have been abundantly recompensed by the Kind partiality with which they have been received."[6]

One way he continued to serve and use his God-given gifts and talents was to encourage others to be grateful and fruitful stewards of God's benevolence. When the legislators from Rhode Island praised him for a successful presidency, Washington responded by insisting that without "the beneficent interposition of the Supreme Ruler of the Universe we could not have reached the distinguished situation which we have attained with such unprecedented rapidity." Americans, therefore, should bow to God "with gratitude and reverence, and endeavor to merit a continuance of his special

3. Henriques, *Realistic Visionary,* 190; Quitt, "English Cleric," 15.

4. Greven, *Protestant Temperament,* 327.

5. Julian Ursyn Niemcewicz, Travels through America, May 21, 1798, in Kaminski, *Founders,* 509.

6. Washington to Alexandria Masons, April 1, 1797, in Abbot and Twohig, *Washington, Retirement Series,* 1:54–55.

favors." He promised Rhode Islanders that he would "supplicate the throne of Grace that the best of Heavens blessings may rest upon your State, and upon your selves individually."[7]

Always a man of action and production, Washington disdained complacency and indolence. A visitor who walked into the most public room of the Mount Vernon mansion would see two key portraits prominently displayed—one of the Virgin Mary and one of St. John, the beloved disciple. Humankind was capable of both brutishness and nobility, so like Mary and John, Washington would serve his family and fellow man with duty and devotion[8] and achieve significant results.

As had been the case since the Revolution, Washington remained confident "that bounteous Providence will continue to bless, & preserve our country in Peace, & in the prosperity it has enjoyed."[9] Even when members of Congress misbehaved in what he felt were treasonous and treacherous ways, in the spring of 1798 (some members were encouraging French officials not to receive United States's envoys), he did not lose faith that God would guard and protect the United States. "It has always been my belief," he assured Henry Knox, the Secretary of War, "that Providence has not led us so far in the path of Independence of one nation, to throw us into the Arms of another." God would bring justice to those attempting to injure the United States, and "the machinations of those, who are attempting it, will sooner or later recoil upon their heads."[10] The retired president believed that God favored the American experiment, even during setbacks and hardship, because the nation embodied and promoted freedom and liberty.[11]

As he aged and endured physical atrophies of all kinds, Washington's Christian faith continued to provide mental and spiritual sustenance. In much of his correspondence, during the last two years of his life, he exhibited a spiritual calm and serenity. To his friend, David Humphreys, for example, he acknowledged the peace he felt living under "the shade of my own Vine & Fig tree" after leaving the "Chair of Government." Of course, he cared deeply for his country and intermittently worried that the sordid state of affairs in Europe might hurt the young republic. Nothing short of a general Peace in Europe will produce tranquility in this country," he opined.

7. Washington to Arthur Fenner and Rhode Island Legislators, April 3, 1797, in ibid., 1:26.

8. Novak and Novak, *Washington's God,* 127.

9. Washington to Massachusetts Masons, March, 1797, in Abbot and Twohig, *Washington, Retirement Series,* 1:117–18.

10. Washington to Secretary of War, March 27, 1798, in Fitzpatrick, *Writings of Washington,* 36:192.

11. Novak and Novak, *Washington's God,* 178.

He had "confidence however, in that Providence, which has shielded the U. States from the Evils which have threatened them hitherto . . . ." He would "view things in the 'Calm lights of Mild Philosophy' and endeavor to finish my course in retirement & ease."[12] God was in control of his life as well as the fate of the United States.

When tensions increased with France in the summer of 1798, President Adams asked his predecessor to abandon retirement and take command of the American army. Insisting that the commander should be younger "and better qualified to encounter the usual vicissitudes of War," Washington informed Adams that he wanted to close the "remnant of my days in my present peaceful abode." He did not want, "at so late a period of life, to leave Scenes I sincerely love, to enter upon the boundless fields of public action—incessant trouble—and high responsibility." If war were inevitable, however, he would serve if called. "We can with pure hearts," he told Adams, "appeal to Heaven for the justice of our cause, and may confidently trust the final result to that kind Providence who has hitherto, and so often, signally favoured the People of the United States."[13]

Not wanting to leave the serenity of retirement, Washington, nonetheless, believed the pending appointment as commander in chief was yet another calling from Providence. "New scenes are opening upon us," he asserted to his longtime friend, John Trumbull, "and a very unexpected one, as it respects myself, is unfolding . . . the final result of these measures is only known to that Providence in whose directions all things are." He further explained, "when I bid adieu last to the Theatre of public life, I thought it was hardly possible that any event would arise, *in my day*, that could induce me to tread that stage again." Nevertheless, in the current "age of Wonders," he once again "consented to become an Actor in the great Drama."[14] Still, he wrote to another friend, he never "imagined when I took my last leave of the walks of Public life and retired to the Shades of my Vine & Fig tree that any event would arise *in my day* that could bring me again on a public theatre." At the age of sixty-six, he had little incentive or ambition to "relinquish the peaceful walks to which I had retired, and in the shades of which I had fondly hoped to spend the remnant of a life worn down with cares in contemplation on the past and in scenes present & to come, of rural growth." It was now time to "let others & especially those who are best acquainted with the Construction of Mind" to lead. However, he believed "that man was not

12. Washington to David Humphreys, June 26, 1797, in Abbot and Twohig, *Washington, Retirement Series*, 1:219–20.

13. Washington to John Adams, July 13, 1798, in ibid., 2:402–03.

14. Washington to Jonathan Trumbull, July 25, 1798, in ibid., 2:457.

designed by the All wise Creator to live for himself alone" and must "prepare for the worst that can happen."[15] If God called him to serve, he would do so despite his own misgivings, health issues, and personal considerations. "The ways of Providence" had always been "inscrutable, and Mortals must submit."[16] He was "grateful to that Providence which has directed my steps, and shielded me in the various changes and chances, through which I have passed, from my youth to the present moment."[17]

Although Washington would never see combat action against the French, due to a successful peace initiative orchestrated by the Adams's administration, his faith and trust in God remained steadfast as the turn of the century approached. The older he became, the more he marveled at God's inscrutable ways and interventions—big and small—in the everyday lives of men.[18]

"When I presented my Valedictory address to the People of the United States, in September 1796," he wrote his childhood friend, the Reverend Bryan Fairfax, in early 1799, "I little thought that any event would occur in my day that could again withdraw me from the Retirement after which I had been so long panting." Life had taught him, however, that "we know little of ourselves, and still less the ways of Providence." Frustrated with French encroachments on American sovereignty and increasing belligerence from the Jefferson and Madison-led Democratic-Republican party, Washington asserted that he "always believed, and trusted" that God, who "has carried us through a long and painful War with one of the most powerful Nations in Europe," would not abandon the American cause nor allow "more than a temporary interruption to the permanent Peace and happiness of this rising Empire." Then he summarized his biblical worldview and leadership motivation explaining that the

> favourable sentiments which others, you say, have been pleased to express respecting me, cannot but be pleasing to a mind who always walked on a straight line, and endeavored as far as human frailties, and perhaps strong passions, would enable him, to discharge the relative duties to his Maker and fellow-men, without seeking any indirect or left handed attempts to acquire popularity.[19]

15. Washington to James Anderson, July 25, 1798, in ibid., 2:452–53.

16. Washington to Thaddeus Kosciusko, August 23, 1797, in ibid., 1:178.

17. Washington to William Gordon, October 15, 1797, *Writings of Washington*, 36:49.

18. Novak and Novak, *Washington's God*, 128–29.

19. Washington to Reverend Bryan, Lord Fairfax, in Fitzpatrick, *Writings of Washington*, 37:91–95.

One of the last letters he ever wrote was to James McHenry, the Secretary of War, approximately one month before he would pass away. Frustrated over the quagmire with France, Washington lamented his helplessness. He had been watching "the political concerns of the United States with an anxious, and painful eye" and "they appear to me, to be moving by hasty strides to some awful crisis." However, he was still confident all would be well or, at the very least, that events would turn out they way they were supposed to according to "that Being, who sees, foresees, and directs all things . . . ." Since "the vessel is afloat, or nearly so, and considering myself as a Passenger only, I shall trust to the Mariners whose duty it is to watch, to steer it into a safe Port."[20]

Anchored in his Christian faith and worldview, Washington "walked on a straight line" knowing life would unfold according to God's plans and design. To the very end of his life, Washington's Christian faith inspired a confidence to live, serve, and lead without reservation and hesitation in both his private and public worlds.

20. Washington to James McHenry, November 17, 1799, in ibid., 37:428–29.

14

The Slavery Issue

Like many founding fathers, Washington's slave ownership remains a significant blemish on his character and leadership legacy. Throughout his life he admitted that the peculiar institution was evil, but he did little to end or publicly condemn the horrific practice. Only at the end of his life, through his will, did he emancipate his own slaves.

Forty percent of the population in Virginia, during the Virginian's lifetime, was made up of slaves and, in many ways, he personified the traditional southern slaveholder. A slave owner at the age of eleven, Washington did and said many things that would be considered "racist" today—calling slaves shiftless, lazy, careless, deceitful, etc. Moreover, his slaveholding practices indicate that he employed cruel measures deemed essential for maintaining order and discipline in a system based on human bondage.[1]

Others assert that Washington treated his slaves more humanly compared to other slaveowners. Many Europeans, who visited Mount Vernon, noticed and commented on his kind and benevolent treatment of the enslaved. When slaves were sick and ailing, the master of Mount Vernon lessened their workload and provided medical care. He did not separate families by sale or purchase. Moreover, archeological digs have uncovered animal and fish remains at Mount Vernon, which suggest that slaves were well fed and lived less restrictive lives compared to the enslaved on other plantations. Furthermore, slaves were allowed to use firearms, hunt, fish, raise poultry, and tend gardens to supplement their food allotment.

1. Henriques, *Realistic Visionary*, 146.

Washington actually purchased vegetables, potatoes, melons, eggs, and teeth from his own slaves.[2]

Though the president did not publicly advocate for the abolition of slavery, his private correspondence reveals a growing disdain for the peculiar institution over time. He never believed, as many other founding fathers and early American slaveholders did, that African-Americans were inherently inferior. This was a matter of nurture over nature. Any deficiencies in black slaves were the result of their enslavement and lack of educational opportunities. If they could be literally and figuratively unshackled, ex-slaves would prosper.[3]

While he never referred to his slaves as his children, Washington did identify them as part of his family—"my Negroes," "my people," or "my black labourers." Whatever their legal status as human chattel, slaves experienced the same range of human emotions as all men, and Washington tried to interact and accommodate accordingly. For example, in opposition to Virginia state law, he recognized the validity of slave marriages. As he aged, he also became increasingly concerned for slave families and their personal relationships. Moreover, unlike Jefferson and other plantation owners, there was never a credible tale or accusation of the president taking advantage of a slave sexually.[4]

The Virginian evolved gradually but substantially on the slavery issue. Over time, he became increasingly antislavery for a variety of reasons and convergence of different factors. For Washington, the institution of slavery was economically inefficient and risky for farmers. The invisible hand of the peculiar institution lured Virginia planters into one-crop tobacco farming—a sort of agricultural and economic bondage. Slavery seemed to make landowners lazy and self-indulgent. Moreover, Washington—a farmer known for his work ethic, diligence, and relentless focus on production—grew disillusioned with the entire institution as he endured and witnessed slaves feigning illness, destroying equipment, embracing idleness, and stealing corn, meat, apples, and liquor. For every glass of wine served at Mount Vernon, he wondered if two glasses had been consumed by unsupervised slaves. Anything not nailed down was in danger of being stolen, including the nails. The economic complacency and lethargy inherent in the peculiar

2. Henriques, *Realistic Visionary,* 154; Twohig, "That Species of Property," 117; Brookhiser, *Founding Father,* 181.

3. Wiencek, *Imperfect God,* 356.

4. Henriques, *Realistic Visionary,* 152; Brookhiser, *Founding Father,* 181.

institution was simply too much to endure for an outcome-oriented entrepreneur like Washington.[5]

The sentiments and ideals of the American Revolution, as well as his service and experiences as commander in chief, also shaped and influenced the general's view on slavery. While he never publicly condemned human bondage, he did sign his name to the Fairfax Resolves in 1774—resolutions that denounced and urged the termination of the slave trade. In late December 1775, he also authorized the enlistment of African American soldiers in the Continental Army for military reasons of necessity. The executive order provided a legal means which many slaves utilized in order to obtain their freedom and, in retrospect, afforded a watershed moment in the long march toward emancipation.[6]

Once he made the decision to allow African Americans to serve in the army, Washington ignored the protests of Southern racists. He did not object to freedom being offered as an incentive for slaves to fight. Having observed African Americans successfully perform military duties alongside New England troops, during the war, Washington was compelled to confront his own personal and institutional prejudices. Soon, he advocated for the recruitment of free blacks into the Continental Army. In 1778, he allowed Rhode Islanders to raise an all-black regiment of soldiers. In 1779, he approved a plan to grant slaves their freedom in exchange for their military service. Throughout the duration of the war, Washington led a racially integrated army composed of as many as five thousand African American soldiers. Slowly and privately, the general reevaluated the slavery issue. By the time he returned to Mount Vernon, at the end of the war, he was convinced the institution should be abolished, not only because of its economic inefficiency but, more importantly, because it dishonored and belied the ideals of the American Revolution.[7]

During the last year of the war, he approved a scheme, designed by his abolitionist friend, John Laurens, which proposed to have Congress purchase slaves from owners and form an African American regiment. At the end of their enlistment, the purchased slaves, or black soldiers, would be freed. The general cautioned Laurens not to get upset if his plan did not find a warm welcome in Congress, however, since it went against southern self-interest.[8]

---

5. Henriques, *Realistic Visionary*, 149; Johnson, *Washington: Founding Father*, 41.

6. Hirschfeld, *Washington and Slavery*, 232.

7. Wood, *Revolutionary Characters*, 39–40; Hirschfeld, *Washington and Slavery*, 224, 232.

8. Jones, *Washington*, 88.

The close friendships formed with strong antislavery men during the Revolutionary War also spurred Washington's growing disdain for the institution of slavery. He admired and respected the compelling opinions of John Laurens, Alexander Hamilton, David Humphreys, and Lafayette—all strong, outspoken antislavery advocates.[9]

During the Confederation period, his growing repugnance toward slavery continued to crystallize. In late spring, 1785, two British evangelists, Reverend Thomas Coke and Reverend Francis Asbury, who had been sent to the United States to help organize the Methodist movement, called on the general at Mount Vernon. The two fiery ministers had been traveling throughout Virginia preaching emancipation, despite threats from mobs, and holding worship services for slaves. They asked Washington to sign a petition advocating for gradual emancipation legislation in the Virginia General Assembly. According to Coke, the general received the two ministers with great politeness, interest, and favorable sentiments toward their anti-slavery advocacy.

Washington failed to lead and confront the slavery issue directly, however, and did not sign the petition. Only if the Assembly members considered the petition would he publicly declare his views by letter. Unanimously, the Virginia House of Delegates refused to consider the petition. Nonetheless, as he told his friend, David Humphreys, he had come to believe that slavery was "displeasing to the justice of the Creator."[10]

In December 1785, Robert Pleasants, a Quaker who freed his own slaves and later become an abolitionist leader in Virginia, sent Washington a letter condemning slavery.

> Seeing the Lord has done great things for thee . . . How strange then it must appear to impartial thinking men, to be informed, that many who were warm advocates for that noble cause during the War, are now sitting down in a state of ease, dissipation and extravagance on the labour of Slaves? And more especially that thou, who could forego all the Sweets of domestic felicity for a number of years, & expose thy Person to the greatest fatigue & dangers in that cause, should now withhold that enestimable blessing from any who are absolutely in thy power, & after the Right of freedom is acknowledg'd to be the natural & unalienable Right of all mankind . . . It is a Sacrifice which I fully believe the Lord is requiring of this Generation; and should we not submit to it, Is there not reason to fear, he will deal with us as he did with Pharaoh on a similar occasion? . . . We Read,

9. Henriques, *Realistic Visionary,* 161.

10. Flexner, *Washington,* 4:121.

"where much is given, the more will be requird" and as thou hast acquired much fame, in being the Successful Champion of American Liberty; It seems highly probable to me, that thy example & influence at this time, towards a general emancipation, would be as productive of real happiness to mankind, as thy Sword may have been: I can wish therefore, that thou may not lose the opportunity of Crowning the great Actions of thy Life, with the satisfaction of, "doing to Others as though would (in the like Situation) be done by," and finally transmit to future ages a Character, equally famous for thy Christian virtues, as they worldly achievements.[11]

John Elliot Jr., who served as a surgeon's mate in a New York regiment during the American Revolution and was later appointed by the president as a surgeon in the United States's Army, also sent a letter to Washington advocating abolition. He wanted American citizens to "become what they profess to be, *Christians*, not in name & profession only, but indeed & in truth followers of a meek & crucified Savoir who laid down this rule for his Disciples." Christians were to follow the inspiration of Christ: "If any man will come after me let him deny himself and take up his Cross & follow me." Employing biblical references, some of the same which Washington often used, Elliot was influenced "with a degree of Gospel love toward my fellow Citizens" and desired "to invite them to gather unto *Shiloh* the peaceable Saviour; who has promised 'to be given for a Light to the Gentiles and to be God's Salvation to the end of the earth.'" Every citizen should be able to sit "'under his Vine & under his Fig tree, and none shall make them afraid'— For those who truly love & fear the Lord have no need to fear what Man can do unto them." Those who followed the admonitions of Jesus and the Holy Bible would "be favoured at the conclusion of time, with the answer of 'Well done good & faithful Servants' and become inheritors of a Crown of Glory in the Mansions of Purity, Peace, and everlasting felicity."[12]

As he approached his twilight years, Washington received many letters from individuals, such as Pleasants and Elliot, who appealed to his Christian convictions in an attempt to persuade him to free his slaves and publicly support abolition. Hoping that he would be an example to the nation, Washington would, instead, disappoint many of his supporters on this most crucial issue until his earthly death. Yet, the cumulative sentiments expressed by fellow Americans, especially those who argued that abolition

11. Robert Pleasants to Washington, December 11, 1785, in Abbot and Twohig, *Washington, Confederation Series*, 3:449–51.

12. John Elliot Jr. to Washington, June 18, 1789, in Abbot, *Washington, Presidential Series*, 3:485–90.

was the just and Christian thing to do, certainly weighed considerably on Washington's mind and consciousness.

In the second year of his presidency, Quakers petitioned to abolish the slave trade before the year 1808, as designated in the Constitution. Congressmen were enraged by the appeal and openly threatened civil war. Although he opposed the slave trade privately, the president was glad the petition did not pass and upset the populace. He was simply too reluctant to confront the slavery issue and antagonize the South. Washington even had his slaves sent back to Mount Vernon, in 1791, fearing that they would accrue enough residence time and earn citizenship in the slave-free, northern capitals of New York and Philadelphia.[13]

While the president would not publicly condemn slavery, he privately prepared to emancipate his own slaves. In a May 6, 1794 letter to his personal secretary, Tobias Lear, Washington laid out plans to sell his western lands—his most valuable economic asset. His "powerful" and earnest "motive" in selling his land holdings was to "liberate a certain species of property which I possess, very repugnantly to my own feelings; but which imperious necessity compels."[14] When his presidential chef and slave, Hercules, ran away in Philadelphia, in 1796, he vowed to never purchase another slave. He hoped to free all of his slaves during his lifetime, even if it meant financing the emancipation of his slaves with his retirement savings.[15]

After completing his two presidential terms in 1797, he quietly but deliberately left behind some house slaves in Philadelphia—in effect granting them *de facto* emancipation in a slave free state.[16] "I wish from my Soul," he asserted, that the Virginia legislature "could see the policy of gradual abolition of Slavery."[17]

While sitting under his own vine and fig tree in retirement, Washington continued to ponder the fate of slavery and his leadership role on the issue. Numerous letters continued to arrive at Mount Vernon imploring him to take a courageous, public stand against slavery. Many appealed to his Christian faith and values in presenting their case for abolition.

John Jones, an iron mill owner who resided in Maryland, reminded Washington, that as the former president approached "the Throne of

13. Jones, *Washington*, 180; Flexner, *Washington*, 4:22, 125.

14. Washington to Tobias Lear, May 6, 1794, in Fitzpatrick, *Writings of Washington*, 33:358.

15. Wiencek, *An Imperfect God*, 274; Randall, *Washington*, 500; Flexner, *Washington*, 4:9.

16. Johnson, *Washington: Founding Father*, 118; Ferling, *First of Men*, 480.

17. Washington to Lawrence Lewis, August 4, 1797, in Abbot and Twohig, *Washington, Retirement Series*, 1:288.

Grace," God would be looking into the "inmost recesses of the Soul" of every man. God called on each human being to remember that "'Whatsoever ye would men should do unto you; do ye even so unto them.'" Indeed, "many things have been permitted to continue for Ages that are offensive to God; amongst which perhaps there is none more so; than the Slavery imposed, by one part of the human Species upon the Other." Jones boldly suggested that Washington return his lands to slave families and let them live and farm as free people. He also encouraged the president to pay overseers who, among other things, would "school their own Children at least to learn them to read the Holy Scriptures." Children "trained up in habits of industry and under a sense of the Obligations of Religion & Morality" would "become useful, and worthy of that freedom they are justly entitled to." Freeing his slaves would add significantly to his "fame" and transmit "to succeeding generations amongst those whom the Father honours; who have honoured his Son."[18]

Nathaniel Luff Jr., a surgeon from Kent County, Delaware, who also served in the Revolutionary War, urged the retired president to confront the slavery issue, at the very least, by freeing his own slaves as a private citizen. Luff keenly understood that it would have been "hurtful" for Washington to have pursued abolition during the nation's tenuous, infant stages and fragmented beginnings. Now that the president had retired from public service, however, the private holding and possessing of slaves "remains indefencible to thy *friends*."[19]

The Master of Mount Vernon had almost always let his actions speak louder than words. He would, eventually and finally, free his slaves, through his will, upon death. Washington updated and penned his final will, in the summer of 1799, after hearing and reflecting upon Patrick Henry's death earlier in the spring.[20] At the very top of the first page, he wrote in large letters: "In the name of God amen." After making sure his entire estate would pass on to Martha, he declared that "upon the decease of my wife, it is my Will and desire that all the Slaves which I hold in *my own right*, shall receive their freedom." Moreover, he made provisions in the will to ensure that the freed slaves would be provided for and supported. "There may be some," he surmised, "who from old age or bodily infirmities, and others who on account of their infancy, that will be unable to support themselves." His "Will and desire" was that

---

18. John Jones to Washington, February 20, 1798, in ibid., 2:95–96.

19. Nathaniel Luff Jr. to Washington, March 3, 1798, in ibid., 2:167–68.

20. Unger, *"Mr. President,"* 232.

all who come under the first and second description as have no parents living, or if living are unable, or unwilling to provide for them, shall be bound by the Court until they shall arrive at the age of twenty five years; and in cases where no record can be produced, whereby their ages can be ascertained, the judgment of the Court upon its own view of the subject, shall be adequate and final. The Negroes thus bound, are (by their Masters or Mistresses) to be taught to read and write; and to be brought up to some useful occupation, agreeably to the Laws of the Commonwealth of Virginia, providing for the support of Orphan and other poor Children.

Unfortunately, "black laws" in Virginia did not allow for the education of Negroes and, hence, the provision could not be carried out. The last of Washington's pensioned Negroes died in 1833.[21]

The familial relationships Washington developed with his house servants and slaves may have also have shaped his outlook on the peculiar institution over the years. His affection and gratitude for his personal body servant, Billy Lee, was obvious to many. He bemoaned the passing of his slave, Paris, and referred to the death of one of his slaves as "trusty old negro Jack."[22] Washington thought highly enough of his slave, Christopher Sheels, that he paid a large sum of money to treat him when he was bitten by a mad dog, and kept him as a personal body servant even after Sheels sought to escape from Mount Vernon. He regularly employed black physicians and overseers on his farms and plantations. Two other slaves, Morris and Dave, were paid and accorded great respect as overseers at Mount Vernon. Washington kept slave families intact and steadfastly assisted in empowering his slaves to develop and learn "marketable" skills (all five of his farms had black overseers by the time he assumed the presidency).[23]

---

21. Washington, Last Will and Testament, July 9, 1799, in Fitzpatrick, *Writings of Washington*, 37:276–77.

22. Henriques, *Realistic Visionary*, 157.

23. Wills, *Certain Trumpets*, 234–35.

WASHINGTON & FAMILY AT MOUNT VERNON.

Washington's legacy, as a political and Christian leader, is tarnished by the fact that he was a slaveowner. Nevertheless, his Christian faith also led him to be one of the few founding fathers who freed his slaves, albeit at his death. Engraved by Thomas Phillibrown, after Alonzo Chappel. (Courtesy of the Mount Vernon Ladies' Association)

No other major founding father set his slaves free, and none ever contemplated educating slaves as Washington did. Out of the nine slave-owning presidents, he was the only one who freed all of his slaves, albeit at his death. Moreover, the strong language used in his will suggests a lack of trust in his family to follow through on his directive to free his slaves.[24] Yet Washington remained undeterred and resolute in emancipating his slaves with no ambiguity in his will. Not only did he free them but, quite contrary to Jefferson, he did not resort to racist language to explain or argue for the innate inferiority of blacks. Moreover, he did not dismiss the idea of free blacks living in harmony with whites.[25]

Keeping humans in bondage gnawed at his conscience as well as his desire for a reputable legacy. Jefferson once reported how Washington threw a newspaper upon the floor cursing "with a 'damn' of the author who had charged him with the crime of being a slaveholder."[26] From the many letters he received, as well as the conversations he held with respected Christian friends and associates, Washington recognized that his slaveholder status

24. Wiencek, *Imperfect God,* 5–6.

25. Henriques, *Realistic Visionary,* 165.

26. Benjamin Rush to John Adams, June 4, 1812, in Kaminski, *Founders,* 518.

threatened to tarnish his legacy and esteemed reputation as a republican and as a Christian. He wanted, and had great incentive, to be on the right side of history and to be right before God.[27]

To free his slaves earlier in life, however, would not have been expedient for Washington or the fragile nation. While he had selfish reasons to keep his slaves, to be sure, he felt compelled to choose the stability of the Union over the chaos of abolition. Emancipating those held in bondage would have created a firestorm with no sound plan in place to deal with a newly altered culture and society. He, therefore, kept his intention to free his slaves secret even to most of his family members. His slaves would be freed after Martha's earthly passing.[28]

Consistently throughout his entire life, Washington remained committed to the tenets and teachings of his orthodox, Anglican faith. He lived and led confidently as inspired by his God and the Holy Scriptures. The evidence suggests that the decision to ultimately free his slaves was strongly influenced by his Christian faith and the desire to seek forgiveness and make right on his debts and trespasses. After all, he admitted and believed the peculiar institution was "displeasing to the justice of the Creator."[29] His gradual change of heart—from slaveholder to emancipator—demonstrates a profound internalization and embrace of Christian repentance. The brutal and ugly realities of slavery had, indeed, bothered and conflicted Washington's conscious for quite some time.[30]

Even within the horrible institution of slavery at Mount Vernon, the influence of Washington's Christian faith is evident. Slaves, for example, were granted Christian holidays. Contrary to other Virginian slaveholders, he allowed and provided opportunities for his slaves to be baptized and educated. We know of at least twelve slaves who were baptized at Mount Vernon according to the documentation available. Furthermore, Christian philanthropy was evident by the care he gave and demanded of his slaves.[31]

The ownership and participation in the institution of human bondage is a major stain on Washington's legacy as a Christian leader. Though he had valid political reasons for not publicly speaking out against the evils of slavery or advocating for the abolition of slavery, these justifications do not propitiate or excuse the gravest wrongdoing of his generation. He was the

---

27. Henriques, *Realistic Visionary,* 163.

28. Twohig, "That Species of Property," 131; Wiencek, *Imperfect God,* 275.

29. Flexner, *Washington,* 4:121.

30. Lillback and Newcombe, *Sacred Fire,* 518–19; Moore, *Family Life,* 207.

31. Johnson, *Washington: Founding Father,* 40; Wiencek, *Imperfect God,* 165; Smith, *Patriarch,* 148.

Indispensable Man and leader of his country, but a flawed and sinful one too.

Yet Washington's Christian faith was a significant force in moving him to free his slaves. He had always favored action over words. While neither he nor Martha mentioned Jesus by name in their wills, adhering to the Anglican way and Latitudinarian approach, their actions and written wills spoke volumes about repentance and forgiveness.[32]

Washington's God looked favorably upon liberty and the freedom of conscience. Perhaps knowing that in death he could do no more to ensure the stability and unity of the nation, he decided to right a great wrong he had upheld for most of his life. Perhaps, he was simply moved, yet again, to do the right thing for the right reason as a follower of Christ—the Savior who had liberated all humankind from their sins.

---

32. Lillback and Newcombe, *Sacred Fire*, 682.

15

Private Integrity

In the same manner that Washington encouraged his fellow Americans to embrace morality and religion in the public sphere, Washington faithfully lived the Christian life in private. At Mount Vernon, visitors, associates, close friends, and family members alike saw how his life revolved around farming, family, and faith. God, church, prayer, Bible study, and devotional time were regimented priorities in his daily and weekly routines. Generosity, integrity, an indomitable work ethic, and service were fruits of his biblical worldview and essential attributes of his character. He lived with conviction and encouraged others to embrace the core values he deemed vital to inner peace and prosperity. He believed "that without Virtue & without integrity, the finest talents & the most brilliant accomplishments can never gain the respect and the Esteem of the truly valuable part of mankind."[1] To Sally Ball Haynie, an impoverished relative of his mother whom he financially supported since 1791, Washington insisted, "industry, economy, and a virtuous conduct" were "commendable" and "indispensably necessary" where "it has pleased Providence to place you."[2]

A faithful and caring husband, stepfather, and stepgrandfather, Washington was able to spend more time with his family in retirement. In the winter and spring of 1798, a series of letters to stepgrandson, George Washington Parke Custis, illustrate the spiritual care and concern he exhibited for his loved ones. Discipline, he contended, and "system in all things should be aimed at; for in execution, it renders everything more easy."[3] He praised

1. Washington to Bartholomew Dandridge Jr., March 8, 1797, in Abbot and Twohig, *Washington, Retirement Series,* 1:23.

2. Washington to Sally Ball Haynie, February 11, 1798, in ibid., 2:83.

3. Washington to George Washington Parke Custis, January 7, 1798, in ibid., 2:4.

his stepgrandson for focusing on his "studies with zeal & alacrity." Quoting the book of Ecclesiastes in Bible, Washington reminded Custis that "there is a *time* for all *things*," and exhorted him to "pursue the *course* of Studies" with all due diligence.[4] When young Custis fell in love and was paying too much attention to "a certain young lady of that place," he encouraged him to make sure "that the hours which might be more profitably employed at your studies" were not "misspent" in pursuit of love. He then reminded his stepgrandson, yet again, using the same reference to Ecclesiastes: "Recollect the saying of the wise man, 'That there is a time for all things.'"[5]

In December of 1798, when it appeared that young Custis would be going off to war to fight the French, Washington worried that his stepgrandson might die in combat. Custis was "an only Son; indeed the only male of his Great great Grandfathers family," he rationalized to a friend. Comforted in his Christian faith, he believed that "the same Providence that wd watch over & protect him in domestic walks, can extend the same protection to him in a Camp, or the field of battle, if he should ever be in one."[6]

The love and concern shown for his stepgrandson was not an aberration. Indeed, during his life and after he passed away, family members, friends, and contemporaries spoke affectionately about Washington the family man and Christian leader.

He was no saint and certainly exhibited sinful behavior. His temper could get the best of him. He had to make tough business decisions that could often be self-serving. He worried about his own reputation and legacy. He held humans in bondage.

Yet, it is also revealing that in 1798, when George and Martha hosted almost 700 overnight guests, not one reference has ever surfaced that he drank in excess or even appeared mildly tipsy. The same holds true for his dining habits: Not one report exists describing the president as a glutton. Numerous accounts, on the other hand, tell of Washington treating guests, and women in particular, with great respect.[7]

More importantly, many contemporaries were impressed by his devoutness, virtue, respect for God, service to his congregations, and the manner in which he carried out his private life in accordance with the Christian faith. The more intimately he was known, the more he was respected,

---

4. Washington to George Washington Parke Custis, March 19, 1798, in ibid., 2:149.

5. Washington to George Washington Parke Custis, June 13, 1798, in ibid., 2:324–25.

6. Washington to David Stuart, December 30, 1798, in ibid., 3:299.

7. Rees, *Leadership Lessons,* 34.

admired, and loved. A rare and exceptional realization in any age, Washington was everything his public image portended him to be and more.[8]

Those who were closest to Washington knew him to be a strong, God-fearing Christian. Many friends and visitors commented on his love and affection for his entire extended family, and the earnestness with which he embraced his role as the spiritual leader of his household.

Washington was a doting father and grandfather who cared for the spiritual well-being of his stepchildren and stepgrandchildren. Picture by Edward Savage. (Courtesy of the Mount Vernon Ladies' Association)

The spiritual well-being of each family member was important to Washington. He may have discouraged his stepsons from attending the College of William and Mary, among other reasons, fearing that they might embrace some of the deistic teachings that had begun to emerge on campus. The curriculum and philosophical trends at William and Mary seemed to be incongruent with the teachings George and Martha's children received from the orthodox Christian scholars and tutors of their early and crucial, faith-formation years.[9]

Washington was a godfather to at least eight young children in his close circle. Anglican christenings, during this time in history, used an

8. Schwartz, *American Symbol*, 181.

9. Lillback and Newcombe, *Sacred Fire*, 252.

order of service from *The Book of Common Prayer* called *The Ministration of Public Baptism of Infants, to Be Used in the Church*. Thus, some eight different times, Washington heard and publicly affirmed the expectations of godparents according to the orthodox teachings of the Anglican/Episcopal Church. Godparents were to renounce the devil, believe in God's Holy Word, keep God's commandments, let the Holy Ghost sanctify the child, and pray that Jesus would receive the child and release him or her from sin. At least eight different times, the Anglican/Episcopal minister publicly asked Washington to speak on behalf of the child when answering a series of questions including if he believed in the Articles of the Christian faith as contained in the Apostles's Creed, and if he was willing to be baptized in the Christian faith; all eight times, he publicly affirmed the orthodox Christian faith with words of the virgin birth, the forgiveness of sins, and Jesus's resurrection. As a godfather, he made a public declaration and embraced the solemn responsibility to oversee and nurture the spiritual growth of the godchild in the Christian faith. In addition to his own responsibilities as a godparent, many other christenings took place at Mount Vernon with his approval and participation.

Washington's public confessions starkly contrast with Jefferson—who repeatedly declined invites to become a godparent because he did not want to give a false representation of his own religious beliefs. As a Unitarian and deist, Jefferson could not in good conscience assent to the orthodox and endorse the trinitarian teachings of the Anglican Church.[10]

A doting stepfather and stepgrandfather of Martha's two children and their four grandchildren, he had ordered, from Great Britain much earlier in his life, beautifully bound and personally embossed Bibles for each of them, and purchased other Christian books and devotional prayers for their spiritual growth. He encouraged and modeled Christian faithfulness, and treated the Sabbath as a day of worship, relaxation, entertainment, and letter writing. By the end of his life, Washington had numerous books devoted to religious topics, plus hundreds of printed sermons—most of which he received from ministers and pastors. Well-read in Christian works, he also exhibited the Anglican habits of moderation, reserve, and privacy.[11]

As the spiritual head of the household, Washington habitually and faithfully led his family in devotions, Scriptural recitations, and sermon readings. Cash records indicate he purchased many of these sermons with regularity, and family members and personal assistants observed and

---

10. Thompson, *Good Providence*, 33–35; Lillback and Newcombe, *Sacred Fire*, 108; Novak and Novak, *Washington's God*, 216.

11. Novak and Novak, *Washington's God*, 164.

recorded his Bible readings and sermon recitations with great fondness. Washington made sure sermons were on hand for worship and study at Mount Vernon; his church often did not have an Anglican preacher available on the Sabbath, and, at times, bad weather or ill health prevented his family from attending church. While he did occasionally travel to locations in preparation of some fox hunting and engaged in horseback riding and entertaining, he often fasted and steadfastly guarded family time for prayers and sermon readings on Sunday evenings.

Indicating the high value and earnest appreciation he had for these works, Washington signed many sermons he purchased or received and sent thank you letters to the pastors and ministers who wrote or sent them. He also bound many and created a personal hardcover collection of sermons, which numbered several volumes in length. Having memorized a few of his favorite sermons, Washington quoted from them regularly in his correspondence. Even when he went to church on Sundays, he still read sermons or a portion of the Bible at night for the benefit of the entire household.[12]

Washington received orthodox Christian sermons from a variety of clergy throughout his life. Many of the sermons he bound were critical of deism and praiseworthy of the Gospel.[13] One came from Reverend Israel Evans, an army general in the Revolutionary War, whose sermon message to Washington and the soldiers noted how:

> You have opened a passage into the wilderness, where the Gospel has never yet received . . . As the Gospel, or Son of Righteousness, has only glanced on the shores of this western world, and it is predicted of it, that is shall be universally propagated, it will probably be like the Sun, travel to the western extremities of the continent. And when men from other nations, prompted by Liberty and love of the pure Gospel of truth, shall cross the ocean to this extensive empire, they will here find a safe asylum from persecution and tyranny. How honorable then must your employment appear, when considered in all these points of view. How happy to have been the instrument in the hand of God, for accomplishing so great a revolution, and extending the Kingdom of the Son so far. Liberty, and Religion shall have their wide dominion across the Atlantic through the great continent

12. M'Guire, *Religious Opinions,* 154–56, 168–70; Thompson, *Good Providence,* 50–74; Lillback and Newcombe, *Sacred Fire,* 641–42, 661; Novak and Novak, *Washington's God,* 162; Johnson, *Washington: The Christian,* 149.

13. Lillback and Newcombe, *Sacred Fire,* 644; Zehariah Lewis to Washington, July 17, 1797, in Abbot and Twohig, *Washington, Retirement Series,* 1:260.

to the western shore . . . promoting the kingdom of our Lord
Jesus Christ.[14]

When his stepgrandson was in college, Washington wrote him insisting that "the more knowledge you acquire, the greater will be the probability
of your succeeding . . . and the greater will be your thirst for more."[15] The
line of reasoning he took with young Custis can also be applied to his own
collection and study of sermons. Washington remained a life-long student
of the Holy Scriptures to the very end of his earthly life.

As general, president, and retired, private citizen, the Sabbath remained important and sacred to Washington. "Having no Church nearer
than Alexandria (nine miles distant) I usually postpone writing, or answering letters that do not require immediate attention, until then," he wrote in
the summer of 1799.[16] The letter indicates Washington's lifelong predilection
and dedication to Sabbath worship, even in retirement. Traveling a great
distance to attend church—even when facing inclement weather, long trips,
and pulpit shortages—was a burden he and his family regularly and willingly confronted and overcame for most of their life. And when they did not
attend church, the Washington family would worship, read the Bible, and
recite sermons at Mount Vernon. Sundays, of course, also provided time
to catch up on the voluminous correspondence that constantly beckoned.

As a man who prided himself on constancy and consistency, his neighbors worshipping at Christ Church in Alexandria regularly saw the retired
president.[17] Christian preachers of many different denominations, close
friends, family members, and his beloved wife all regarded him as a model
Christian. His forebears were Christian as was his progeny.[18] His faithful
church attendance, throughout the entirety of his life, was nothing out of
the ordinary for one who was baptized, raised, married, and would later
be buried, under the auspices of the Anglican Church. Professing to be an
Anglican Christian, he lived, worshipped, and acted as one.

If Washington had been duplicitous in exhibiting or embracing a
Christian faith when did not have one, or if he had manipulated his image
and reputation for political purposes, his character would not have been
viewed in such a reputable and noble manner by his peers and the American
people. Nor should historians esteem his character and integrity as the great

---

14. Lillback and Newcombe, *Sacred Fire*, 187.

15. Washington to George Washington Parke Custis, November 14, 1796, in Fitzpatrick, *Writings of Washington*, 35:282.

16. Washington to Secretary of State, August 4, 1799, in ibid., 37:323.

17. M'Guire, *Religious Opinions*, 154–55; Schwartz, "Character of Washington," 213.

18. Novak and Novak, *Washington's God*, 226; Gaustad, *Faith of Our Fathers*, 76.

majority have for over two centuries. The truth is that the private and public Washington were one in the same. His thoughts, words, and deeds speak for themselves and need no revision.

16

Confident and Courageous Exit

On December 9, 1799, Gouverneur Morris asked Washington to run for a third presidential term in 1800. "Recollect Sir, that each Occasion which has brought you back on the public Stage has been to you the Means of new and greater Glory," he argued.

> If General Washington had not become Member of the Convention he would have been considered only as Defender and not as the Legislator of his Country. And if the president of the Convention had not become president of the United States he would not have added the Character of Statesman to those of a Patriot and Hero . . . But you may perhaps say that you stand indirectly pledged to private life. Surely Sir you neither gave nor meant to give such Pledge to the Extent of possible Contingencies . . . Nay, you stand pledged by your former Conduct that when Circumstances arise which may require it you will act again. Those Circumstances seem to be now imminent, and it is meet that you consider them . . . Ponder them I pray.[1]

The letter from Morris arrived at Mount Vernon on December 16, 1799. Washington had been dead for two days.[2]

---

1. Gouverneur Morris to Washington, December 9, 1799, in Abbot and Twohig, *Washington, Retirement Series*, 4:452–53.

2. Unger, *Unexpected Washington*, 260–61.

The many years of public service took a toll on the physical health and appearance of America's Indispensable Man. He would only live for a few short years after he retired from the presidency. Picture by Charles Willson Peele. (Courtesy of the Mount Vernon Ladies' Association)

Ironically, Washington's health, in early December of 1799, was actually quite good considering his past ailments. He had been busy making plans for the future and wrote a jocular pact not to die until the new century. On December 12, 1799, however, he rode and checked his farms for five hours during a storm of constant rain, hail, and high wind. He eventually contracted acute epiglottis—a virulent bacteria, possibly Haemophilus Influenzae Type b. The epiglottis is a cartilaginous place located at the base of the tongue and at the entrance to the larynx or voice box. Over the next two days, the president's airway would slowly but steadily became blocked as the epiglottis ballooned. After intentionally being bled five times by doctors in a twelve-hour period and losing over five pints of blood in the process, he would, under great duress and pain, literally suffocate to death.[3]

The earliest recording of the Virginian's thoughts on the afterlife is in an April 25, 1773 letter to Burwell Bassett, who had lost his daughter at an early age. Washington offered compassion and hope to his friend. "That we sympathize in the misfortune, and lament the decree which has deprived

3. Henriques, "Final Struggle," 254–55.

you of so dutiful a child, and the world of so promising a young lady, stands in no need, I hope, of argument to prove," he condoled. Since "the ways of Providence" were "inscrutable, and the justice of it not to be scanned by the shallow eye of humanity, nor to be counteracted by the utmost efforts of human power or wisdom," humans should live "as far as the strength of our reason and religion can carry us" and with "a cheerful acquiescence to the Divine Will."[4]

Washington understood that human grief could best be solaced through the comfort of religious faith. When Samuel Washington's wife passed away, George consoled and encouraged his younger brother "to look with calmness upon losses wh. distress us although they are acts of Providence, and in themselves unavoidable." Indeed, to "acquiescence to the divine will is not only a duty, but is to be aided by every manly exertion to forget the causes of such uneasiness."[5] When Governor Jonathan Trumbull's wife suffered a fatal stroke, he acknowledged to his friend that while "calamities of this kind are what we should all be prepared to expect, yet few, upon their arrival, are able to bear them with a becoming fortitude." The Governor's "determination however to seek assistance from the great disposer of all human events is highly laudable, and is the source from whence the truest consolation is to be drawn."[6] When his good friend, Henry Knox, grieved over the death of his son, the general encouraged him to "submit patiently to the decrees of the Allwise disposer of Human events," where one would "find the only true, and substantial comfort under the greatest of calamities."[7] To Pierre L'Enfant, who lost his father, he offered consolation insisting, "there is a good Providence which will never fail to take care of his Children."[8] When yet another one of Henry Knox's sons died, the general lamented "the death of your promising Son with great concern, and sincerely condole with you and Mrs. Knox on the melancholy occasion." He conceded that personal pain, grief, and "parental feelings are too much alive in the moment of these misfortunes to admit the consolations of religion and philosophy." Yet, he was "persuaded reason will call one or both of them to your aid as soon as the keenness of your anguish is abated." Only God, the

---

4. Washington to Burwell Bassett, April 25, 1773, in Fitzpatrick, *Writings of Washington*, 3:133.

5. Washington to Samuel Washington, August 10, 1777, in ibid., 9:39.

6. Washington to Jonathan Trumbull, June 11, 1780, in ibid., 18:511.

7. Washington to Henry Knox, September 12, 1782, in ibid., 25:150.

8. Washington to Pierre Charles L'Enfant, April 28, 1788, in ibid., 29:481.

giver of all life, "has a right to take away," but God's "ways are wise, they are inscrutable, and irresistible."[9]

A man of deep-rooted feelings and emotion, Washington coped with tragedies and death with a fortified biblical worldview and a mature submission to God's divine plan. In early 1793, the president expressed concern over his nephew's deteriorating health. Nevertheless, "the will of Heaven is not to be controverted or scrutinized by the children of this world," he admitted. "It therefore becomes the Creatures of it to submit with patience and resignation to the will of the Creator whether it be to prolong, or to shorten the number of our days." Only God could "bless them with health, or afflict them with pain."[10] To his nephew, Burwell Bassett, Washington "sincerely" lamented "the death of your amiable Sister." Her passing was "one of those events which is dispensed by an All-wise and uncontroulable Providence." Yet, "as I believe no person could be better prepared to meet it, it is the duty of her relatives to submit, with as little repining as the Sensibility of our Natures is capable of."[11] After Henry Knox's third child passed away, in early 1797, Washington wrote that he had "participated in the sorrows which I know you must have felt for your late heavy losses." He reminded his friend, "it is not for a man to scan the wisdom of Providence." Instead, "the best he can do, is to submit to its decrees. Reason, religion, and Philosophy, teaches us to do this, but 'tis time alone' that can ameliorate the pangs of humanity, and soften its woes."[12]

Earthly departures were painful for loved ones left behind, but Washington had no doubt that the afterlife presented a glorious destination for Christians. "Awful and affecting as the death of a parent is," he reflected after his mother passed away in August of 1789 at the age of 83, "there is consolation in knowing that Heaven has spared ours to an age beyond which few attain, and favored her with the full enjoyment of her mental faculties and as much bodily strength as usually falls to the lot of fourscore." His mother had been "translated to a happier place," and it was the "duty of her relatives to yield due submission to the decrees of the Creator."[13] When friends and other loved ones passed away, he referred to the "happier clime" and "land of spirits" they now inhabited.[14]

9. Washington to Henry Knox, September 8, 1791, in ibid., 31:360.

10. Washington to George Augustine Washington, January 27, 1793, in ibid., 32:315–16.

11. Washington to Burwell Bassett, April 24, 1796, in ibid., 35:27.

12. Washington to Henry Knox, March 2, 1797, in ibid., 35:409.

13. Freeman, *Washington*, 7:229.

14. Grizzard, *Ways of Providence*, 9.

After he retired from the presidency, Washington made reference to Ps 90:10 that he was not far from his "three score and ten"[15] or end of his life. Many of his family members were passing. After his sister, Betty, died, he explained, "the debt of nature however sooner or later must be paid by us all." Moreover, "although the separation from our nearest relatives is a heart rending circumstance, reason, religion & Philosophy, teach us to bear it with resignation." The passage of time would "ameliorate, & soften the pangs we experience at parting."[16] Grieving with his nephew, William Augustine Washington—whose son, Augustine, and eldest daughter, Hannah, both died in 1797—Washington noted that such deaths were "the decrees of an Allwise Providence, against whose dictates the skill, or foresight of Man can be of no avail." It was "incumbent upon him therefore, to submit with as little repining as the sensibility of nature will admit." Indeed, "this will have its course, but may be greatly ameliorated by philosophical reflection & resignation."[17] When his youngest brother, Charles, died in the fall of 1799, the president conceded that "the death of near relations always produces awful and affecting emotions, under whatsoever circumstances it may happen." He was "the *first*, and now the *last*, of my fathers Children by the second marriage who remain." His future was "known only to the giver of life." Contemplating his own earthly passing and foreshadowing his own courageous behavior, he insisted, "when the summons comes I shall endeavor to obey it with good grace."[18] Death certainly brought mourning and anguish to loved ones left behind, but Heaven remained a comforting and consoling destination.

Washington's depictions of the afterlife reflect an orthodox, Christian understanding and biblical worldview of death. Having employed the word "Heaven" over 130 times in his writings, as well as his frequent usage of phrases like "raise the dead," "send to life eternal," "throne of grace," "reward of good and faithful servant," "separation of wheat and tares," "blessings of a gracious God upon the righteous," "wise man counts the cost," "the millennial state," "last trump," "until the globe itself is dissolved" demonstrate a profound and reverent understanding of the last things, what theologians would label the study of eschatology.[19] Trusting in the promises of Scripture, Washington revealed that the afterlife was not anything to be feared, but an

15. Freeman, *Washington*, 7:582.

16. Washington to George Lewis, April 9, 1797, in Abbot and Twohig, *Washington, Retirement Series*, 1:90.

17. Washington to William Augustine Washington, February 27, 1798, in ibid., 2:109.

18. Washington to Burgess Ball, September 22, 1799, in Fitzpatrick, *Writings of Washington*, 37:372.

19. Lillback and Newcombe, *Sacred Fire*, 677–78.

expected destination for a faithful follower. Heaven was a happier clime and the home where his kind and inscrutable God awaited him after his earthly passing.

In the hours before he took his last breath, Washington displayed a stoic, Christian courage and "good grace" that inspired those who tended to him. Even as he was slowly suffocating to death, he would not let Martha run to retrieve further medical help in the middle of the night fearing she would acquire a cold. He used precious energy and time to calm the fears of his overseer, George Rawlins, who first drew blood from him. He apologized for bothering and fatiguing his personal secretary, Tobias Lear, who was trying to shift and prop up the general in bed so that he could breathe more easily. He thanked the many doctors for their exertions and assistance. He also urged his personal body servant, Christopher Sheels, who had been standing by his bedside for hours, to sit down.[20]

After Washington asked Lear if his papers and affairs were in order, he spoke his last words: "Tis well." Martha—who had remained at her husband's bedside where she rested her head on the family Bible and prayed throughout the ordeal—responded with the very same words when her husband breathed his last.[21]

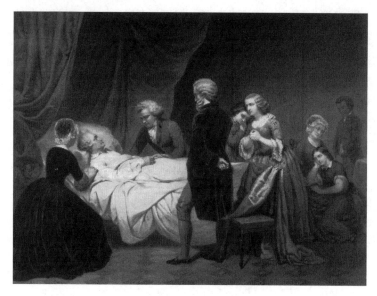

Washington's last hours were excruciating. He could barely talk and had great difficulty breathing. His stoic, peaceful resolve on his deathbed demonstrated a mature Christian faith. Lithography by Claude Regnier, after Junius Brutus Stearns. (Courtesy of the Mount Vernon Ladies' Association)

20. Henriques, "Final Struggle," 256.

21. Lear, *Letters and Recollections*, 129–35.

The courage and dignity Washington showed during his last hours was nothing new or out of character. When he was deathly sick in mid-June of 1789, and many Americans worried that their nation's indispensable leader might pass away before the new Constitutional government could take root, he demonstrated the same stoic calm and peacefulness. Dr. Samuel Bard, a prominent New York physician who stayed at the president's bedside for days after diagnosing a cutaneous form of anthrax, was thoroughly impressed with his patient's bravery and mettle. "Whether tonight, or twenty years hence, makes no difference," he remembered Washington stating during the peak of his life-threatening sickness. "I know that I am in the hands of a good Providence."[22]

Over a decade later, the president was back on his deathbed, in the hands of the same good Providence, exhibiting the same courage, poise, fortitude, and Christian peace of mind. In addition to having blood repeatedly drawn from his body, he was gagged on throat cantharides and given a tartar emetic—both now known to be poisonous.[23] He also inhaled steam from a vinegar concoction, and nearly suffocated when he gargled sage tea mixed with vinegar. A tracheotomy was overruled due to his weakened condition. He took medications and treatment to primarily oblige Martha, and tried to reassure his doctors that they could rest easy. They had done all they could, and he knew he would not last long.

During these last hours, the Master of Mount Vernon asked Lear to arrange and oversee his vast correspondence. Martha was instructed to dig out a pair of wills from his desk drawer. When Lear insisted that the end was not near, Washington reassured his personal secretary that he was resigned to his imminent death. "Doctor, I die hard; but I am not afraid to go," he told Dr. Craik.[24] He did request that he not be buried until three days after his body expired (being buried alive was a common fear of many in the era).

There was no need to call for a priest and ask for some religious ritual or form of last rites, for he was not Catholic. The closest Anglican minister was at least nine miles away and need not be bothered, for Washington believed he was passing quickly. His friends and family members knew of his lifelong Christian faith so no deathbed conversion or formal testimony was necessary. Come-to-Jesus-moments or deathbed conversion experiences are for those who are not of the faith. His debilitating condition worsening by the minute, Washington could barely talk anyway in his last few hours. Martha kneeled and reclined her head on her Bible, which lay on her husband's bed. If

22. Chernow, *Washington*, 586.

23. Unger, "*Mr. President*," 232.

24. Lear, *Letters and Recollections*, 133.

anything, a peaceful room meant that he could pray silently to his God. He did, in fact, ask everyone to leave the room so he could be alone for a few moments (to pray?) during his last hours. Shortly after checking his own pulse, he would breath his last much quicker than those gathered anticipated (perhaps yet another reason no summons was given for a minister). The Father of His Country passed away at the age of 67, on December 14, 1799, with great self-control, awareness, and without a sigh.[25]

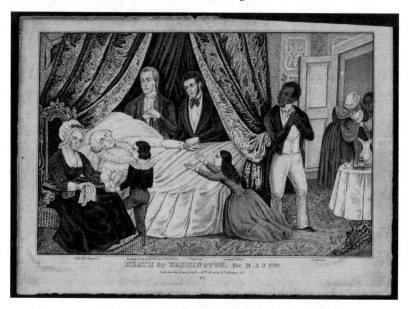

Washington died on December 14, 1799. While Martha's grieving was severe, she found comfort and assurance in the Christian faith she and her deceased husband both shared. Lithograph by James Baillie. (Courtesy of the Mount Vernon Ladies' Association)

Dr. Craik was not surprised at his long-time friend's courage and calmness during his last moments. He knew of Washington's unwavering Christian faith, and thought the president displayed the ideal, peaceful demeanor of a mature Christian. Dr. Craik would later recall that "during the short period of his illness," Washington "economised his time, in the arrangement of such few concerns as required his attention, with the utmost serenity." He also "anticipated his approaching dissolution with every demonstration of that equanimity for which his whole life as been so uniformly and singularly

25. Lear, *Letters and Recollections,* 133–35; M'Guire, *Religious Opinions,* 348–55; Meade, *Old Churches,* 255; Chernow, *Washington,* 807–09; Thompson, *Good Providence,* 169–75; Schwartz, *American Symbol,* 185; Novak and Novak, *Washington's God,* 208.

conspicuous."[26] In the eyes of those who knew him and surrounded his bed-side in these last hours, Washington died as a he lived—a Christian who knew of the promises of salvation, a happier clime, and eternal life.

Five days after Washington's death, John Marshall spoke for many Americans before the House of Representatives in Philadelphia:

> Our Washington is no more! The hero, the sage, and the patriot of America—the man on whom in times of danger every eye was turned and all hopes were placed, lives now only in his own great actions, and in the hearts of an affectionate and afflicted people.

Washington was one of those "whom Heaven had selected as its in-struments for dispensing good to men . . . More than any other individual . . . has he contributed to found this our wide spreading empire, and to give to the western world its independence and freedom."[27]

President Adams declared a time of national mourning until Wash-ington's birth date on February 22. (When Ben Franklin died and Jefferson suggested to set aside a period of national mourning, Washington declined insisting that it was unwise to set a precedent). Newspaper articles frequently mentioned the president's Christian fortitude and witness for which he had been eminently known. Hundreds of eulogies were offered from New York, to London, to Amsterdam, to Paris. Church bells were muffled, mourning rings were worn, black clothing or black sleeve bands were displayed—by some for as long as six months.

The eulogizers, in the unifying spirit of Washington, were both numer-ous and diverse. They included Federalists and Democratic-Republicans; those who knew him well and those who did not; lawyers, statesmen, and clergymen; northerners and southerners; Congregationalists and Presbyte-rians along with Quakers, Episcopalians, Unitarians, deists, and Masonic grandmasters.[28] One proclaimed that Washington had "changed mankind's ideas of political greatness."[29] Gouverneur Morris commended his judg-ment, which "was always clear, because his mind was pure . . . In him were the courage of a soldier, the intrepidity of a chief, the fortitude of a hero."[30]

Eulogists praised Washington's character, integrity, morality, piety, as well as his motivation to be an instrument or agent of God's will. His

26. Lillback and Newcombe, *Sacred Fire,* 671.

27. John Marshall, Speech in House of Representatives, 1799, in Kaminski, *Found-ers,* 509–10.

28. Gaustad, *Faith of Our Fathers,* 74; Schwartz, *American Symbol,* 98.

29. Smith, *Patriarch,* 359.

30. Novak and Novak, *Washington's God,* 21.

Christian character was something every American could emulate. As Henry "Light-Horse Harry" Lee's eulogy declared, Washington was

> first in war, first in peace and first in the hearts of his countrymen, he was second to none in the humble and endearing scenes of private life. Pious, just, humble, temperate and sincere—uniform, dignified, and commanding . . . Such was the man for whom our nation mourns.[31]

Christian clergy and religious leaders commended and honored Washington throughout the nation. While everyone wanted to claim a piece of America's first national hero, Christians felt a special bond and closeness to the man they perceived as one of their own. Reverend J. T. Kirkland exclaimed that the "virtues of our departed friend were crowned by piety." He was "known to have been habitually devout. To Christian institutions he gave the countenance of his example, and no one could express, more fully, his sense of the Providence of God, and the dependence of man."[32] William Linn emphasized that

> neither in the parade of military life, nor in the cares of civil administration; neither in a state of depression, nor amidst the intoxicating sweets of power and adulation; did he forget to pay homage to the "Most High, who doeth according to his will in the army of heaven, and among the inhabitants of the earth."[33]

Richard Furman, a Baptist pastor, spoke of Washington's

> high sense of the importance and excellence of religion, his public declarations on almost every occasion abundantly manifested. God's superintending Providence; his special interposition in favor of the just and innocent; his attention to the prayers of his supplicating people; and the necessity of religion, for the support of morality, virtue, and the true interests of civil society; are articles which he has fully stated in them, and zealously supported.[34]

Another added that he "had all the genuine mildness of Christianity, with all its force." He was "neither ostentatious nor ashamed of his Christian profession."[35] Reverend Devereux Jarratt was more succinct: Washington

---

31. M'Guire, *Religious Opinions,* 357–58.
32. Schroeder, *Maxims of Washington,* 274.
33. Ibid., 275.
34. Hamburger, *Separation,* 176.
35. Schroeder, *Maxims of Washington,* 297.

"was a professor of Christianity."[36] One eulogist insisted that his "expressions of his dependence on Providence should never be forgotten."[37]

Beyond clergy, other contemporaries also acknowledged his devout Christian faith. Timothy Dwight, president of Yale College, explained how impressed he was with Washington's

> numerous and uniform public and most solemn declarations
> of his high veneration for religion, his exemplary and edifying
> attention to public worship, and his constancy in secret devo-
> tion, as proofs, sufficient to satisfy every person willing to be
> satisfied. I shall only add that if he was not a Christian, he was
> more like one than any man of the same description whose life
> has hitherto recorded.[38]

Washington's good friend, John Marshall, stated, "without making ostentatious professions of religion, he was a sincere believer in the Christian faith, and a truly devout man."[39] Abigail Adams noted that "simple truth" was the president's "greatest eulogy."[40] According to Mrs. Adams,

> no man ever lived, more deservedly beloved and Respected . . .
> He never grew giddy but ever maintained a modest diffidence
> of his own talents . . . and Retired from his exalted station with
> a Character which malice would not wound, nor envy tarnish.
> If we look through the whole tenor of his Life, History will not
> produce to us a Parallel.[41]

To another contemporary, Washington was Moses, Noah, and Joshua all wrapped into one because he had been "an instrument of God's providence" and delivered his people "from the hands of degeneracy and oppression." While the Virginian was "ardent and intrepid as Caesar in the field," he had also "kneeled" as "a humble suppliant to the God of armies." Americans admired and loved the "sound policy of the GENERAL," as well as his "incorruptible integrity" as a "CHRISTIAN."[42]

Over the years, no one had worked more closely with Washington than Alexander Hamilton.

36. Ibid.

37. Carroll, *Eulogy,* 15.

38. Lillback and Newcombe, *Sacred Fire,* 719.

39. Novak and Novak, *Washington's God,* 161.

40. Hay, "American Moses," 145.

41. Abigail Adams to Mary Cranch, December 22, 1799, in Kaminski, *Founders,* 511.

42. Lambert, *Founding Fathers,* 272–73.

'Tis only for me to mingle my tears with those of my fellow soldiers, cherishing with them the precious recollection, that while others are paying a merited tribute to "*The man of the age,*" we in particular allied as we were to him by a close tie, are called to mourn the irreparable loss of a kind and venerated Patron and father![43]

A few weeks later, the former Treasury Secretary stated that his heart was still filled with "bitterness" at his Commander in Chief's passing. "Perhaps no man in this community has equal cause with myself to deplore the loss." He was "very indebted to the kindness of the general, and he was an Aegis very essential to me." Hamilton asserted, "If virtue can secure happiness in another world he is happy. In this the Seal is now put on his Glory. It is no longer in jeopardy from the fickleness of fortune."[44]

Ten days later, Hamilton penned a touching letter to Martha Washington insisting that "no one, better than myself, knows the greatness of your loss, or how much your excellent heart is formed to feel it in all its extent." He knew that Martha could not "receive consolation" fitting for such a loss and, thus, he would "attempt to offer none." Yet, he encouraged Martha by reminding her of the Christian faith she shared with her deceased husband: "Resignation is the will of Heaven, which the practice of your life ensures," and will "alone alleviate the sufferings of so heart-sending an affliction." No one could expect to "be exempt" from calamity. "Perhaps it is even a privilege," he concluded, "to have a claim to a larger portion of it than others."[45]

Tobias Lear, Washington's personal secretary, also had a close relationship and a firsthand look at the president's private life. Lear never expressed any doubt or reservation of the man's Christian faith. Lear told Hamilton that their dear friend endured "his distressed situation with the fortitude of a Hero" and "retained his composure and reason to the last moment." He died "as he had lived, truly a great man."[46] On Christmas Day, 1799, after witnessing the closing of the general's coffin, Lear reflected that he had "beheld for the last time that face which shall be seen no more here; but which I hope to meet in Heaven."[47]

Martha had no doubt of her husband's Christian faith and place in Heaven. Indeed, after George's passing, she was comforted by many friends who reminded her of her husband's devout, Christian faith and ultimate

43. Alexander Hamilton, General Orders, in Kaminski, *Founders,* 511.

44. Hamilton to Tobias Lear, January 2, 1800, in Syrett, *Papers of Hamilton,* 24:155.

45. Hamilton to Martha Washington, January 12, 1800, in ibid., 24:185.

46. Lear to Hamilton, December 15, 1799, in ibid., 24:101.

47. Lear, *Letters and Recollections,* 141.

resting place. Although her grieving was severe—she would never again sleep in their bedroom[48]—the faith that she and her husband shared sustained and reassured her. Lear, writing to a friend on behalf of Martha shortly after Washington's passing, noted that while the

> respect and veneration paid to the memory of our illustrious Chief, make the most grateful impression on the heart of Mrs. Washington, she finds that the only source of Consolation is from that Divine Being who sends Comfort to the Afflicted, and has promised to be the Widow's God. Your prayers for her health and happiness are received with gratitude, and reciprocates with sincerity.[49]

One month after George's death, Martha lifted up her husband's faith as a source of inspiration and comfort in her time of mourning and grieving. She explained, "When the mind is deeply afflicted by those irreparable losses which are incident to humanity, the good Christian will submit without repining to the dispensations of divine Providence." Indeed, Christians could "look for consolation to that Being who alone can pour balm into the bleeding heart, and who has promised to be the widow's God." She insisted that "the loss is ours; the gain is his." She would endure her husband's death "with humble submission to the will of that God who giveth, who taketh away, looking forward with faith and hope to the moment when I shall be again united with the partner of my life."[50]

Thanking her friend, Catherine Garreston, for her "kind sympathy" and "fervent prayers," Martha insisted that

> the precepts of our holy Religion have long since taught me, that in the severe and trying scenes of life, our only sure Rock of comfort and consolation is the Divine Being who orders and directs all things for our good. Bowing with humble submission, to the dispensations of his Providence, and relying upon that support which he has promised to those who put their trust in him, I hope I have borne my late irreparable loss with Christian fortitude. To a feeling heart, the sympathy of friends, and the evidences of universal respect paid to the memory of the deceased are truly grateful. But while these alleviate our grief, we find that the only sense of comfort is from above. It gives me great pleasure to hear that your good Mother yet retains her health and faculties unimpaired, and that you experience those

48. Henriques, *Realistic Visionary,* 104.

49. Lillback and Newcombe, *Sacred Fire,* 686.

50. Novak and Novak, *Washington's God,* 209.

comforts, which the Scriptures promise to those who obey the Laws of God. That you may continue to enjoy the blessings of this life and receive hereafter the portion of the Just is the prayer of your sincere friend.[51]

Four months after George's death, Martha asserted, "There is but one source from whence comfort can be derived under afflictions like ours." Christians "must look with pious resignation and with that pure confidence which our holy religion inspires."[52]

In addition to Martha, many other members of Washington's immediate family also testified and hailed his Christian faith. George Washington Parke Custis later stated that his stepgrandfather was "always a strict and decorous observer of the Sabbath" and regular church attendee. With the exception of Jonathan Trumbull, a dear friend and Speaker of the House of Representatives, Washington would not entertain unexpected visitors or guests on the Sabbath. "In the evenings," Custis remembered, "the president read to Mrs. Washington, in her chamber, a sermon, or some portion from the sacred writings."[53]

Eleanor "Nelly" Parke Custis Lewis, Washington's stepgranddaughter, said he was a private man—silent and thoughtful—who spoke very little of himself. Just as he rarely talked about his Revolutionary War experiences, he did not talk publicly about his specific, religious faith either. Nelly, however, noted that he had a pew at Pohick Church and one at Christ Church in Alexandria. He was instrumental in establishing Pohick Church and "subscribed largely" to it. "No one in church," she contended, "attended to the services with more reverential respect." Her stepgrandfather "stood during the devotional parts of the service," which became a customary practice in the Episcopal Church in the 1780s and 1790s. Each night he retired to his library, "at nine or ten o'clock, where he remained for an hour before he went to his chamber." In the mornings, he "rose before the sun, and remained in his library until called for breakfast." Nelly "never witnessed his private devotions" and "never inquired about them." She just knew him to be a man of faith and the Scriptures. There was no reason "to doubt his firm belief in Christianity," for "his life, his writings, prove that he was a Christian. He was not one of those who act or pray, 'that they may be seen of men.' He communed with his God in secret." According to Nelly, Martha and George were so "perfectly united and happy, that he must have been a Christian," for Martha

51. Lillback and Newcombe, *Sacred Fire*, 687.
52. Ibid., 240.
53. Ibid., 253.

had no doubts and no fears for him. After forty years of devoted affection and uninterrupted happiness, she resigned him without a murmur into the arms of his Savior and his God, with the assured hope of his eternal felicity. Is it necessary that any one should certify, "General Washington avowed himself to me a believer in Christianity?" As well may we question his patriotism, his heroic, disinterested devotion to his country. His mottos were, "Deeds, not Words"; and, "For God and my Country."[54]

The women in Washington's life knew him well.

On December 18, 1799, Reverend Thomas Davis, rector of Christ Church in Alexandria where George and Martha were members, presided over the funeral reading from the Episcopal Order of Burial. Family ancestors eventually put the very first words of the funeral service, taken from the *Book of Common Prayer*, on Washington's tombstone: "I am the resurrection, and the life: he that believeth in me, though he were dead, yet shall he live: And whosoever liveth and believeth in me shall never die" (John 11:25 KJV). George Washington's earthly life had come to an end, but his testaments and legacy live on.

54. Grizzard, *Ways of Providence,* 47–50.

PART VI

Legacy

17

The Washington that Still Matters

George Washington was far from perfect. Flawed and sinful, as all humans are, he worried about his legacy and fame too much and about slavery too little. He acted selfishly, lost his temper, and craved wealth and status. He may have been leading a religiously inspired and informed life, but he did not always act or behave the way Jesus did or the Bible commanded.

Yet, as one recent biographer summarized, "history records few examples of a leader who so earnestly wanted to do the right thing, not just for himself but his country."[1] Despite his sinful ways and flaws, Washington was centered, grounded, faithful, and consistently upheld the highest moral and ethical standards. He avoided many temptations and abuses that would have sacked lesser men. A few years after the general's death, Gouverneur Morris told John Marshall that Washington's character and self-command were of a "higher grade."[2]

The Christian faith, which the Virginian so consistently and earnestly embraced, shaped and inspired his worldview, leadership, and character. "A good & faithful Servant is never afraid or unwilling to have his conduct looked into, but the reverse," Washington once told his personal secretary Tobias Lear, "because the more it is inspected the brighter it shines."[3]

1. Chernow, *Washington*, 812.
2. Gouverneur Morris to John Marshall, June 26, 1807, in Kaminski, *Founders*, 513.
3. Washington to Tobias Lear, *Letters and Recollections*, 43.

Portraits like this one were once prevalent in schools and public buildings throughout the United States. The personal sacrifices, leadership, and achievements of Washington should be learned by each generation. Picture by James Reid Lambdin, after John Trumbull. (Courtesy of the Mount Vernon Ladies' Association)

While numerous historians and biographers regard him as one of the United States's greatest presidents, many Americans have little or no familiarity with the nation's first hero and most important founding father. Portraits of the man, once mounted on almost every classroom wall, are now rarely seen hanging anywhere. History textbooks cover as little as ten percent of his life compared to what was presented about him just a few decades ago. These works are more inclined to talk about Washington's teeth rather than his religion. Washington's birthday, one of the most important and celebrated holidays of the year for many decades, has been replaced by a generic Presidents's Day. Skits that used to be performed across the country on his birthday—specifically focusing on the man's honesty, goodness, and character—have been supplanted with, as one historian puts it, "ridiculous costumed versions of George Washington and Abraham Lincoln hawking new cars and appliance sales during a three-day shopping extravaganza."

And even though the White House is just sixteen miles away from Washington's home in Mount Vernon, Bill Clinton broke a long-standing presidential tradition by being the first president of the United States never to visit the national shrine.[4] He has become as common and forgettable as the one-dollar bill, which adorns his marble-like, stale portrait.

This historical amnesia is a lamentable reality because Washington's legacy does shine so brightly and is worthy of study and emulation. His leadership generated remarkable results and long-lasting achievements. More than any other American, he brought to the fruition the creation, implementation, and stabilization of the United States of America. He truly was America's Indispensable Man.

Just as important, he was also a great and good man—a leader who inspired contemporaries and those who examine his life today. Benevolent, humble, courageous, hard-working, resolute, authentic, trustworthy, resilient, learned, diverse, perceptive, inspiring, empowering, and confident—Washington was blessed with all of these venerable attributes, traits, and qualities.

All too often, however, today's portrayals of Washington are incomplete and unfulfilling. Historians and biographers underemphasize, ignore, or suppress evidence of a devout, Anglican Christian faith and the impact it had on his life and leadership, even though his "moral stamina" was conspicuously evident throughout his entire life.[5] Indeed, Washington's Christian faith was a constant, guiding force and motivation.

Though he did not crawl out of his cradle dreaming of becoming an American Moses, his submission to biblical teachings and trusting relationship with God eventually made him into one. He was raised and nurtured in the Christian faith by family, peers, associates, and friends, and his own personal faith deepened over time. Over 700 times in his writings, Washington refers to "God," "Divine," "Heaven," "Providence," and other honorific titles for God. In addition, he alluded to the Bible over 200 times, composed over one hundred prayers, frequently called on Americans to embrace Christianity, and repeatedly claimed to be a Christian. For a man who was neither a scholar nor a theologian, these regular and seamless references to religious themes present quite a striking portrayal and worldview in and of themselves.[6]

While he was a man of deep religious conviction, Washington did not flaunt his specific denomination and biblical worldview or allow the republic

4. Rees, *Leadership Lessons*, xii–xiv.

5. Fischer, *Washington's Crossing*, 13.

6. Lillback and Newcombe, *Sacred Fire*, 713.

to become intolerant of different religious practices and expressions. Everyone had a right to their own religion and faith life. "To expect that all men should think alike upon political, more than on Religious, or other subjects," he wrote to a friend in 1798, "would be to look for a change in the order of nature."[7]

Nevertheless, without compromising or watering down his own biblical worldview, Washington's Christian witness inspired a trust and confidence that brought people together. He went out of his way to lift up faith and religious practice in general, not just his own theological views. Both his military and political callings were well suited for his Latitudinarian disposition and approach. Employing language that all Americans could accept, he spoke in Hebraic terms that reminded Jews, Catholics, and Protestants of the religious common ground they shared. He never wanted religion to become a point of contention or division and avoided rousing up doctrinal debate and rivalry. While morality and religious faith were inextricable, Washington made great efforts not to publicly state or endorse one particular religious faith as a better path of morality over another. He enjoyed attending many different Christian churches and congregations. God was omnipresent in the houses of worship of all Christian denominations.

Anglican teachings eschewed public use of the words "Jesus Christ" outside of worship settings, so Washington purposely used benign references such as "Almighty," "Merciful Sovereign of the Universe," "Creator," "Divine Author of Our Blessed Religion," "Hand of Heaven," "Father of All Mercies," "God," Great Lord and Ruler of Nations," "Lord of Hosts," "Supreme Being."[8] Adhering to the Anglican way and Latitudinarian worldview, he achieved and succeeded as a peacemaker, unifying agent, and as non-threatening leader who happened to be deeply religious. Even deists and infidels praised his piety and morality, especially since he displayed a balanced, moderate, and harmonious disposition.[9]

While Washington was well aware of the contentious differences that sometimes separated religious sects and denominations, he believed, in the end, that religious people had a better chance of establishing a harmonious society than people who were not religious. If religion and morality were key pillars in a republican society, then they were also desirable attributes in republican leaders and citizens.

Washington recognized that all human beings were frail, sinful, and mistake-prone. "Providence," he once noted, "for purposes beyond the reach

7. Washington to Joseph Hopkinson, May 27, 1798, in Abbot and Twohig, *Washington, Retirement Series*, 2:300–01.

8. Novak and Novak, *Washington's God,* 122; Unger, *Unexpected Washington,* 194; McBrien, *Caesar's Coin,* 27.

9. Schwartz, "Character of Washington," 215.

of mortal scan, has suffered the restless and malignant passions of man, the ambitious and sordid views of those who direct them." Man's imperfection and sinful nature kept the "world in a continual state of disquietude."[10] As a leader, he calculated for and anticipated mistakes, shortcomings, and indecision. His grasp of humankind's sinful nature and propensity for disappointment, as well as his own firsthand experiences with failure, significantly contributed to his own humility and resiliency. Human execution and outcomes would rarely, if ever, be achieved in a flawless or even near perfect manner. No one was perfect—such was the state of a fallen world.

Many years after his death, Jefferson asserted that Washington "was naturally distrustful of men, and inclined to gloomy apprehensions."[11] Indeed, he was cynical toward man's behavior because he knew of his own sinful nature and had witnessed and experienced the immorality of others in a wide variety of settings and experiences. He learned and understood well the doctrine of original sin and the depravity of human nature as taught to him by his orthodox, Anglican Church.

Acknowledging and understanding humankind's sinful nature did not make him a social and political killjoy or even a melancholy leader. On the contrary, the realization humbled Washington and compelled him to faithfully rely on his benevolent and perfect God. Throughout his life, he frequently admitted his own shortcomings, incapability, and limitations. At the same time, he incessantly praised and lifted up the superior ways and omnipotence of Providence.[12] His God sent a Savior—the "Divine Author of our blessed Religion"—to forgive people of their sins. Realizing that he did not have to be perfect, and could not be perfect, provided a cathartic effect on a man who tried to walk the straight line, but knew he would veer off the straight and narrow from time to time.

Washington's Christian faith provided energy and a bias toward action in his daily walk and psyche. Inspired by his faith and biblical worldview, he built an impressive mental stamina and became a resilient, resourceful leader. He understood that God's benevolence and plans would become clear no matter what mistakes were made or successes achieved. Only God was in control. Only God could bring order out of chaos. Only God could use the infallibility and mistakes of men and use them for fruitful, God-pleasing outcomes.

Leaders, however, were called to take action and use the gifts that God had so generously bestowed upon them. A man of action—who was more

---

10. Washington to Earl of Buchan, May 26, 1794, in Fitzpatrick, *Writings of Washington,* 33:383.

11. Jefferson to Walter Jones, January 2, 1814, in Peterson, *Jefferson: Writings,* 1320.

12. Novak and Novak, *Washington's God,* 188.

afraid of idleness than failure, Washington knew he had been called and equipped to lead by example.[13] If God was constantly intervening in his created world to bring his unfolding plans to fruition, then Washington was to be action-oriented and forward-leaning too. This understanding explains why the Virginian encouraged and applauded Americans who, as good stewards, took action and carried out their republican duties, especially in the name of liberty and freedom.[14]

The humility which Washington possessed, especially considering all of his accomplishments, is yet another impressive legacy. He pleaded for patience when contemporaries placed him in formal leadership positions and roles. When he took command of the Continental Army and was elected president, his humility was palpable to all on the scene. Army officers, cabinet officials, family members, and close family friends were rarely jealous of him, but consistently praised his self-deprecation, modesty, and reserve. After almost every battle during the Revolution, his resignation from the army, the creation of a new Constitution, and every major undertaking during his presidency, Washington instinctively praised and expressed profound, heartfelt gratitude to God.[15] He believed God controlled the outcome of his life and of all life in general. After the Whiskey Rebellion had been put down, he explained, "The Great ruler of events, not to any exertions of mine, is to be ascribed the favorable termination of our late contest for liberty." He "never considered the fortunate issue of any measure adopted by me in the progress of the Revolution in any other light than as the ordering of a kind Providence."[16] God deserved the glory, not him.

Certainly Washington had an ego and ambition. Of course he desired fame, took pride in his contributions to history, and carefully guarded his legacy. Yet, Washington knew that his vanity and selfishness were part of his sinful nature and mortality. In confessing his sins regularly in church, he acknowledged that his Savior's moral standards were far superior to his own. Therefore, when successes came, he gave credit to God from whom he believed these earthly gifts and blessings had come. Washington was a man made humble by his Christian faith.[17]

Americans gravitated to the Indispensable Man because he was a God-fearing, humble, servant of God dedicated to the well-being and liberty of

13. Brookhiser, *Founding Father*, 12–13.

14. Novak and Novak, *Washington's God*, 179.

15. Lillback and Newcombe, *Sacred Fire*, 177.

16. Washington to Jonathan Williams, March 2, 1795, in Fitzpatrick, *Writings of Washington*, 34:130.

17. Schwartz, "Character of Washington," 215.

American citizens. When he ordered prayers after every military victory, the general eschewed any accolades for himself. At every opportunity, from his First Inaugural Address to his Farewell Address, he publicly venerated God. His submission to Providence paralleled his submission to the will of the people[18] and reflected an inner strength and confidence not lost among his countrymen. A submissive leader was a trustworthy one.

Although far from perfect, the integrity with which he lived, both in his personal and public life, was highly lauded and praised by his contemporaries as well as those who came after him. His character, perhaps, remains his most impressive legacy and gift to the American people. The great statesman and senator, Daniel Webster, once said of Washington: "America has furnished to the world the character of Washington, and if our American institutions had done nothing else, that alone would have entitled them to the respect of mankind."[19] One historian asserts that in over 20,000 individual letters Washington wrote, there is no evidence that he lied even once, save for some subjective character assessments of contemporaries.[20] He wanted to be known as an honest and noble man and reflected on his rectitude often. He used the word "character" over 1,500 times in his writings.[21]

Since so many historians and biographers laud his character, arguments for the deistic Washington must be respectfully scrutinized and challenged. If he was a deist: Why would he faithfully attend and remain a member of orthodox Anglican congregations throughout his entire life? Why would he praise orthodox Christianity and disdain deism in his correspondence? Why would he allow most Americans to believe that he was a Christian? Why would he sign an oath of membership to the Anglican Church—an oath that called on him to believe and endorse orthodox, Christian views such as the forgiveness of sins, justification by grace, and the Triune God—if he did not assent to these core teachings? Why would he become a Christian godfather, giving public testimony and affirmation to the orthodox tenets of the Christian faith, to eight different babies?

Washington lived and led with integrity because he was a Christian, not simply one who desired to be perceived as a Christian. He would have little integrity to claim if, as a deist, he went about the business of duping Americans to think he was a Christian. He was either an authentic Anglican Christian or he intentionally fooled and manipulated contemporaries and the American people for political expediency.

---

18. Schwartz, *American Symbol,* 172.
19. Rees, *Leadership Lessons,* x.
20. Ibid., 13.
21. Lillback and Newcombe, *Sacred Fire,* 193.

Washington, however, was a man of character. He led by example and believed that one's actions and integrity reveal one's convictions and commitment. The general would never have called on his own soldiers, for example, to be authentic Christians if he was not trying to live as one too.[22]

Reverend Eliab Stone once stated that he had four indisputable proofs that Washington had lived and died as a Christian: 1) On his inauguration day, he promised to never do secular business on the Sabbath, and he never did. 2) He was regular and constant in his attendance at public worship, and his manner was "serious and engaged." 3) He "maintained daily intercourse with Heaven by prayer," regularly facilitated family prayer, and throughout the War of Independence, was "know to have observed stated seasons of retirement for secret devotion." 4) In both private and public communications, he expressed "his deep sense of a superintending providence, and of his own dependence upon the divine care and direction."[23]

Reverend Alexander MacWhorter, a Presbyterian minister from Newark, New Jersey who had served with Washington during the Revolutionary War, wrote that

> General Washington was a uniform professor of the Christian religion . . . steadily discountenanced vice; abhorred the principles of infidelity, and the practice of immorality. He was a constant and devout attendant upon divine worship. In the army he kept no chaplain of his own, but attended divine services with his brigades, in rotations, as far as conveniency would allow, probably to be an example to his officers, and encouraged his soldiers to respect religion. He steadily attended the worship of God when president. He was not in this respect like too many, who practically declare themselves superior to honoring their Maker in the offices of religion. He firmly believed in the existence of God and his superintending providence. This appears in almost all of his speeches. He was educated in the Episcopal Church, and always continued a member thereof, and was an ornament to the same. He was truly of the catholic faith, and considered the distinction of the great denominations of Christianity rather as shades of difference, than anything substantial or essential to salvation.[24]

One eulogist wrote, "The language uniformly held by Washington, the maxim invariably inculcated and repeated by him in almost every public manifestation of his sentiments, was the acknowledgment of a superintending providence." God was "preparing, regulating and governing all human

22. Ibid., 32–34.

23. Novak and Novak, *Washington's God*, 221–22.

24. Ibid., 221.

events for the accomplishment of its eternal purposes, and the predisposing of the instruments, by which they are to be affected." Certainly "religion and observation" had taught Washington "that God's provident wisdom *reacheth from end to end mightily, and disposeth all things sweetly.*" The eulogist noted that the nation's first president referred

> every human event to the moral government of a supreme intel-
> ligent Being. This became the polar star, by which he was guided
> in his progress through life, and in all his anxious folicitude for
> maintaining the liberty, perfecting the policy, preserving the
> peace, insuring the stability of his country on the foundations
> of order and morality, and guarding it against the turbulence of
> faction, licentiousness, foreign hostility and artifice. This virtu-
> ous maxim of religious, moral, and political wisdom, so deeply
> impressed him, never perhaps more illustrated, than by the
> course of providence in preparing and adapting his body and
> mind to suit the destinies of his life. He was to be himself a most
> luminous proof of that truth which was so rooted in his soul.[25]

Washington carried himself with great integrity because his Christian faith compelled him to do so. He was a lifelong member of Anglican parishes—baptized, married, and buried according to the teachings and rituals of the Anglican Church. He gave large sums of money to religious organizations and churches and spent more money on his pew, at Christ Church in Alexandria, for example, than any other member of the congregation. He constantly gave money and goods to the less fortunate. He served as a vestryman at his local parish and became a godfather to eight children—the latter two roles requiring vows and oaths of belief in Christian orthodox teaching. He referred to himself as a Christian in his writings, while never explicitly stating he was not one. Individuals who knew him well and best, as well as the vast majority of the Christian clergy, supported and admired him for his Christian faith.[26] While Jefferson was constantly criticized, sometimes vilified, as a closet atheist, Washington had no such charges or public attacks made against him. Instead, he would acquire, in his own lifetime, an almost mythic status as a Christian servant-statesman.[27]

He lived his Christian faith in private as he encouraged all Americans to live in public. His guiding principles were well known and understood. Trustworthy and transparent, he did not compartmentalize his core convictions, which were grounded in his Christian faith. Contemporaries earnestly

25. Carroll, *Eulogy,* 5–6.
26. Henriques, *Realistic Visionary,* 174.
27. Novak and Novak, *Washington's God,* 161, 216–17.

respected and venerated him for his honesty and forthrightness. There was nothing pretentious about him, especially his faith.

The vast majority of Americans, associates, and comrades believed Washington to be a devout Christian, as did his family. Moreover, the fruits of his life exhibit the life of a Christian servant leader. The more contemporaries got to know him, the more impressed they were with his character, integrity, and devotedness. Picture by Thomas Pritchard Rossiter. (Courtesy of the Mount Vernon Ladies' Association)

Washington's close family members testified on his active and personal Christian faith. They had witnessed his prayer life, church attendance, Sunday evening sermon recitations, Bible study, and devotions. His faith was lived and practiced in both the private and public domains. Picture by Thomas Pritchard Rossiter. (Courtesy of the Mount Vernon Ladies' Association)

The certainty he exuded in the American experiment was palpable and empowering to those around him. Contemporaries sensed Washington's genuine confidence in the promises of America—freedom, liberty, independence—and how his confidence was inspired by his religious faith. He repeatedly wrote and spoke of the sureness he had in the American cause because he believed it was God's plan. His message was consistent: God was guiding America's fortunes and smiling favorably upon America's noble pursuit of freedom and liberty. Thus, he held that it was right and proper to "offer up our prayers to the Sovereign Dispenser of life and health" when facing challenges. God's "favor . . . on our endeavors, the good sense and firmness of our fellow Citizens, and fidelity in those they employ, will secure to us a permanence of good government."[28]

Washington's Christian faith inspired his greatest leadership strength—confidence. There are many lessons that can be learned from studying the life of Washington and what made him so effective. Picture by Rembrandt Peale. (Courtesy of the Mount Vernon Ladies' Association)

28. Washington to Trustees of Public School of Germantown, November 6, 1793, in Fitzpatrick, *Writings of Washington,* 33:149.

Of all the leadership attributes he possessed, confidence was king. This confidence—inspired and derived from his Christian faith—bore fruit in his prodigious productivity, effectiveness, and influence. Moreover, his Christian faith provided a comfort and security that he was leading and acting in history as God both allowed and directed him to do. His letters and writings show how he reflected upon his accomplishments and setbacks from a biblical worldview. No matter the circumstances, his intervening God was with and always around him.[29] Furthermore, the decisiveness, mental stamina, stoic courage, calmness, and honesty he possessed—just a few of his commendable leadership attributes—were directly informed and bolstered by his faith.

Washington's courage to forge ahead, no matter the odds or challenges, reveals an inner strength and confidence touched by the transcendent force of a religious faith. Whether charging enemy lines, launching a new government, coming out of retirement, or confronting the daily physical challenges, Washington relied on his Christian faith to provide clarity and direction in his life. "I look upon every dispensation of Providence as designed to answer some valuable purpose," he once told his cousin, Lund Washington, "and I hope I shall always possess a sufficient degree of fortitude to bear without murmuring any stroke which may happen, either to my person or estate, from that quarter."[30]

When William Pearce's crops were destroyed by drought, Washington encouraged his friend never to complain "at disappointment and losses which are the effects of Providential acts." He was "sure the alwise disposer of events knows better than we do, what is best for us, or what we deserve."[31] A few months later, when Pearce's seed was washed away by storms, the president explained that "these are effects of Providential dispensations" and "resignation is our duty."[32] When yet another calamity befell Pearce's crops from rain and floods, Washington maintained that "it is our duty to submit" to God's unfolding plans, even tragedies. "I never repine at these acts of Providence," he insisted, "because I always suppose, however adverse they may be to our wishes, they are always for the best."[33] Later, he sympathized with another Pearce hardship—winter grain had spoiled and fences were destroyed from strong winds. "These being acts of Providence and not

---

29. Connell, *Faith*, xix.

30. Washington to Lund Washington, May 29, 1779, in Fitzpatrick, *Writings of Washington*, 15:180.

31. Washington to William Pearce, May 25, 1794, in ibid., 33:375.

32. Washington to William Pearce, September 14, 1794, in ibid., 33:499.

33. Washington to William Pearce, June 21, 1795, in ibid., 34:217.

within our controul, I never repine at them."[34] Though God's plans may be inscrutable at the time, Washington was confident that they were always purposeful and for one's ultimate good.

Throughout his life, as he aged but continued to endure crushing responsibilities, Washington became more grateful and dependent on his Christian faith and relationship with God.[35] He was doing everything he could to preserve "the civil and religious liberties of the American people" with "the assistance of divine providence." Therefore, "it always affords me satisfaction," he asserted, "when I find a concurrence in sentiment and practice between all conscientious men in acknowledgements of homage to the great Governor of the Universe, and in professions of support to a just civil government." He trusted "people of every denomination, who demand themselves good citizens," and would "always strive to prove a faithful and impartial Patron of genuine, vital religion." He thanked church members for "presenting your prayers at the Throne of Grace for me."[36]

Washington's confidence was palpable to his peers. Indeed, this confidence—the charisma, calmness, clarity, focus, mental stamina, and fortitude no matter the odds—revealed itself when his vocation called for him to be a military commander, farmer, entrepreneur, delegate, chairman, president, statesman, friend, husband, father, and grandfather. He led boldly and decisively in all of his vocations. Confidence was compelling. Taken together, Washington's character and confidence produced his charisma. It was a powerful and compelling combination.

Washington and Jefferson shared and exuded confidence that served them well as leaders, but they were confident in different things. Jefferson predicted, incorrectly as it turned out, that most Americans would be Unitarian within decades after the founding. Revealed, inspired religion was destined to simply wear out, fade away, and become obsolete. Jefferson envisioned an uncomplicated rational man, inhabiting a moral universe.

Washington's vision, on the other hand, demonstrated a reliance on the inscrutability of God, human neediness, and the profound importance of a religious character.[37] Morality could only come from religion. For problems and challenges that may not appear to have immediate, clear-cut answers or outcomes, Washington's dependence upon God provides a sense of hope

34. Washington to William Pearce, March 27, 1796, in ibid., 34:507.

35. Smith, *Patriarch,* 148.

36. Washington to Bishops of the Methodist Episcopal Church, May 29, 1789, in Abbot, *Washington, Presidential Series,* 2:411–12.

37. Novak and Novak, *Washington's God,* 225.

and comfort. For leaders, character matters far more than the illusion of having all the right answers.

The subject of religion, no doubt, stirs up great controversy, debate, and suspicion. Recent United States presidents have been scrutinized for their religious faith and practices, or lack thereof, and the impact they may have had on policy and vision. Perhaps the strong emotions and convictions, which the subject of religion elicits, have made it harder for religiously inspired and motivated leaders to emerge, especially in the public square.

Washington would truly be saddened and distraught by such a state of affairs. His character and effectiveness as a leader, at all different stages in his life, were significantly shaped and informed by his Christian faith and biblical worldview. He left a rich legacy as a man and a leader who lived with purpose, confidence, and character. The manner in which he lived out his religious faith—in public and private—compels us to examine and apply the lessons that can be learned from the life of this most Indispensable Man. 'Tis well.

Bibliography

Abbot, W. W. "George Washington, the West, and the Union." In *George Washington Reconsidered*, edited by Don Higginbotham, 198–211. Charlottesville, VA: University Press of Virginia, 2001.

———, ed. *The Papers of George Washington, Presidential Series*. 16 vols. Charlottesville, VA: University Press of Virginia, 1987.

———. "An Uncommon Awareness of Self: The Papers of George Washington." In *George Washington Reconsidered*, edited by Don Higginbotham, 275–86. Charlottesville, VA: University Press of Virginia, 2001.

Abbot, W. W., & Dorothy Twohig, eds. *The Papers of George Washington, Confederation Series*. 6 vols. Charlottesville, VA: University Press of Virginia 1992.

———, eds. *The Papers of George Washington, Colonial Series*. 10 vols. Charlottesville, VA: University Press of Virginia, 1983.

———, eds. *The Papers of George Washington, Retirement Series*. 4 vols. Charlottesville, VA: University Press of Virginia, 1998.

Ahlstrom, Sydney. *A Religious History of the American People*. New Haven, CT: Yale University Press, 1972.

Albanese, Catherine. *Sons of the Fathers: The Civil Religion of the American Revolution*. Philadelphia: Temple University Press, 1976.

Alden, John. *George Washington: A Biography*. Baton Rouge, LA: Louisiana State University Press, 1984.

Ambler, Charles Henry. *George Washington and the West*. New York: Russell & Russell, 1936.

Bailey, Thomas. *Presidential Greatness: The Image and the Man from George Washington to the Present*. New York: Appleton-Century, 1966.

Bailyn, Bernard. *The Ideological Origins of the American Revolution*. Enlarged ed. Cambridge, MA: Harvard University Press, 1992.

Beck, Glenn. *Being George Washington: The Indispensable Man, as You've Never Seen Him*. New York: Threshold, 2011.

Ballagh, James, ed. *The Letters of Richard Henry Lee*. 2 vols. New York: Da Capo, 1970.

Bellah, Robert, and Phillip Hammond. *Varieties of Civil Religion*. San Francisco: Harper & Row, 1980.

Berns, Walter. *The First Amendment and the Future of American Democracy*. Chicago: Gateway, 1985.

Bloch, Ruth. "Religion and Ideological Change in the American Revolution." In *Religion American Politics: From the Colonial Period to the 1980s,* edited by Mark Noll, 44–61. New York: Oxford University Press, 1990.

———. "Religion, Literary Sentimentalism, and Popular Revolutionary Ideology." In *Religion in a Revolutionary Age,* edited by Ronald Hoffman and Peter Albert, 308–30. Charlottesville, VA: University Press of Virginia, 1994.

———. *Visionary Republic: Millennial Themes in American Thought, 1756–1800.* Cambridge, MA: Cambridge University Press, 1985.

Boller, Paul, Jr. "To Bigotry No Sanction." In *Character Counts: Leadership Qualities in Washington, Wilberforce, Lincoln, and Solzhenitsyn,* edited by Os Guinness, 41–64. Grand Rapids: Baker, 1999.

———. "George Washington and Religious Liberty." *William and Mary Quarterly* 17 (1960), 486–506.

Bonick, Colin. *The American Revolution.* Charlottesville, VA: University Press of Virginia, 1991.

Borden, Morten. *Great Lives Observed: George Washington.* Englewood Cliffs, NJ: Prentice Hall, 1969

———. *Jews, Turks, and Infidels.* Chapel Hill, NC: University of North Carolina Press, 1984.

Boorstin, Daniel. *The Americans: The National Experience.* New York: Random House, 1965.

Bourne, Miriam. *First Family: George Washington and His Intimate Relations.* New York: Norton, 1982.

Bowen, Catherine Drinker. *Miracle at Philadelphia: The Story of the Constitutional Convention, May to September 1787.* Boston: Little, Brown, 1966.

Boyd, Julian, ed. *The Papers of Thomas Jefferson.* 21 vols. Princeton, NJ: Princeton University Press, 1950.

Brady, Patricia, *George Washington's Beautiful Nelly: The Letters of Eleanor Parke Custis Lewis to Elizabeth Bordley Gibson, 1794–1851.* Columbia, SC: University of South Carolina Press, 1991.

Brookhiser, Richard. "The Forgotten Character of George Washington." In *Patriot Sage: George Washington and the American Political Tradition,* edited by Gary Greg, Matthew Spalding, and William Bennett, 299–308. Wilmington, DE: ISI, 1999.

———. *Founding Father: Rediscovering George Washington.* New York: Free Press, 1996.

———. *George Washington on Leadership.* New York: Basic, 2008.

———. *What Would the Founders Do? Our Questions, Their Answers.* New York: Basic, 2006.

Bryan, Helen. *Martha Washington: First Lady of Liberty.* New York: John Wiley, 2002.

Buchanan, John. *The Road to Valley Forge: How Washington Built the Army that Won the Revolution.* Hoboken, NJ: John Wiley, 2004.

Burns, James, and Susan Dunn, *George Washington.* New York: Henry Holt, 2004.

Bush, George W. *Decision Points.* New York: Crown, 2010.

Bush, Laura. *Spoken from the Heart.* New York: Scribner, 2010.

Butler, Jon. *Becoming America: The Revolution before 1776.* Cambridge, MA: Harvard University Press, 2000.

———. "Coercion, Miracle, Reason: Rethinking the American Religious Experience in the Revolutionary Age." In *Religion in a Revolutionary Age,* edited by Ronald

Hoffman and Peter Albert, 1–30. Charlottesville, VA: University Press of Virginia, 1994.

Callahan, North. *George Washington: Soldier and Man.* New York: William Morrow, 1972.

Carroll, John. *Eulogy on George Washington—Delivered in St. Peter's Church, Baltimore—February 22, 1800.* New York: P. J. Kennedy, 1931.

Carter, Stephen. *God's Name in Vain: The Wrongs and Rights of Religion in Politics.* New York: Basic, 2000.

Catanzariti, John, ed. *The Papers of Thomas Jefferson.* Vols. 25–28. Princeton, NJ: Princeton University Press, 1990.

Chernow, Ron. *Washington: A Life.* New York: Penguin, 2010.

Chestnutt, David, and James Taylor, eds. *The Papers of Henry Laurens.* Vols. 11–16. Columbia, SC: University of South Carolina Press, 1990.

Clark, Harrison. *All Cloudless Glory: The Life of George Washington.* 2 vols. Washington, D.C.: Regnery, 1995.

Clary, David. *Adopted Son: Washington, Lafayette, and the Friendship that Saved the Revolution.* New York: Bantam Dell, 2007.

Cleland, Hugh. *George Washington in the Ohio Valley.* Pittsburgh: University of Pittsburgh Press, 1955.

Clinton, Bill. *My Life.* New York: Vintage, 2004.

Connell, Janice. *Faith of Our Founding Father: The Spiritual Journey of George Washington.* New York: Hatherleigh, 2004.

Cope, Kevin, ed. *George Washington in and as Culture.* New York: AMS, 2001.

Corbin, John. *The Unknown Washington: Biographic Origins of the Republic.* New York: Charles Scribner's Sons, 1930.

Cousins, Norman, ed. *'In God we trust': The Religious Beliefs and Ideas of the American Founding Fathers.* New York: Harper & Brother, 1958.

———, ed. *The Republic of Reason: The Personal Philosophies of the Founding Fathers.* San Francisco: Harper & Row, 1988.

Crackel, Theodore, ed. *The Papers of George Washington, Digital Edition.* George Washington's Mount Vernon Estates and Gardens (2007). http://rotunda.upress.virginia.edu:8080/pgwde/dflt.xqy.

Crutchfield, James. *George Washington: First in War, First in Peace.* New York: Tom Doherty Associates, 2005.

Cullen, Charles, ed. *The Papers of Thomas Jefferson.* Vols. 22–23. Princeton, NJ: Princeton University Press, 1986.

Cunliffe, Marcus. *George Washington: Man and Monument.* Rev. ed. Mount Vernon, VA: Mount Vernon Ladies' Association, 1982.

Cunningham, Homer. *The Presidents' Last Years: George Washington to Lyndon B. Johnson.* Jefferson, NC: McFarland, 1989.

DeConde, Alexander. *Entangling Alliance: Politics and Diplomacy under George Washington.* Durham, NC: Duke University Press, 1958.

De Tocqueville, Alexis. *Democracy in America.* Rev. ed. Translated by Henry Reeve. Vol. 1. New York: Vintage, 1957.

Draper, Theodore. *A Struggle for Power: The American Revolution.* New York: Random House, 1996.

Eck, Diana. *A New Religious America: How a "Christian Country" has now become the World's Most Religiously Diverse Nation.* San Francisco: HarperCollins, 2001.

Eidsmoe, John. *Christianity and the Constitution: The Faith of Our Founding Fathers.* Grand Rapids: Baker, 1987.

Elkins, Stanley, and Eric McKitrick. *The Age of Federalism: The Early American Republic, 1788–1800.* New York: Oxford University Press, 1993.

Ellis, Joseph. *Founding Brothers: The Revolutionary Generation.* New York: Alfred A. Knopf, 2000.

———. *His Excellency: George Washington.* New York: Alfred A. Knopf, 2004.

Emery, Noemie. *Washington: A Biography.* New York: G.P. Putnam's Sons, 1976.

Evans, Bette Novit. *Interpreting the Free Exercise of Religion: The Constitution and American Pluralism.* Chapel Hill, NC: University of North Carolina Press, 1997.

Farrand, Max, ed. *The Records of the Federal Convention of 1787.* 4 vols. Rev. ed. New Haven, CT: Yale University Press, 1966.

Fay, Bernard. *George Washington: Republican Aristocrat.* Boston: Houghton Mifflin, 1931.

Ferling, John. *The First of Men: A Life of George Washington.* Knoxville, TN: University of Tennessee Press, 1988.

———. *A Leap in the Dark: The Struggle to Create the American Republic.* New York: Oxford University Press, 2003.

Fields, Joseph, ed. *"Worthy Partner:" The Papers of Martha Washington.* Westport, CT: Greenwood, 1994.

Finke, Roger, and Rodney Stark. *The Churching of America, 1776–1990: Winners and Losers in Our Religious Economy.* New Brunswick, NJ: Rutgers University Press, 1992.

Fischer, David. *Washington's Crossing.* New York: Oxford University Press, 2004.

Fishman, Ethan, William-Pederson, and Mark Rozell, eds. *George Washington: Foundations of Presidential Leadership and Character.* Westport, CT: Praeger, 2001.

Fitzpatrick, John. *George Washington Himself: A Common Sense Biography Written from His Manuscripts.* Indianapolis: Bobbs-Merrill, 1933.

———, ed. *The Writings of George Washington from the Original Manuscript Sources, 1745–1799.* 39 vols. Washington, D.C.: United States Government Printing Office, 1931.

Fleming, Thomas, ed. *Affectionately Yours, George Washington: A Self-Portrait in Letters of Friendship.* New York: Norton, 1967.

———. *Washington's Secret War: The Hidden History of Valley Forge.* New York: HarperCollins, 2005.

Flexner, James. *George Washington, 1732–1799.* 4 vols. Boston: Little, Brown, 1965.

———. *Washington: The Indispensable Man.* Boston: Little, Brown, 1974.

Ford, Paul. *George Washington.* Philadelphia: J. B. Lippincott, 1896.

Ford, Worthington. *George Washington.* 2 vols. New York: Charles Scribner's Sons, 1900.

Fowler, William, Jr. *American Crisis: George Washington and the Dangerous Two Years after Yorktown, 1781–1783.* New York: Walker, 2011.

Freeman, Douglas. *George Washington: A Biography.* 7 vols. Volume 7 completed by John Alexander Carroll and Mary Wells Ashworth. New York: Charles Scribner's Sons, 1948.

Freeman, Joanne, ed. *Alexander Hamilton: Writings.* New York: Library of America, 2001.

Gaustad, Edwin. *Faith of Our Fathers: Religion and the New Nation.* San Francisco: Harper & Row, 1987.

———. *Sworn on the Altar of God: A Religious Biography of Thomas Jefferson.* Grand Rapids: Eerdmans, 1996.

Genovese, Michael. *The Power of the American Presidency, 1789–2000.* New York: Oxford University Press, 2001.

Gilbert, Felix. *To the Farewell Address: Ideas of Early American Foreign Policy.* Princeton, NJ: Princeton University Press, 1961.

Gregg, Gary, and Matthew Spalding, eds. *Patriot Sage: George Washington and the American Political Tradition.* Wilmington, DE: ISI Books, 1999.

Greven, Philip. *The Protestant Temperament: Patterns of Child-Rearing, Religious Experience, and the Self in Early America.* New York: Alfred A. Knopf, 1977.

Grizzard, Frank, Jr., *The Ways of Providence: Religion & George Washington.* Charlottesville, VA: Mariner, 2005.

Hamburger, Philip. *Separation of Church and State.* Cambridge, MA: Harvard University Press, 2002.

Hamilton, Stanislaus, ed. *The Writings of James Monroe.* 7 vols. New York: AMS, 1969.

Hatch, Nathan. *The Democratization of American Christianity.* New Haven, CT: Yale University Press, 1989.

———. "The Democratization of Christianity and the Character of American Politics." In *Religion and American Politics: From the Colonial Period to the 1980s,* edited by Mark Noll, 92–120. New York: Oxford University Press, 1990.

———. *The Sacred Cause of Liberty: Republican Thought and the Millennium in Revolutionary New England.* New Haven, CT: Yale University Press, 1977.

Hay, Robert. "The American Moses." In *American Life, American People, Volume 1,* edited by Neil Shumsky & Timothy Crimmins, 143–51. San Diego: Harcourt Brace Jovanovich, 1988.

Heimert, Alan. *Religion and the American Mind: From the Great Awakening to the Revolution.* Cambridge, MA: Harvard University Press, 1966.

Henriques, Peter. "The Final Struggle between George Washington and the Grim King." In *George Washington Reconsidered,* edited by Don Higginbotham, 250–71. Charlottesville, VA: University of Virginia Press, 2001.

———. *Realistic Visionary: A Portrait of George Washington.* Charlottesville, VA: University of Virginia Press, 2006.

Herold, J. Christopher. *The Age of Napoleon.* Boston: Houghton Mifflin, 1987.

Higginbotham, Don. *George Washington and the American Military Tradition.* Athens, GA: University of Georgia Press, 1985.

———, ed. *George Washington Reconsidered.* Charlottesville, VA: University of Virginia Press, 2001.

———. "George Washington and Revolutionary Asceticism: The Localist as Nationalist." In *George Washington Reconsidered,* edited by Don Higginbotham, 141–64. Charlottesville, VA: University of Virginia Press, 2001.

———. *George Washington: Uniting a Nation.* Lanham, MD: Rowman & Littlefield, 2002.

Hirschfeld, Fritz. *George Washington and Slavery: A Documentary Portrayal.* Columbia, MO: University of Missouri Press, 1997.

Hobson, Charles, ed. *The Papers of John Marshall.* Vols. 6–11. Chapel Hill, NC: University of North Carolina Press, 1990.

Hoffer, Peter. *Revolution and Regeneration: Life Cycle and the Historical Vision of the Generation of 1776.* Athens, GA: University of Georgia Press, 1983.

Hoffman, Ronald, and Peter Albert, eds. *Religion in a Revolutionary Age.* Charlottesville, VA: University Press of Virginia, 1994.

Hofstadter, Richard. *The American Political Tradition and the Men Who Made It.* New York: Vintage, 1958.

Hofstra, Warren, ed. *George Washington and the Virginia Backcountry.* Madison: Madison House, 1998.

Holifield, E. Brooks. *Theology in America: Christian Thought from the Age of the Puritans to the Civil War.* New Haven, CT: Yale University Press, 2003.

Holmes, David. *The Faiths of the Founding Fathers.* New York: Oxford University Press, 2006.

Horwitz, Robert, ed. *The Moral Foundations of the American Republic.* 3rd ed. Charlottesville, VA: University Press of Virginia, 1986.

Hughes, Rupert. *George Washington, 1732–1781.* 3 vols. New York: William & Morrow, 1926.

Hutchinson, William, and William Rachal, eds. *The Papers of James Madison.* Vols. 1–8. Chicago: University of Chicago Press, 1962.

Hutson, James, ed. *Religion and the New Republic: Faith in the Founding of America.* Lanham, MD: Rowman & Littlefield, 2000.

Jackson, Donald, and Dorothy Twohig, eds. *The Diaries of George Washington.* 6 vols. Charlottesville, VA: University Press of Virginia, 1976.

Johnson, Herbert, ed. *The Papers of John Marshall.* Vol. 1. Chapel Hill, NC: University of North Carolina Press, 1974.

Johnson, Paul. *George Washington: The Founding Father.* New York: HarperCollins, 2005.

———. *A History of Christianity.* New York: Macmillan. 1976.

Johnson, William. *George Washington: The Christian.* Arlington Heights, IL: Christian Liberty, 1919.

Jones, Robert. *George Washington: Ordinary Man, Extraordinary Leader.* New York: Fordham University Press, 2002.

Kaminski, John, ed. *The Founders on the Founders: Word Portraits from the American Revolutionary Era.* Charlottesville, VA: University of Virginia Press, 2008.

Kaminski, John, Jill McCaughan, and Don Higginbotham. *A Great and Good Man: George Washington in the Eyes of His Contemporaries.* Madison: Madison House, 1989.

Kaufman, Burton. *Washington's Farewell Address: The View from the 20th Century.* Chicago: Quadrangle, 1969.

Kelly, J. N. D. *Early Christian Doctrines.* 2nd ed. New York: Harper, 1960.

Ketcham, Ralph. *From Colony to Country: The Revolution in American Thought, 1750–1820.* New York: Macmillan, 1974.

———. *Presidents Above Party: The First American Presidency, 1789–1829.* Chapel Hill, NC: University of North Carolina Press, 1984.

Knollenberg, Bernhard. *George Washington: The Virginia Period, 1732–1775.* Durham, NC: Duke University Press, 1964.

Koch, Adrienne. *Power, Morals, and the Founding Fathers: Essays in the Interpretation of the American Enlightenment.* Ithaca, NY: Cornell University Press, 1961.

LaHaye, Tim. *Faith of Our Founding Fathers.* Green Forest, AR: Master, 1994.

Lambert, Frank. *The Founding Fathers and the Place of Religion in America.* Princeton, MA: Princeton University Press, 2003.

Landy, Mark, and Sidney Milkis, *Presidential Greatness.* Lawrence, KS: University Press of Kansas, 2000.

Lear, Tobias, and George Washington. *Letters and Recollections of George Washington: Being Letters to Tobias Lear and Others between 1790 and 1799, Showing the First American in the Management of His Estate and Domestic Affairs. With a Diary of Washington's Last Days, Kept by Mr. Lear.* New York: Doubleday, 1906.

Leibiger, Stuart. *Founding Friendship: George Washington, James Madison, and the Creation of the American Republic.* Charlottesville, VA: University Press of Virginia, 1999.

Lemay, J. A. Leo, ed. *Benjamin Franklin: Writings.* New York: Library of America, 1987.

Lengel, Edward. *General George Washington: A Military Life.* New York: Random House, 2005.

———. *Inventing George Washington: America's Founder, in Myth & Memory.* New York: HarperCollins, 2011.

Levy, Leonard. *The Establishment Clause: Religion and the First Amendment.* New York: Macmillan, 1986.

Lewis, Thomas. *For King and Country: The Maturing of George Washington, 1748–1760.* New York: Harper Collins, 1993.

Lillback, Peter, and Jerry Newcombe. *George Washington's Sacred Fire.* Bryn Mawr, PA: Providence Forum, 2006.

Lodge, Henry Cabot. *George Washington.* 2 vols. Boston: Houghton Mifflin, 1898.

Longmore, Paul. *The Invention of George Washington.* Berkeley: University of California Press, 1988.

Lossing, Benson. *George Washington's Mount Vernon.* New York: Fairfax, 1870.

Madison, James. *Notes of Debates in the Federal Convention of 1787 Reported by James Madison.* New York: Norton, 1966.

Maier, Pauline. *American Scripture: Making the Declaration of Independence.* New York: Alfred A. Knopf, 1997.

Manschreck, Clyde. *A History of Christianity in the World: From Persecution to Uncertainty.* Englewood Cliffs, NJ: Prentice-Hall, 1974.

Mansfield, Stephen. *Ten Tortured Words: How the Founding Fathers Tried to Protect Religion in America . . . and What's Happened Since.* Nashville: Thomas Nelson, 2007.

Mapp, Alf, Jr. *The Faith of Our Fathers: What America's Founders Really Believed.* Lanham, MD: Rowman & Littlefield, 2003.

Marty, Martin. *Religion, Awakening, and Revolution.* New York: Oxford University Press, 1977.

May, Henry. *The Enlightenment in America.* New York: Oxford University Press, 1976.

Mayo, Bernard. *Myths and Men: Patrick Henry, George Washington, Thomas Jefferson.* Athens, GA: University of Georgia Press, 1959.

McBrien, Richard. *Caesar's Coin: Religion and Politics in America.* New York: Macmillan, 1987.

McDonald, Alonzo. "A Leader for the Multitude." In *Character Counts: Leadership Qualities in Washington, Wilberforce, Lincoln, and Solzhenitsyn,* edited by Os Guiness, 25–40. Grand Rapids: Baker, 1999.

McDonald, Forrest. *The American Presidency: An Intellectual History.* Lawrence, KS: University Press of Kansas, 1994.

————. *Novus Ordo Seclorum: The Intellectual Origins of the Constitution.* Lawrence, KS: University of Kansas Press, 1985.

————. *The Presidency of George Washington.* Lawrence, KS: University Press of Kansas, 1974.

McDowell, Stephen. *Apostle of Liberty: The World-Changing Leadership of George Washington.* Nashville: Cumberland House, 2007.

Meacham, Jon. *American Gospel: God, the Founding Fathers, and the Making of a Nation.* New York: Random House, 2006.

Mead, Sidney. *The Lively Experiment: The Shaping of Christianity in America.* New York: Harper & Row, 1963.

Meade, William. *Old Churches, Ministers, and Families of Virginia.* 2 vols. Westminster, MD: Heritage, 1857.

Meyer, Donald. *The Democratic Enlightenment.* New York: Capricorn, 1976.

M'Guire, Edward. *The Religious Opinions and Character of Washington.* New York: Harper & Brothers, 1836.

Milkis, Sidney, and Michael Nelson. *The American Presidency: Origins & Development, 1776–1998.* 3rd ed. Washington, D.C.: Congressional Quarterly, 1999.

Miller, William. *The First Liberty: Religion and the American Republic.* New York: Alfred A. Knopf, 1986.

Moore, Charles. *The Family Life of George Washington.* Boston: Houghton Mifflin, 1926.

Morgan, Edmund. *The Genius of George Washington.* New York: Norton, 1980.

————. *The Meaning of Independence: John Adams, George Washington, and Thomas Jefferson.* New York: Norton, 1978.

Moynahan, Brian. *The Faith: A History of Christianity.* New York: Doubleday, 2002.

Muhlenberg, Henry. *The Notebook of a Colonial Clergyman.* Edited and translated by Theodore Tappert and John Doberstein. Minneapolis: Fortress, 1998.

Murrin, John. "Religion and Politics in America from the First Settlements." In *Religion and American Politics: from the Colonial Period to the 1980s,* edited by Mark Noll, 19–43. New York: Oxford University Press, 1990.

Nelson, James. *George Washington's Great Gamble: And the Sea Battle that Won the American Revolution.* New York: McGraw-Hill, 2010.

Nettels, Curtis. *The Emergence of a National Economy, 1775–1815.* New York: Holt, Rinehart, and Winston, 1962.

————. *George Washington and American Independence.* Boston: Little, Brown, 1951.

Neuhaus, Richard. *The Naked Public Square: Religion and Democracy in America.* Grand Rapids: Eerdmans, 1984.

Noll, Mark. *America's God: From Jonathan Edwards to Abraham Lincoln.* New York: Oxford University Press, 2002.

————. *One Nation Under God? Christian Faith and Political Action in America.* San Francisco: Harper & Row, 1988.

————, ed. *Religion and American Politics: From the Colonial Period to the 1980s.* New York: Oxford University Press, 1990.

————. *Turning Points: Decisive Moments in the History of Christianity.* Grand Rapids: Baker, 1997.

Noll, Mark, Nathan Hatch, and George Marsden. *The Search for Christian America.* Westchester, IL: Crossway, 1983.

Nordham, George. *The Age of Washington: George Washington's Presidency, 1789–1797.* Chicago: Adams, 1989.

Novak, Michael. "The Influence of Judaism and Christianity on the American Founding." In *Religion and the New Republic: Faith in the Founding of America,* edited by James Hutson, 159–85. Lanham, MD: Rowman & Littlefield, 2000.

Novak, Michael, and Jana Novak. *Washington's God: Religion, Liberty, and the Father of Our Country.* New York: Basic, 2006.

Oberg, Barbara, ed. *The Papers of Thomas Jefferson.* Vols. 29–32. Princeton, NJ: Princeton University Press, 2002.

Paine, Thomas. *The Age of Reason: The Definitive Edition.* Ann Arbor: Michigan Legal, 2014.

Palmer, David. *George Washington and Benedict Arnold: A Tale of Two Patriots.* Washington, D.C.: Regnery, 2006.

Parry, Jay, et al. *The Real George Washington.* Malta, ID: National Center for Constitutional Studies, 1991.

Peterson, Barbara. *George Washington, America's Moral Exemplar.* New York: Nova History, 2005.

Peterson, Merrill, ed. *Thomas Jefferson: Writings.* New York: Library of America, 1984.

Pfeffer, Leo, ed. *Church, State, and Freedom.* Rev. ed. Boston: Beacon, 1967.

Phelps, Glenn. *George Washington and American Constitutionalism.* Lawrence, KS: University Press of Kansas, 1993.

———. "The President as a Moral Leader: George Washington in Contemporary Perspective," In *George Washington: Foundation of Presidential Leadership and Character,* edited by Ethan Fishman, William Pederson, and Mark Rozell, 3–17. Westport, CT: Praeger, 2001.

Quitt, Martin. "The English Cleric and the Virginia Adventurer: The Washingtons, Father and Son," In *George Washington Reconsidered,* edited by Don Higginbotham, 15–37. Charlottesville, VA: University of Virginia Press, 2001.

Rakove, Jack, ed. *James Madison: Writings.* New York: Library of America, 1999.

———. *Original Meanings: Politics and Ideas in the Making of the Constitution.* New York: Alfred A. Knopf, 1996.

Randall, Willard. *George Washington: A Life.* New York: Henry Holt, 1997.

Rasmussen, William, and Robert Tilton. *George Washington: The Man Behind the Myths.* Charlottesville, VA: University Press of Virginia, 1999.

Rees, James. *George Washington's Leadership Lessons: What the Father of Our Country Can Teach Us about Effective Leadership and Character.* Hoboken, NJ: John Wiley, 2007.

Reichley, James. *Religion in American Public Life.* Washington, D.C.: Brookings Institution, 1985.

Rice, Condoleezza. *No Higher Honor: A Memoir of My Years in Washington.* New York: Crown, 2011.

Richey, Russell, and Donald Jones, eds. *American Civil Religion.* New York: Harper & Row, 1974.

Rutland, Robert, ed. *The Papers of George Mason, 1725–1792.* 3 vols. Chapel Hill, NC: University of North Carolina Press, 1970.

———. *The Papers of James Madison.* Vols. 9–16. Chicago: University of Chicago Press, 1975.

Rutland, Robert, and Thomas Mason, eds. *The Papers of James Madison: Presidential Series.* Vol. 1. Charlottesville, VA: University Press of Virginia, 1984.

Saint Peter's Church. "The Venerable Doctor Abercrombie." http://www.stpetershistory. org/stpetershistoryabercrombiehtml.html.

Schroeder, John, ed. *Maxims of Washington: Political, Social, Moral, and Religious.* Mount Vernon, VA: Mount Vernon Ladies' Association, 1942.

Schwartz, Barry. "The Character of Washington: A Study in Republican Culture," *American Quarterly* 38:2 (1986), 202–22.

———. *George Washington: The Making of an American Symbol.* New York: Free Press, 1987.

———. "George Washington and the Whig Conception of Heroic Leadership," *American Sociological Review* 48:1 (1983), 18–23.

Smith, Richard. *Patriarch: George Washington and the New American Nation.* Boston: Houghton Mifflin, 1993.

Smyth, Albert, ed. *The Writings of Benjamin Franklin.* 10 vols. New York: Haskell House, 1970.

Sparks, Jared. *The Life of George Washington.* New York: A.L. Burt, 1902.

Stagg, J. C. A., ed. *The Papers of James Madison: Congressional Series.* Vols. 16–17. Charlottesville, VA: University Press of Virginia, 1989.

———. *The Papers of James Madison: Presidential Series.* Vols. 2–5. Charlottesville, VA: University Press of Virginia, 1994.

Stazeksy, Richard. "George Washington, Genius in Leadership." In *The Papers of George Washington, Articles* (2000). http://gwpapers.virginia.edu/history/articles/george-washington-genius-in-leadership/.

Stout, Harry, and D.G. Hart, eds. *New Directions in American Religious History.* New York: Oxford University Press, 1997.

Sweet, William. *Religion in the Development of American Culture, 1765–1840.* New York: Charles Scribner's Sons, 1952.

Syrett, Harold, ed. *The Papers of Alexander Hamilton.* 26 vols. New York: Columbia University Press, 1969.

Taranto, James, and Leonard Leo, eds. *Presidential Leadership: Rating the Best and the Worst in the White House.* New York: Free Press, 2004.

Tebbel, John. *George Washington's America.* New York: E. P. Dutton, 1954.

Thayer, William. *George Washington.* Boston: Houghton Mifflin, 1931.

Thompson, Mary. *"In the Hands of a Good Providence": Religion in the Life of George Washington.* Charlottesville, VA: University of Virginia Press, 2008.

Thorsmark, Thora. *George Washington.* Chicago: Scott, Foresman, 1931.

Turner, Nancy. *The Mother of Washington.* New York: Dodd, Mead, 1930.

Twohig, Dorothy. "The Making of George Washington." In *George Washington and the Virginia Backcountry,* edited by Warren Hofstra, 3–34. Madison: Madison House, 1998.

———. "That Species of Property: Washington's Role in the Controversy Over Slavery." In *George Washington Reconsidered,* edited by Don Higginbotham, 114–38. Charlottesville, VA: University of Virginia Press, 2001.

Unger, Harlow. *"Mr. President": George Washington and the Making of the Nation's Highest Office.* Boston: Da Capo, 2013.

———. *The Unexpected George Washington: His Private Life.* Hoboken, NJ: John Wiley, 2006.

Walker, Williston, et al. *A History of the Christian Church.* 4th ed. New York: Charles Scribner's Sons, 1985.

Wall, Charles. *George Washington: Citizen-Soldier.* Charlottesville, VA: University Press of Virginia, 1980.

Weems, Mason. *The Life of Washington.* Edited by Marcus Cunliffe. Cambridge, MA: Harvard University Press, 1962.

West, John, Jr. "George Washington and the Religious Impulse." In *Patriot Sage: George Washington and the American Political Tradition,* edited by Gary Gregg and Matthew Spalding, 267–86. Wilmington, DE: ISI, 1999.

White, Leonard. *The Federalists: A Study in Administrative History.* New York: Macmillan, 1956.

Wiencek, Henry. *An Imperfect God: George Washington, His Slaves, and the Creation of America.* New York: Farrar, Straus, & Giroux, 2003.

Wills, Garry. *Certain Trumpets: The Call of Leaders.* New York: Simon & Schuster, 1994.

———. *Cincinnatus: George Washington and the Enlightenment.* Garden City, NY: Doubleday, 1984.

———. *Under God: Religion and American Politics.* New York: Simon & Schuster, 1990.

Wilson, John. *Public Religion in American Culture.* Philadelphia: Temple University Press, 1979.

Wood, Gordon. *American Revolution: A History.* New York: Modern Library, 2002.

———. *The Radicalism of the American Revolution.* New York: Vintage, 1991.

———. "Religion and the American Revolution." In *New Directions in American Religious History,* edited by Harry Stout and D.G. Hart, 173–205. New York: Oxford University Press, 1997.

———. *Revolutionary Characters: What Made the Founders Different.* New York: Penguin, 2006.

Woodward, Bob. *The War Within: A Secret White House History, 2006–2008.* New York: Simon & Schuster, 2008.

Woodward, W. E. *George Washington: The Image and the Man.* New York: Boni & Liveright, 1926.

Zagarri, Rosemarie, ed. *David Humphreys' "Life of General Washington" with George Washington's "Remarks."* Athens, GA: University of Georgia Press, 1991.

Zall, Paul, ed. *Washington on Washington.* Lexington, KY: University Press of Kentucky, 2003.

Index